CAROLINA WHITEWATER

A Canoeist's Guide to the Western Carolinas

Bob Benner
&
David Benner

MENASHA RIDGE PRESS

Birmingham
Alabama

ISBN 0-89732-008-5
LCC card No. 84-115920

Menasha Ridge Press
3169 Cahaba Heights Road
Birmingham, AL 35243

CAROLINA WHITEWATER
A Canoeist's Guide
to the Western Carolinas

Dedicated to Ramone Eaton

A man who canoed as he lived—with grace and charm laid his paddle to rest on April 25, 1980. It will be awhile before another like him will paddle with us.

Table of Contents

Acknowledgments

The authors would like to acknowledge the many people whose assistance made such an undertaking possible. There are so many, too numerous to mention, who have lent a helping hand in some way or another. A few whose efforts require a special note of thanks are:

Members of the Blue Ridge Outing Club and the Carolina Canoe Club for providing invaluable feedback for the new edition. Vann and Laura Evans for their notes on the Haw River. Leonard Baker and R. B. Binegar for their willingness to go well beyond the call of duty. Donna Benner for her patience in typing the work in progress — little pay but many thanks.

And last, but certainly not least, all of the many friends for joining in "interesting" exploratory trips, undoubtedly questioning the advisability of the friendship at times when such trips turned into hikes down dry stream beds, ice breakers, and major engineering feats — but always turned into memorable outings.

We have all followed the wild goose and hopefully are the better for having done so.

Part 1

Introduction

This guide, originally written for the use of the recreational open boater, has been expanded with this edition to include stretches of water that will challenge the most advanced decked canoe and kayak paddler. Much of the water, however, is suitable for the novice paddler. The more difficult runs are not recommended for those thrill-seekers who wish to try their wings. One's wings need to be fully grown before attempting these highly technical, and quite often dangerous, stretches. In classifying rapids it is quite difficult to remain totally objective because one's judgment is generally relative to one's experience. In any case, it is hoped that the system will be found consistent.

As the sport of canoeing grows one sees more and more clubs being organized with canoeing as their main interest. Some long-time paddlers question the need for such growth or organization and rightly so, but this is one of the few safe proving grounds available for aspiring canoeists. It is primarily through clubs that one can obtain competent instruction toward improving skills and learning safe canoeing practices. Also, it is only by organization that our free-flowing rivers are going to be saved for future generations.

Information on safety has been included because of the certain hazards involved in the sport. Hopefully the suggestions made will lessen the possibilities of accidents other than normal swampings and dunkings that are likely to occur.

Along with these suggestions are rules which will be helpful for the canoeist who decides that Labor Day shouldn't necessarily mean the end of his season. More and more paddlers are venturing forth in the middle of winter to experience a completely different world. The risks increase as the air and water temperatures decrease. A familiarity with certain facts relating to exposure can cut down considerably on these inherent risks.

The average canoeist in North Carolina seems to harbor the idea that he has an inalienable right to paddle on any stream that has enough water to float his canoe. This most certainly is a misconception under present interpretation of state law and an attempt to clarify what the rights of the canoeist may be is discussed.

An explanation of the overall format has been included so that the reader can fully understand the organization of the materials on the streams and the various sections that it may be divided into. In "Canoeing White Water," Randy Carter established such an understandable outline in describing rivers that it has been followed very closely.

Finally, the major organization of the book contains six sections on rivers. The first four consist of groups of rivers in neighboring counties in the foothills and mountains of the state. The fifth section contains the Chattooga, the Chagua, the Doe and the Elk, which are located in neighboring states. The Haw River, a stream of the Piedmont, has been included due to its extreme popularity. The last section has very little whitewater. It has been included to offer the paddler a selection of some 200 miles suitable for camping trips.

The maps of the various streams in each section are drawn to scale. Scale: $1'' = 2$ miles.

The original reason for undertaking such a work as this was to provide a source of information for those who would like to take their pleasure in paddling the many beautiful rivers of Western Carolina. The effort will have been worthwhile if any small portion of the great pleasure the authors have experienced on the several hundred miles contained herein is imparted to the reader.

Carolina Overview

 Physiologically, North and South Carolina are sisters. Both are bordered on the west by the Blue Ridge Mountains and on the east by the Atlantic Ocean. Moving west to east in either state, three major physiographic regions are encountered: The Blue Ridge Mountains, the Piedmont, and the Coastal Plain. In both states the coastal plain is locally referred to as the "lowlands," while the Piedmont and Mountain regions are collectively known as "uplands" or "highlands."

The Blue Ridge Mountains are the eastern part of the Appalachian Mountain System, extending from Southeastern Pennsylvania across Maryland, Virginia, North Carolina, South Carolina and Northern Georgia. In North Carolina, the Blue Ridge forms the eastern section of a mountain chain more than seventy-five miles wide, where cross ridges connect the more westerly Black Mountains and Great Smokies. In this area, known as the "Land of the Sky," are forty three peaks of over 6,000 feet, and 125 others of more than 5,000 feet. Mountain valleys here are characteristically narrow, deep, and densely forested with elevations consistently above 2,000 feet.

By contrast, Western South Carolina extends only slightly into the Blue Ridge Mountains, where a small number of peaks not exceeding 3,600 feet rise rather abruptly from the foothills. Where mountains occupy approximately 6,000 square miles in North Carolina, there are only about 500 square miles of mountain terrain in South Carolina. The highest point in South Carolina is Sassafrass Mountain (3,560 feet), situated on the North Carolina/South Carolina state line.

The coolest and wettest portion of both states, the Blue Ridge Mountain region is not farmed extensively nor densely populated, with the steepness of the terrain making the land more suitable for forest than for farms.

Geologically, the region is underlain by "crystalline" rocks such as granite, slate, and gneiss, which are dense and hard. The mountains are usually steep with V-shaped valleys. Slopes are covered with thick soil and luxurious forests which retard run-off.

Many rivers are born high in the mountains of the Carolinas, flowing down in all directions like chocolate on a sundae. Typically running along steep, rocky channels, the streams roll swiftly down the mountains over an abundance of rapids and falls, broadening when they reach the valley floors. West of the Blue Ridge the streams flow north and west, forming a major part of the Tennessee River Drainage. To the north are the headwaters of the New, which eventually empties into the Ohio. On the southeastern slopes of the Blue Ridge the Broad, Catawba, and Yadkin are born. These merge with other drainages after crossing into South Carolina and finally find their way to the Atlantic Ocean. To the south are the headwaters of the Savannah River, which follows the South Carolina/Georgia border to the sea.

Beyond the Blue Ridge to the east the Carolinas drop out of the mountains and out onto the rolling plateau of the Piedmont. Extending from the Blue Ridge Escarpment to the fall line where the topography suddenly drops off onto the flat expanse of the Coastal Plain, the Piedmont descends at roughly 3.5 ft. per mile with the terrain changing gradually from rolling hills to flat upland. Deeply cut by rivers and creeks, the hills of the Piedmont rise from 400 to 1,500 feet above sea level. Though the Piedmont is underlain by the same crystalline rock as the Blue Ridge region, it lacks the mountains' high relief. Only occasionally are the rolling plains punctuated by a prominent hill. Comprising about forty percent of the area of both Carolinas, the Piedmont is generally well developed and populated. Rivers flowing through the Piedmont, while lacking the high gradient and pristine setting of the mountains, are generally attractive and some are endowed with a variety of rapids and falls.

The Coastal Plain region of the Carolinas begins at the fall line, where the underlying geology abruptly changes from hard crystalline rock to sandy loam over marl. Known locally as the "low country," the plain was at the bottom of the Atlantic Ocean in the past geologic ages. The Fall Line, where a dramatic drop in elevation occurs as one moves east from the Piedmont into the Coastal Plain, runs very roughly on the line of Falls-of-the-Roanoke to Durham to Columbia to Augusta (Ga.). Near the Fall Line the Coastal Plain consists of small hills. Moving toward the ocean, the terrain flattens. Swamp and marsh characterize the coastline corridor to the far east with many natural lakes occurring. Below the mouth of the Cape Fear River the coastal environs assume a more tropical look with black water (caused by tannic acid from decaying vegetation), thick groves of palmettos, magnolias, tall cypress draped with Spanish Moss, and live oak.

The Carolinas are alive with beautiful and diverse flora and fauna. Because of their great variety of climate and soil they have the greatest variety of plant life of any area in the Eastern U.S. Longleaf pine dominates the upper coastal plain along with water oaks, and hickories. In the Piedmont, pine remains plentiful but hardwood forests are the order of the day with deciduous oak being most prevalent followed by beech, birch, ash, maple, black walnut, sycamore, and yellow poplar. On the mountains the forest is generally comprised of oak, chestnut, laurel, white pine, and hemlock. Wildlife is abundant and varied, especially birds, many of which winter and breed in the coastal marshes.

Climate in the Carolinas is equable and pleasant, being cool in the mountains and almost subtropical on the Coastal Plain with the Piedmont representing the middle of the spectrum. Temperatures average approximately 10 degrees cooler in the mountains than in the low country. The mean annual temperature for North Carolina is about 59 degrees and for South Carolina 63 degrees, with January being the coldest month and July the warmest. North Carolina receives more rain than South Carolina owing to its larger mountain region. Averages for both states approximate fifty-four inches in the mountains, forty-seven inches in the Piedmont, and forty-eight inches in the Coastal Plain. On the east slope of some of the mountains the precipitation is exceptionally heavy. Heavy snow is unusual except in the mountains. Winds are variable and seldom violent except during the storms of fall along the coast.

Clubs and Organizations

There are a number of local and national organizations that the paddler should be aware of. We have attempted to list those groups that we are acquainted with that are active in the surrounding area.

Most local clubs have as their main objectives the training of members toward safer canoeing, and the preservation of the streams on which they paddle. Generally they have regularly scheduled trips throughout most of the year and periodically publish newsletters which are in themselves a valuable source of information for the canoeist.

For those who wish to improve their skills in the canoe it is almost a necessity to paddle with those of greater experience. In many areas "the local club" will be the only source of such experience.

Many of us begin paddling to get away from the hustle and bustle of today's busy life; to get back to nature; to see things that few others see; or to engage in an activity that few people do. For this reason joining a club and participating in organized trips might seem alien to us. However, the fact remains, without organizations that are willing to work and fight toward preserving our free-flowing streams, there may be none to enjoy in the future. We don't care to see our rivers become the "L.A. Freeway" at rush hour, but can we afford to be so selfish as to want to keep our favorite streams all to ourselves? How much weight will a handful carry when the "Corps" begins surveying for the best damsite? Your "bag" may be an occasional quiet float trip down your favorite stream with one or two close friends, but we hope you will see fit to support the organization in your area that may help you save that stream some day. We can save our rivers only if our numbers are large and we are well organized. Not quantity alone, but quantity with quality will be needed. A good source for determining whether or not there is a club in your area might be your canoeing outfitter.

Local and Area

Carolina Canoe Club
P.O. Box 12932
Raleigh, NC 27605

Blue Ridge Outing Club
P.O. Box 1938
Morganton, NC 28655

Catawba Valley Outing Club
c/o Outdoor Supply
774 4th Street Dr. SE
Hickory, NC 28601

Piedmont Paddlers
P.O. Box 11526
Charlotte, NC 28220

Triad River Runners
P.O. Box 11283
Winston-Salem, NC 27116
(Bethabara Station)

Float Fishermen of Virginia
Richard Abeyta, Treasurer
417 Beauregard Ave.
Petersburg, VA 23803

Georgia Canoeing Association
P.O. Box 7023
Atlanta, GA 30309

Tennessee Scenic Rivers Association
P.O. Box 3104
Nashville, TN 37219

National

American Whitewater Affiliation
P.O. Box 1483
Hagerstown, MD 21740

Composed of boating clubs and individuals interested in white water paddling. It promotes conservation, cruising, and wild water and slalom competition on national and international levels. "American Whitewater," the journal of the Affiliation, is published six times yearly. Dues $6.00/year.

American Canoe Association
4260 East Evans Avenue
Denver, CO 80222

Comprised of individual members and clubs organized into regional division. The ACA conducts canoe and kayak cruises, promotes canoe sailing, encourages and sanctions competition, and has conservation as one of its prime areas of interest. "Canoe," the official magazine, is published six times a year. Dues: $15.00, Magazine Subscription Rate: $20.00.

Conservation Organizations

We are losing our free-flowing rivers and streams one by one in the frantic push for development. Whether that development be by damming, channelization or dredging, many miles of wild, wonderful water will soon be lost forever. One of our most precious resources is literally going down the drain slowly but surely. We all must stand up and be heard if we are to stem the tide and save some of these waters for our future generations to know and enjoy.

There are many national and local organizations that have as one of their primary objectives the preservation of free-flowing waters. We list only a few of these in hopes the reader might see fit to join in and support the cause.

American Rivers
801 Pennsylvania Ave SE
Suite 303
Washington, D.C. 20003

Founded in 1973, the American Rivers Conservation Council publishes a quarterly newsletter which contains articles about recent action in Congress dealing with wild and scenic rivers and with water resource projects. Also covered are the progress of wild and scenic river studies being performed by federal agencies and state scenic river programs.

In addition to reporting on current events, the newsletter gives suggestions on how individuals can take action to help protect rivers.

Conservation Council of North Carolina
P.O. Box 37564
Raleigh, NC 27627

The Conservation Council of North Carolina is a statewide organization which coordinates activities of the many conservation groups within North Carolina. A monthly newsletter is published commenting on the various environmental concerns in the state. Among the many special committees of CCNC is the River Preservation Committee.

Sierra Club
Dept. J-045
P.O. Box 7959
San Francisco, CA 94120

The Joseph LeConte Chapter of the Sierra Club is composed of members in North Carolina and currently has active groups within the chapter in most of the more populous areas of the state. Many of the groups have canoeing activities throughout the year.

■

Exertion brings vital physiological reactions when there are worthwhile goals to achieve. Without weariness there can be no real appreciation of rest, without hunger no enjoyment of food, without the ancient responses to the harsh simplicities of the environment that shaped mankind, a man cannot know the urges within him. Having known this during a period of life when I could satisfy the needs, I think I understand what wilderness can mean to the young men of today.   *Sigurd F. Olson*

North Carolina Natural and Scenic Rivers

A Natural and Scenic Rivers System was created by the General Assembly in 1971 to preserve and protect certain free flowing rivers in their natural state. A thirteen mile segment of the Linville River and some 26.5 miles of the New and the South Fork of the New became the first rivers to be included in the system in 1976. Currently, the state is treading lightly around the troubled waters of establishing scenic rivers. Opposition, primarily from land owners, has arisen in every case that has come up for study in the recent past. However, progress is being made toward studying the Dan for inclusion in either the state or federal system.

Information regarding trips on these streams can be quite useful. Such information as: date of trip, put in and take out, length of trip (time and distance), number of participants, and anything unusual can prove important. Jot it down on a card and send it to the author in care of Pisgah Providers. Such reports will be tabulated and forwarded to the North Carolina Department of Natural Resources and Community Development. This type of data can be most helpful in making decisions on these streams.

State Water Trails

In 1973 a state trails committee was established by the General Assembly to represent the citizen's trail interests. Included in the area are trails for hikers, O.R.V.'s, horseback riders, bicyclists, and canoeists. Out of this committee and from interest by the North Carolina Department of Natural Resources and Community Development has grown the North Carolina Trails Association. This organization, still somewhat in the embryo stage, is composed of individuals and groups interested in the promotion of trails and trail related activities. In 1978 some 62 miles of the Lumber River received recognition as the state's first water trail. Also a stretch of the French Broad received such recognition later that year. In addition to these, approximately 1,400 miles of other streams and lakes are deemed to have·potential for establishment as State Water Trails.

If interested in working toward a better system of trails in North Carolina contact:

North Carolina Trails Association
P.O. Box 1033
Greensboro, NC 27402

Paddler Information

The most widely publicized of the *paddler* self-evaluations was created by the Keel-Haulers Canoe Club of Ohio. This system brings the problem of matching paddlers with rivers into perspective but seems to overemphasize nonpaddling skills. A canoe clinic student who is athletically inclined but almost totally without paddling skill once achieved a rating of 15 points using the Keel-Haulers system. His rating, based almost exclusively on general fitness and strength, incorrectly implied that he was capable of handling many Class II and Class III rivers. A second problem evident in the system is the lack of depth in skill category descriptions. Finally, confusion exists in several rating areas as to whether the evaluation applies to open canoes, decked canoes, or both.

To remedy these perceived shortcomings and to bring added objectivity to paddler self-evaluation, Bob Sehlinger* has attempted to refine the paddler rating system. Admittedly the refined system is more complex and exhaustive, but not more so than warranted by the situation. Heavy emphasis is placed on paddling skills, with description adopted from several different evaluation formats, including a non-numerical system proposed by Dick Schwind.**

* Sehlinger, Bob; *A Canoeing and Kayaking Guide to the Streams of Tennessee*, Thomas Press.
** Schwind, Dick; "Rating Systems for Boating Difficulty," *American Whitewater Journal*, Volume 20, Number 3, May/June 1975.

Rating the Paddler

Instructions: All items, except the first, carry points that may be added to obtain an overall rating. All items except "Rolling Ability" apply to both open and decked boats. Rate open and decked boat skills separately.

---

1. Prerequisite Skills. Before paddling on moving current, the paddler should:
  a. Have some swimming ability.
  b. Be able to paddle instinctively on nonmoving water (lake). (This presumes knowledge of basic strokes.)
  c. Be able to guide and control the canoe from either side without changing paddling sides.
  d. Be able to guide and control the canoe (or kayak) while paddling backwards.

e. Be able to move the canoe (or kayak) laterally.

f. Understand the limitations of the boat.

g. Be practiced in "wet exit" if in a decked boat.

2. Equipment. Award points on the suitability of your equipment to white-water. Whether you own, borrow, or rent the equipment makes no differ-ence. *Do not* award points for both *Open Canoe* and *Decked Boat*.

Open Canoe

0 Points: Any canoe less than 15 ft. for tandem; any canoe less than 14 ft. for solo.

1 Point: Canoe with moderate rocker, full depth, and recurved bow; should be 15 ft. or more in length for tandem and 14 ft. or more in length for solo and have bow and stern painters.

2 Points: Whitewater canoe. Strong rocker design, full bow with recurve, full depth amidships, no keel; meets or exceeds minimum length requirements as described under "1 Point"; made of hand-laid fiberglass, Kevlar, Marlex, or ABS *Royalex;* has bow and stern painters. Canoe as described under "1 Point" but with extra flotation.

3 Points: Canoe as described under "2 Points" but with extra flotation.

Decked Boat (K-1, K-2, C-1, C-2)

0 Points: Any decked boat lacking full flotation, spray skirt, or foot braces.

1 Point: Any fully equipped, decked boat with a wooden frame.

2 Points: Decked boat with full flotation, spray skirt and foot braces; has grab loops; made of hand-laid fiberglass, Marlex, or Kevlar.

3 Points: Decked boat with foam wall reinforcement and split flotation; Neoprene spray skirt; boat has knee braces, foot braces, and grab loops; made of hand-laid fiberglass or Kevlar only.

■

This earth is something you protect every day of the year. A river is something you defend every inch of its course.

James A. Michener, *from* Centennial

Table 1: Rating the River

Points	Secondary Factors — Factors Related Primarily to Success in Negotiating			Primary Factors — Factors Affecting Both Success and Safety			Secondary Factors — Factors Related Primarily to Safe Rescue				
	Obstacles, rocks and trees	Waves	Turbulence	Bends	Length (feet)	Gradient (feet/mile)	Resting or rescue spots spots	Water Velocity (mph)	Width and depth depth	Temp. (F)	Accessibility
0	None	Few inches high, avoidable	None	Few, very gradual	<100	<5, regular slope	Almost anywhere	<3	Narrow (<75 feet), and shallow (<3 feet)	>65	Road along river
1	Few, passage almost straight through	Low (up to 1 ft.) regular, avoidable	Minor eddies	Many, gradual gradual	100-700	5-15, regular slope		3-6	Wide (>75 feet), and shallow (<3 feet)	55-65	<1 hour travel by foot or water
2	Courses easily recognizable	Low to med. (up to 3 ft.), regular, avoidable	Medium eddies	Few, sharp, blind. Scouting necessary	700-5,000	15-40, ledges or steep drops		6-10	Narrow (<75 feet) and deep (>3 feet)	45-55	1 hour to 1 day travel by foot or water
3	Maneuvering, course not easily recognizable avoidable	Med. to large (up to 5 ft.), mostly regular,	Strong eddies and cross		>500	>40, steep drops, small falls	A good one below every danger spot	>10 or flood	Wide (>75 feet) and deep (>3 ft.)	<45	>1 day travel by foot or water
4	Intricate maneuvering, course hard to recognize large, unavoidable	Large, irregular, avoidable or med. to cross currents	Very strong eddies, strong								
5	Course tortuous, frequent scouting	Large, irregular, unavoidable	Large scale eddies and cross currents, some up and down								
6	Very tortuous; always scout from shore	Very large (>5 ft.), irregular, unavoidable, special equipment required						Almost none			

Source: Prepared by Guidebook Committee—AWA (From "American White Water," Winter, 1957).

NOTE: RATING | APPROXIMATE DIFFICULTY

RATING	APPROXIMATE DIFFICULTY
I	Easy
II	Requires Care
III	Difficult
IV	Very Difficult
V	Exceedingly Difficult
VI	Utmost Difficulty-Near Limit of Navigability

TOTAL POINTS (from above)	APPROXIMATE SKILL REQUIRED
0-7	Practiced Beginner
8-14	Intermediate
15-21	Experienced
22-28	Highly Skilled (Several years with organized group)
29-35	Team of Experts

3. Experience. Compute the following to determine *preliminary points,* then convert the preliminary points to *final points* according to the conversion table.

Conversion Table	
Preliminary Points	Final Points
0-20	0
21-60	1
61-100	2
101-200	3
201-300	4
301-up	5

Note: This is the only evaluation item where it is possible to accrue more than 3 points.

Number of days spent each year paddling

Class I rivers	× 1	=	_____
Class II rivers	× 2	=	_____
Class III rivers	× 3	=	_____
Class IV rivers	× 4	=	_____
Class V rivers	× 5	=	_____

Preliminary   Points Subtotal   _____

Number of years paddling

experience _____ × subtotal   =

Total Preliminary Points   _____

4. Swimming
0 Points:	Cannot swim
1 Point:	Weak swimmer
2 Points:	Average swimmer
3 Points:	Strong swimmer (competition level or skin diver)

5. Stamina
0 Points:	Cannot run mile in less than 10 minutes
1 Point:	Can run a mile in 7 to 10 minutes
2 Points:	Can run a mile in less than 7 minutes

6. Upper Body Strength
0 Points:	Cannot do 15 push-ups
1 Point:	Can do 16 to 25 pushups
2 Points:	Can do more than 25 push-ups

7. Boat Control
0 Points: Can keep boat fairly straight
1 Point: Can maneuver in moving water; can avoid big obstacles
2 Points: Can maneuver in heavy water; knows how to work with the current
3 Points: Finesse in boat placement in all types of water, uses current to maximum advantage

8. Aggressiveness
0 Points: Does not play or work river at all
1 Point: Timid; plays a little on familiar streams
2 Points: Plays a lot; works most rivers hard
3 Points: Plays in heavy water with grace and confidence

9. Eddy Turns
0 Points: Has difficulty making eddy turns from moderate current
1 Point: Can made eddy turns in either direction from moderate current; can enter moderate current from eddy
2 Points: Can catch medium eddies in either direction from heavy current; can enter very swift current from eddy
3 Points: Can catch small eddies in heavy current

10. Ferrying
0 Points: Cannot ferry
1 Point: Can ferry upstream and downstream in *moderate* current
2 Points: Can ferry upstream in *heavy* current; can ferry downstream in *moderate* current
3 Points: Can ferry upstream and downstream in *heavy* current

11. Water Reading
0 Points: Often in error
1 Point: Can plan route in short rapid with several well-spaced obstacles
2 Points: Can confidently run lead in continuous Class II; can predict the effects of waves and holes on boat
3 Points: Can confidently run lead in continuous Class III; has knowledge to predict and handle the effects of reversals, side currents, and turning drops

12. Judgement
0 Points: Often in error
1 Point: Has average ability to analyze difficulty of rapids

2 Points: Has good ability to analyze difficulty of rapids and make independent judgements as to which should not be run

3 Points: Has the ability to assist fellow paddlers in evaluating the difficulty of rapids; can explain subtleties to paddlers with less experience

13. Bracing

0 Points: Has difficulty bracing in Class II rivers

1 Point: Can correctly execute bracing strokes in Class II water

2 Points: Can correctly brace in intermittent whitewater with medium waves and vertical drops of 3 ft. or less

3 Points: Can brace effectively in continuous whitewater with large waves and large vertical drops (4 ft. and up)

14. Rescue Ability

0 Points: Self-rescue in flatwater

1 Point: Self-rescue in mild whitewater

2 Points: Self-rescue in Class III; can assist others in mild whitewater

3 Points: Can assist others in heavy whitewater

15. Rolling Ability

0 Points: Can only roll in pool

1 Point: Can roll 3 out of 4 times in moving current

2 Points: Can roll 3 out of 4 times in Class II whitewater

3 Points: Can roll 4 out of 5 times in Class III and IV whitewater

Winter Canoeing

Winter canoeing can be beautiful but it also can be quite dangerous unless certain precautions are taken. Some rules that should be followed by open boaters are:

1. Canoe those streams on which you can walk to shore at any point. It is best to stay off the larger rivers and those even nearing flood stage.
2. Always have at least three canoes in the party.
3. Everyone should have a *complete* change of clothing in a waterproof container that will withstand pressures of immersion.
4. Each participant should carry on his person a supply of matches in a waterproof container.
5. Remember that the classification of any particular river is automatically upgraded when canoeing in cold weather. This is due to the extreme effects on the body upon immersion in cold water.

Cold Weather Survival

With more and more paddlers going out in cold weather to engage in their sport a basic knowledge in cold water and cold weather survival is necessary.

When immersed in water the loss of heat from the body becomes much more rapid and survival times without suitable clothing in cold water become very short. For instance, wet clothes lose about 90 percent of their insulating value, and can cause heat loss 240 times faster than dry clothing.

The following table gives the approximate survival times of humans immersed in water at various temperatures.

Water Temp. F.	Exhaustion or Unconsciousness	Survival Time
32.5	Less than 15 min.	Less than 15-45 min.
32.5-40	15-30 min.	30-90 min.
40-50	30-60 min.	1-3 hrs.
50-60	1-2 hrs.	1-6 hrs.
60-70	2-7 hrs.	2-40 hrs.
70-80	3-12 hrs.	3 hrs.-indefinite

The greatest change in survival time occurs as the water temperature drops below 50°F.

Swimming in cold water increases the flow of water past the body and pumps heat out of the clothing so that in spite of heat production the body loses heat more rapidly. If there is no prospect of getting out of the water immediately, survival time will be longer if one does not swim but relies on his life jacket to hold him up. Better still, assume the HELP position (Heat Escape Lessening Position) in which the knees are tucked close to the chest. This allows one to retain body heat longer. It is, therefore, imperative that a life jacket with adequate flotation be worn. Swim only if there is danger downstream.

In recent years a number of new materials have been developed that tend to make cold weather paddling more comfortable and certainly more safe. Materials such as polypropylene, pile, and fleece tend to wick wetness away from the body and dry very quickly. Wool has the ability to provide warmth when wet, but the newer materials do it better. Worn under a paddling jacket and pants, they can be very effective. For the decked boater who is more likely to get wet, a wet or dry suit is highly recommended. Also, a polypro or wool cap can help tremendously because a great deal of body heat is lost through an unprotected head or neck.

Dry clothing should definitely be carried in a waterproof bag on all winter trips and changed into if one gets wet. Quite often you must insist that the victim change clothing and render assistance in changing because of his lack of coordination. The victim more than likely will be totally unaware of his poor reactions.

Symptoms of exposure occur generally as follows: uncontrollable shivering; vague, slow, slurred speech; memory lapses; slowing of reactions, fumbling hands, and apparent exhaustion. Unconsciousness will follow and then death. The mental effects will be similar to those observed in states of extreme fatigue.

In cases of extreme exposure build a fire, give the victim a warm drink, if he is able to swallow; strip him and put him into a sleeping bag with another person who is also stripped. Remember that the victim must be warmed from an outside heat source since he cannot generate his own body heat. Do not give the victim any form of alcohol.

■

It is difficult to find in life any event which so effectively condenses intense nervous sensation into the shortest possible space of time as does the work of shooting, or running an immense rapid. There is no toil, no heart-breaking labour about it, but as much coolness, dexterity, and skill as man can throw into the work of hand, eye, and head; knowledge of when to strike and how to do it; knowledge of water and rock, and of the one hundred combinations which rock and water can assume . . .

Sir William Francis Butler (1872)

Legal Rights of the Canoeist

In any discussion of the legal rights of canoeists the question of navigability arises. It is generally assumed that if a stream is navigable one has the legal right to float a canoe on it. Basically this is correct in the state of North Carolina.

However, the question remains as to what constitutes "navigability" under the laws of the state. One old case defined a stream which loggers used to float their timber down to be navigable; but it is believed that this case defined a limited type of navigable purpose. The general idea seems to be that if a waterway is suitable as a "highway" of commerce it is navigable and the public has a right to use it. When a navigable stream crosses an owner's land the state owns the bottom and the owner cannot legally block use of the stream for navigation or fishing.

In a recent decision, when a land owner attempted to block a waterway, declaring it non-navigable, the California Court of Appeals determined that the test of navigability is met if the stream is capable of boating for pleasure. In making his decision the judge pointed out that the streams of California are a vital recreational resource of the state. Perhaps this case may set a precedent that will be followed in the future in determining the right of the canoeist. Although with the strong laws protecting the property rights of the individual owner in North Carolina this may never be pertinent.

When a person owns land over which a "nonnavigable" stream flows, he owns the land under the stream and has the right to control the surface of the water. For this reason when canoeing on streams of questionable navigability, it is best to observe one's manners to the fullest. If you must cross private property for any reason request the owner's permission before doing so. Generally speaking, the land owner will be a reasonable person if approached courteously and respectfully. More often than not the unreasonable property owner is one whose property rights have been abused in the past.

With the popularity of canoeing growing tremendously, travel on our streams is increasing also. Prime examples of such heavy usage can be found already on the Nantahala and the Chattooga. Be sure that you aren't the proverbial straw that breaks the camel's back by committing some careless act that might cause a landowner along a stream of questionable navigability to block access to it, or perhaps to take the next guy to court for trespass. Make sure that you leave the door open for the next guy.

Safety

A section on safety has been included because of the great interest in white water canoeing and rafting among the uninitiated. The fact is there are potential hazards involved in the sport which in many instances is the very reason many are attracted to it. However, with normal precautions and good judgement in determining one's level of skill it can be a safe sport under normal conditions.

A few tips for the paddler to follow to insure that his trip is an enjoyable one and above all a safe one, are listed. If each and every one of these rules is followed while on the river, you won't become the proverbial "accident looking for a place to happen."

1. Never boat alone. Three boats are generally considered a minimum on anything but small low water streams.

2. Always carry a life jacket. Wear it unless you are a capable swimmer and even then have it on when in water difficulit enough that there is any possibility of upset.

3. Know your ability and don't attempt water beyond this ability. In considering whether or not to run a particular rapid ask:
    a. Is it much greater in difficuilty than anything I've attempted before?
    b. If I try it and don't make it will I place others in a difficult or dangerous situation in order to rescue me or my boat?
If the answer to either one is yes, don't try it. No experienced paddler will ever accuse you of being "chicken" when you back off, but he will respect your good judgement.

4. Be adequately equipped. Have an extra paddle in the canoe, if not an extra one for each paddler. Have bow and stern lines 8-15 ft. long tied on securely to the ends of the craft.

Never tie the ends of these lines in the boat. At the same time be sure no lines are positioned so that they might entangle the canoeist's feet. The author observed a canoe swamp in Nantahala Falls which in itself was certainly not too unusual nor was it very dangerous. The paddler came in for what was a terrifying moment when he came up wearing his bailer line around his neck—with the other end still tied onto the boat. He simply had far too much line tied to his bailer.

A good standard First Aid Kit should be carried in a waterproof container, and a throw line at least 3/8 in. in size, 60-70 ft. long, preferably polypropylene, can become a necessity on all except the small shallow streams.

5. If traveling with a group, or club, know the plans of the group, the organization of the trip, and follow the decisions of the leader. Most clubs have standard trip rules established which determine the trip leader's responsibilities as well as those of each paddler individually.

One rule generally followed on the river is that each canoe is responsible for keeping the canoe following in sight. This same rule should apply when a caravan or cars are traveling to or from the put in or take out.

6. Scout unfamiliar rapids before running them. Even those that are familiar can change considerably at different water levels.

7. Stay off flooded streams. The great increase in drownings from canoeing and rafting accidents has resulted almost entirely from mishaps on swollen rivers.

8. Do not attempt to run dams or abrupt ledges. Quite often a hydraulic jump is formed in which the surface water flows back upstream, causing a rolling action. This rolling action tends to hold a boat or a person in, tumbling **them around and around. The only escape is to swim out to the end and dive toward the bottom into the downriver current.**

9. If you spill, get to the upstream end of the boat and if possible, stay with it. Don't risk the possibility of being pinned against a rock. If others spill, rescue the boaters and then go after the boat and equipment.

10. If you get broadside on a rock or other obstacle, lean toward the obstacle—downstream from the direction of the current. It is the unnatural reaction, but the correct thing to do in order to prevent the upstream gunwhale from dipping into the current and swamping the boat.

In running smaller low water streams, the possibility of personal danger is usually not as great as in large volume rivers, but there are many things to watch for that might prove dangerous if not approached with caution. Some of the most common things that the paddler needs to beware of are logs and trees blocking the passage, barb wire fences which can prove difficult to see, and low water bridges which may be just high enough to lure the unwary paddler into attempting a run under them. If in doubt when approaching the latter, pull to shore well above it and check out the clearance. The American Whitewater Affiliation has a safety code which is quite inclusive and the aspiring boater should become familiar with the aspects of it.

Explanation

Description

A brief description of the stream as a whole or of the particular section is given.

Topographic Maps

"Topo Maps" are listed in the order in which the river flows. Unless otherwise noted all maps are located on the North Carolina Index. If there is not a local source for maps they are available on order from:

Branch of Distribution
U.S. Geological Survey
Box 25286 Denver Federal Center
Denver, CO 80225

Counties

Each stream will have the county in which a particular section is located, and where it flows through more than one they will be listed in the order in which the river flows.

Put In

The exact put in is listed, such as a particular highway or secondary road bridge. Where more than one section is listed, the put in for the following section will be the take out for the preceding section.

Gradient

The total gradient of a section has been given rather than breaking it down into an average number of feet per mile. This has been done since quite often on a long stretch the gradient might be rather great in one portion and not on another. Where the drop is quite rapid it will be listed as (1@40') which indicates one mile in the section will drop at the rate of 40' within that mile.

Difficulty

This refers to the rating of difficulty of the rapids located within the particuliar section of the stream. The rating system used is based on that of the *International Scale for Grading the Difficulty of River Cruising Routes.*

International Scale for Grading the Difficulting of River Cruising Routes

Rating	River or Individual Rapids Characteristics	Approximate Minimum Experience Required
Smooth Water		
A	Pools, lakes, rivers with velocity under 2 m.p.h.	Beginner

| B | Rivers, velocity 2-4 m.p.h. | Beginner with river instructions |
| C | Rivers, velocity above 4 m.p.h., (max. back paddling speed). May have some sharp bends or obstructions. | Instructed and practiced beginner |

White Water

1	Easy—sand banks, bends without difficulty, occasional small rapids with waves regular and low. Correct course may be easy to find but care is needed with minor obstacles like pebble banks, fallen trees, etc., especially on narrow rivers. River speed less than hard back paddling speed.	Practiced beginner
2	Medium—fairly frequent but unobstructed rapids, usually with regular waves, easy eddies and easy bends. Course generally easy to recognize. River speeds occasionally exceeding hard back paddling speed.	Intermediate
3	Difficult—maneuvering in rapids necessary. Small falls, large irregular waves covering boat, numerous rapids. Main current may swing under bushes, branches, or overhangs. Course not always easily recognizable. Current speed usually less than fast forward paddling speed.	Experienced
4	Very Difficult—long extended stretches of rapids, high irregular waves with boulders directly in current. Difficult broken water, eddies and abrupt bends. Course often difficult to recognize and inspection from the bank frequently necessary. Swift current. Rough water experience indispensable.	Highly skilled (several years experience with organized group)
5	Exceedingly Difficuilt—long rocky rapids with difficult and completely irregular broken water which must be run head on. Very fast eddies, abrupt bends and vigorous cross currents. Difficult landings increase hazard. Frequent inspections necessary. Extensive experience necessary.	Team of experts
6	Limit of navigability—all previously mentioned difficulties increased to the limit. Only negotiable at favorable water levels. Cannot be attempted without risk of life.	Team of experts

It is important to know the difficulty rating of a particular river before setting out on it. The ratings used here are based on normal or ideal water heights.

The ratings will vary somewhat as the water level in the stream fluctuates.

The authors have attempted to be as objective as possible in declaring whether or not a rapid is Class 3 or Class 4. Such a judgment will vary considerably from person to person according to his skill or experience.

Where a section has only one rapid of a higher difficulty than others it is listed 2-3/4, with the final number representing the one more difficult rapid as a Class 4.

For the past several years, whitewater cruising has witnessed an ever-expanding willingness and ability, by top experts, to tackle increasingly difficult rapids. There are individual drops, as well as extended stretches, being run that were thought doable only in some abstract sense as recently as five years ago. Welcome to the hardwater boating scene of the present! Many factors have played a part in bringing the sport to this juncture. There are four areas that stand out:

(1) Equipment — Today decked boats are being built and marketed with primary design functions that aid paddlers on steep, technical descents. These boats are generally short, high-volume, and heavily rockered in the bow, with large cockpits — all helpful performance and safety features. Open boats are shorter, narrower, dryer, and more maneuverable. Many experts can roll open boats in difficult water because they are essentially outfitted as C-1s and chock-full of flotation. Drysuits and synthetic undergarments, vast improvements over wetsuits and wool, allow the paddler more comfort and freedom of movement in cold weather (when the steep stuff normally runs). Life vests with exotic safety features, while not widely seen in the the US are becoming commonplace in Europe. Skirts are dryer and more bombproof, with rubber gaskets gripping the cockpit rims. Paddles are lighter and stronger. Helmets with chin and face guards are being used by more paddlers. Hand and elbow armor will not be far behind.

(2) Experience — The experts paddling hair runs today often have an experience backlog of 10, 15, and 20 years on difficult water. Whitewater sport being the relatively recent phenomenon it is, we can look back to the 70s and find very few expert hardboaters with the experience level that so many have today. These days more informed decisions can be made on marginal runs because there is more information (prior probing) available. A certain psychological edge is developed from years of paddling difficult water. This mental toughness is a very real aid in making cool, objective decisions on the river. Instruction is more effective and efficient, allowing paddlers to get on more difficult water sooner. The Class 5 rapids of the 70s will not feed the adrenaline rat of the veteran hairhead today.

(3) Avocational boating — There are increasing numbers of paddlers who look upon the sport as more than a weekend pastime. These folks tend to put more energy, time, and effort into the sport than the weekend warrior, eschewing "real" jobs and "normal" lifestyles to pursue whitewater paddling full time. Much as surfing, rock climbing, and other sports have their devotees, these acolytes of the boating subculture are often on, or creating, the "edge" of the sport.

(4) Unspoken competition — Finally, there is a good deal of unspoken competition at this level of paddling. While this is not new to the sport, it has certainly had an effect on it. This one-upmanship, if you will, has a much larger ante today than ten years ago.

For years the terms "hard" and "easy" have been used as adjuncts in describing whitewater difficulty. We've all heard "easy Class 5" or "hard Class 4" used as a means of further delineating differences between rapids. Largely as a result of the more extreme water being paddled nowadays, rapids graded at the Class 4 and 5 level have by far a broader range of difficulty, within and between them, than the other classes. The much more difficult Class 5 water of today is put in the same category as rapids that were considered extreme 10 years ago. Sometimes this results in shoving the "old" Class 5 rapid down into a lesser category. More often, rapids with large difficulty differences are placed in the same category. With the current ICF scale, this "crowding" is inevitable, and it can be very confusing. There is a need for further, and more precise, delineation in classifying rapids at the Class 4 and 5 level. The old "measuring stick" needs a new coat of paint, one that shows the inch, as well as the foot, markers.

The mechanics of such a scale are relatively simple. It has been suggested to expand the ICF 1-6 scale by adding Class 7, Class 8, etc. — similar to what was done on many western rivers years ago. This seems too radical a departure because almost everything would have to be re-rated. A simpler method would be to add gradations within the Class 4 and 5 levels of difficulty. There is some precedent here. Rock climbing has seen an explosion of increasingly difficult moves and routes. Climbers have answered this by steadily upgrading the scale of difficulty to correspond to the more gymnastic or aid-requiring moves that are becoming the new standards. Why not follow the rock climbing lead?

What we've done with the rating system in the book is to break Class 4 and 5 rapids down into three sub-classes. Starting with Class 4 and moving into Class 5 in order of increasing difficulty, the scale reads: 4, 4.1, 4.2, 5, 5.1, and 5.2. Three sub-classes within each class, at this time, seems to satisfy the variance of difficulty of the rapids.

We understand the subjectivity involved in rating whtewater, with one man's Class 3 being another man's Class 5. However, we have tried to maintain as objective a stance as possible in rating the rivers contained in this book against each other. The reader can be reasonably certain, by the ratings reflection, that Linville Gorge is a tougher run than the Broad River Gorge, and Watauga Gorge is a stiffer paddle, on the whole, than the North Fork of the French Broad (but the North Fork has one rapid tougher than anything in the Watauga Gorge).

The current ICF system does not allow for such delineation and doesn't give the reader as much information as this revamped scale does. This is certainly not an ideal solution, but hopefully a step in the right direction. For instance, we have not attempted to define a Class 5.2 rapid, but will rely on the ICF definition of a Class 5 rapid and only suggest that a 5.2 drop is at the extreme end of what is considered Class 5. We have not broken down Class 1, 2, 3, or 6 rapids. We feel there isn't much variation of difficulty within Class 1, 2, or 3 rapids. What most experts consider Class 6 is run so infrequently that there is too little basis to make valid comparisons or quality differences between them. We welcome any dialogue or criticism toward realizing a more informative and realistic scale of difficulty in today's brave, new whitewater world.

Distance
Measured in miles from county and U.S.G.S. maps and generally rounded off.

Time
This is actual paddling time on the river including time for scouting when necessary. When paddling with a group larger than 2 or 3 canoes and when a lunch stop will be made additional time should be planned for.

Scenery
AA Unusually beautiful even to the spectacular, generally remote and wild.

A Generally remote and wild. Perhaps some signs of civilization but mostly uninhabited.

B More pastoral type of country with more settled areas.

C Fair amount of development, general signs of civilization such as garbage dumps, autos left on the side of the stream, visual pollution.

Water Quality

Excellent	Where water shed is protected and water generally remains "clear as crystal."
Good	Where some small amount of sediment appears but on the whole the water would be considered clean.
Fair	Heavier sediment in stream but no evident pollution.
Poor	Signs of human or industrial pollution to the extent water is actually discolored.

Gage

Where there is a U.S.G.S. gage located close enough to the put in or take out on a particular section, readings have been taken from it. Wherever possible a minimum level for solo paddling has been extablished. Generally a reading of .20 or two tenths of a foot above that listed for solo would be enough for tandem paddling. (Example: 1.54 minimum solo level; 1.74 for tandem).

On streams where a high level can be extremely dangerous a maximum reading is given whenever one has been established.

Where no U.S.G.S. gage is available gages have been painted, usually on a bridge, at a put in or take out. Generally a level of 6" below "0" can be considered a minimum for solo paddling.

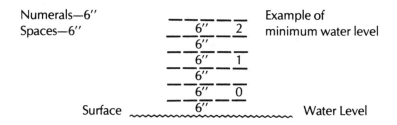

Numerals—6"		Example of
Spaces—6"		minimum water level

Gage Illustration

Whenever information can be obtained by phone, such as dam controlled streams and those entering into the Tennessee Valley, a telephone number has been given which can be called.

A recorded message giving stream flow in the Valley can be obtained by calling 615-632-6065 between the hours of 8:30 AM and 4:30 PM (Eastern Time) Monday through Friday.

Difficulties

A brief description of specific points that might present problems for the paddler are listed, hopefully in enough detail to recognize them, but not so much as to take away the thrill of running a new river.

Directions

Detailed directions have been given to find the put in and the take out. Where there are several sections of a particuliar stream included only the put in on the first section and the take out on the last section are described. It is assumed that one who intends paddling a good bit of a river will obtain county road maps. These maps are available from the local county office of the State Highway Engineer or from:

Head of Location and Survey Unit
N.C. Department of Transportation
Division of Highways
P.O. Box 25201
Raleigh, N.C. 27611

Where a river flows through several counties reference will be made to a county route by name and number (Burke Co. Rt. 1100) initially. Thereafter only route number will be referred to until another road in the next county is introduced.

The author will appreciate any pertinent comments, corrections or suggestions which might prove valuable in any future editions.

■

Once there was a legend that told of a river that went to hear a fountain sing. The song was so beautiful that the river decided to sing it to the ocean. All the way to the shores of the ocean the river sang. Soon, the mountains heard of the song that the river was singing and came from all over the land to listen. And because the song was so beautiful the mountains settled down and stayed to listen forever. *Algonquin Indian Legend*

Part 2
Section 1

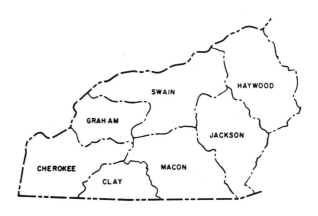

Alarka Creek

Alarka Creek

Alarka Creek heads up in Nantahala National Forest on the slopes of the Alarka Mountains. It is a small fast stream flowing over ledges under low hanging branches. It might carry through a backyard and seconds later through inpenetrable laurel thickets that completely enclose the paddler.

On one trip a Copperhead dropped into the bow of a canoe passing downstream so the heavy foliage bears watching also. This is the only such instance the author has observed or heard of so don't let it discourage what can be a most delightful trip.

Topo Maps   Alarka, Bryson City

County   Swain

(1)   Rt. 1140 bridge to old Rt. 1309 bridge

Drop	Difficulty	Distance	Time	Scenery	Water Quality
200'	2-3	4.5 mi.	2 hrs.	A-B-C	Good

Gage   U.S.G.S. below 1307 bridge (.8 mi. below take out). Minimum for solo run is a reading of 2.50. Can be run in later winter, spring and early summer except after an unusually dry spring.

Difficulties   The narrow passages and low overhanging branches can present problems. There are two ledges that should be scouted. They are easily recognized. As with all small streams of this nature, watch for strainers. For those into running waterfalls, there are two located in the next three or so miles to the backwaters of Lake Fontana. The first, a 12-footer, is about 200 yds. below the recommended take out. The banks are extremely steep making it very difficult to carry. At a level approaching 3.0, one may well be committed to run it without the option of scouting. If so, enter left of center moving to the right immediately, then stay right. The fall is located at the rear of a private home, so do not trespass to scout. J. Johnson Falls, an 8-footer, is 1.5 mi. below 1307 bridge. It can be scouted on river left.

Directions   **Put In**—Rt. 1140 southeast off U.S. 19 west of Bryson City to the first bridge crossing the creek west of the community of Alarka.
Take Out—Rt. 1309 northwest off U.S. 19 (.1 mi. west of Rt. 1140) to old Rt. 1309 bridge (immediately below the new 1309 bridge).

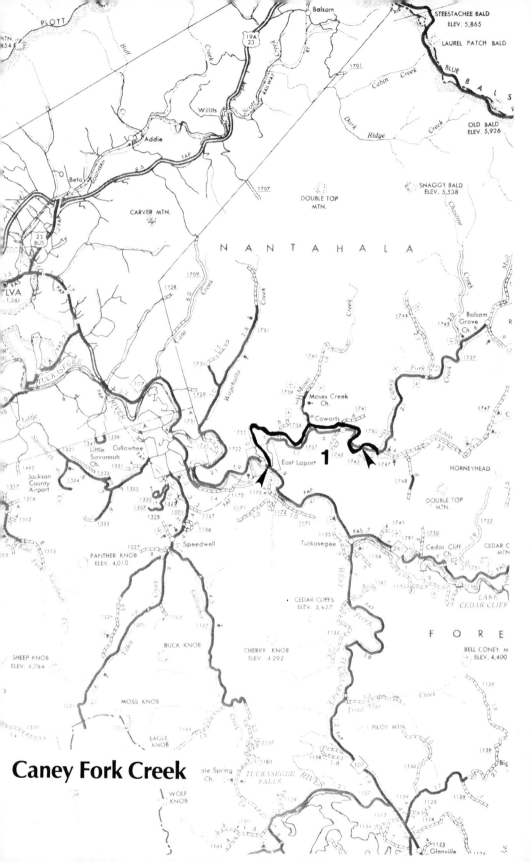

Caney Fork Creek

Caney Fork Creek

The Caney Fork has its headwaters in Nantahala National Forest and is joined by many smaller rivulets as it cuts between Coward Mountain to the north and Shelton and Rich Mountains to the south and southeast. It drops over many ledges before confluencing with the Tuckaseigee River at the community of East Laport.

One may want to take a short side trip here to Judaculla Rock just north of the creek. The Rock has elaborate Indian hieroglyphics which to this time have not been interpreted. Simply follow the signs from N.C. 107.

Topo Maps   Tuckasegee, Sylva South

County   Jackson

(1)   Jackson County Rt. 1737 bridge (second bridge above N.C. 107) to 107 bridge

Drop	Difficulty	Distance	Time	Scenery	Water Quality
145'	2	4.5 mi.	2 hrs.	A-B	Good
.8 mi. @ 50'/mi.					

Gage   U.S.G.S. located alongside Rt. 1737 approximately 2.1 mi. above the put in. Minimum for solo is 3.10. Generally runnable December through the middle of May and following rains.

Difficulties   There is a cable just below the second bridge which can present problems at higher water levels. At normal levels one can easily pass under it. Also, there are a couple of ledges that drop off gradually which could present stoppers at just slightly higher water levels. This in effect would increase the run to good Class 2-3. Beware of strainers.

Directions   Put In—North on Rt. 1737 off N.C. 107 at the community of East Laport.
Take Out—N.C. 107 bridge at East Laport or East Laport River access at mouth of creek.

This run can be extended 2.1 mi. with a reading of 3.20 on the gage. Put in at the gaging station.

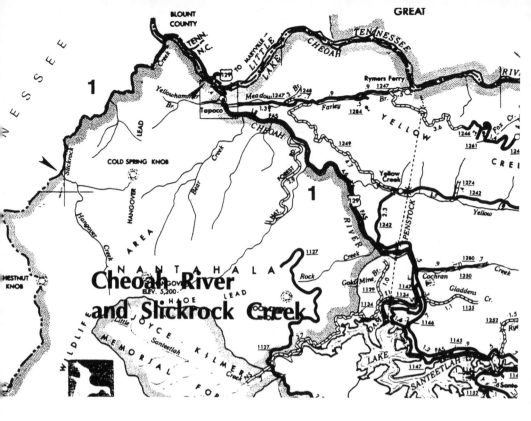

Cheoah River

The Cheoah River is a normally dry stream bed which runs from Santeetlah Dam to the Little Tennessee River. It enters the Little Tennessee within spitting distance of the Cheoah Dam. TVA pipes water from Santeetlah Lake into the Little Tennessee/Lake Cheoah inundation for the obvious reasons, leaving the resultant dry stream bed. The Cheoah below Santeetlah Lake is just west of the Cheoah Mountains in southwestern North Carolina. The river runs only after extended rainfall. If the lake is spilling over the dam there may be more water on the last two mi. than most paddlers want. Most of the run can be seen from N.C. 129 north of Robbinsville.

Topo Maps   Tapoco, NC-TN, Fontana Dam

County   Graham

(1)   Santeetlah Dam to N.C. 129 bridge (just below Cheoah Dam)

Drop	Difficulty	Distance	Time	Scenery	Water Quality
640'	3-4-4.2	9.2 mi.	4.5 hrs.	A	Good

Gage   None. Runnable only after heavy, extended rainfall.

Difficulty   The first seven mi. of this run are primarily Class 2-3. The water here is flowing over small to moderate boulder fields and through shrubs and small trees, as the river bed is normally dry. There is one four-ft. ledge just downstream of the overhead pipe carrying water to Lake Cheoah. The more enjoyable run for advanced boaters is to put in three mi. above the take out. This section picks up volume (due to several creeks entering) and gradient quickly. The action here is more continuous, with only a few flat stretches. The boulders are larger and the view is often blocked. At moderate levels everything can be boat-scouted with the exception of one 10-ft. drop, best run on the far right. The last two mi. drop at a rate of 100 ft. per mi. At higher levels (water spilling over the dam) the extra push would make for some grade 5 drops.

Directions   **Put In**—There are any number of places to put in on this run, as N.C. 129 follows the river for most of its length. For those wanting to do the entire run, take N.C. 129 north of Robbinsville to the Cheoah Point Recreation Area and scramble down to the base of the dam.

        Take Out—Follow N.C. 129 north of Robbinsville to bridge over the Little Tennessee River (just downstream of the Cheoah Dam).

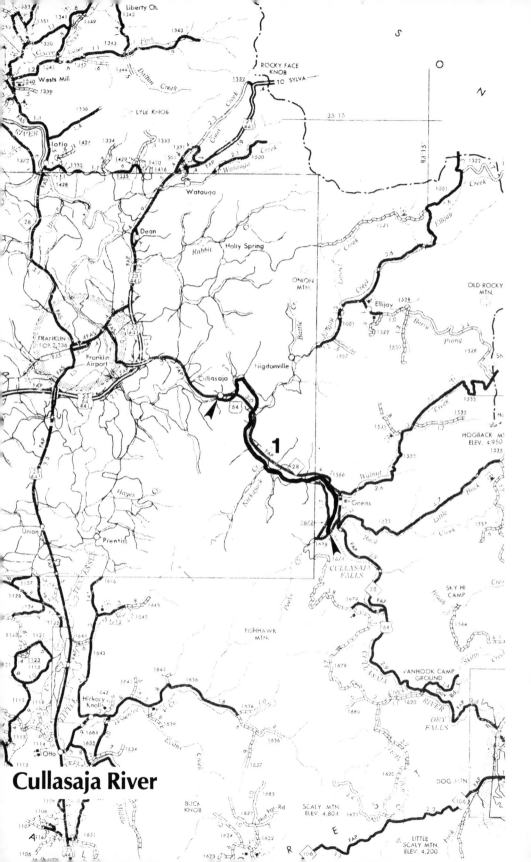

Cullasaja River

Cullasaja River

The Cullasaja rises in the Nantahala National Forest and drops over many falls and cascades before slowing down and entering the Little Tennessee. Three of the better known falls are Bridal Veil, Dry Falls and Cullasaja. The latter drops some 400 spectacular feet to a point about .5 mi. above the put in. U.S. 64 follows alongside the river throughout most of this area and is well worth a drive up through the gorge toward the resort village of Highlands.

Topo Maps   Scaley Mountain, Corbin Knob

County   Macon

(1)   Rt. 1678 bridge to Rt. 1668

Drop	Difficulty	Distance	Time	Scenery	Water Quality
120'	2-3	5.3 mi.	2.5 hrs.	B-C	Excellent to Good

Gage   U.S.G.S. on Rt. 1524 (Sugar Fork Rd.) about 40 yds. above U.S. 64 on the east bank. Minimum for solo is a reading of 2.30.

Difficulties   A fairly steep cut through a rock garden, about 150 yds. down from the put in, which is followed by a series of ledges. At higher water levels it would be best to scout this stretch.

Directions   **Put In**—Rt. 1678 (Peeks Creek Rd.) south off U.S. 64 to bridge. **Take Out**—Rt. 1668 west off U.S. 64 (just south of 64 bridge) .4 mi. to Rt. 1698.

Deep Creek

Deep Creek has its headwaters below Indian Gap (elevation 5,286') and flows through the valley between Noland Divide and Thomas Divide, which rise above it. The watershed is completely within Great Smoky Mountains National Park, thus providing it with excellent water quality. Deep Creek continues as a small, fast-moving stream with a steady gradient until just before joining the Tuckaseigee River, when it flattens out somewhat.

Tubing is one of the main forms of recreation for campers—young and old—at Deep Creek Campground, as well as for the local populace. The run is short but delightful for the experienced open boater.

Topo Map Bryson City

County Swain

(1) Government road on west side of creek at gate above campground to Rt. 1340 bridge

Drop	Difficulty	Distance	Time	Scenery	Water Quality
66'	2	2 mi.	1 hr.	A-B	Excellent

Gage Northwest corner of Rt. 1340 bridge. 5'' below "0" is minimum for solo paddling. With a reading of 3'' below "0" put in .5 mi. farther upstream, above the next bridge, for a run through a small but beautiful gorge. It can be run all year except after long dry spells.

Difficulties Many, but none that are dangerous. At low water this requires the utmost in skill to read the small passages, to push, pull, lean and anything else to squeeze through. This is definitely not a trip for the heavy water lover. One should be on the alert for tubers during the summer.

Directions **Put In**—Follow signs out of Bryson City to Deep Creek Campground (Rt. 1337). Continue on west side of creek to gate and put in. If gate is open proceed to first or second bridge, depending on the water level. If putting in at the second bridge, cross it and put in above 50 yds. above it. This bridge crosses Indian Creek. Deep Creek is on your left after crossing the bridge. The 1/2 mi. through the gorge drops at the rate of 50' per mi.

Take Out—Cross bridge entering into the main entrance of the campground from Rt. 1337 and turn right on Rt. 1339. Proceed approximately 2 mi. to Rt. 1340 and the take out. Ask permission at the residence behind the Baptist Church before taking out on the west bank.

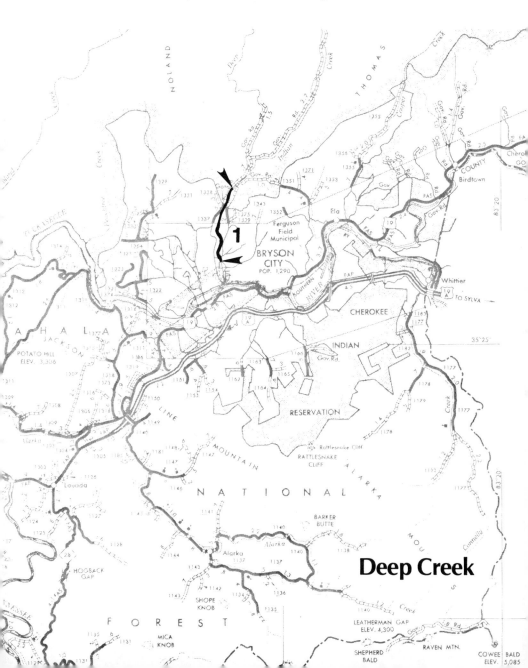

Deep Creek

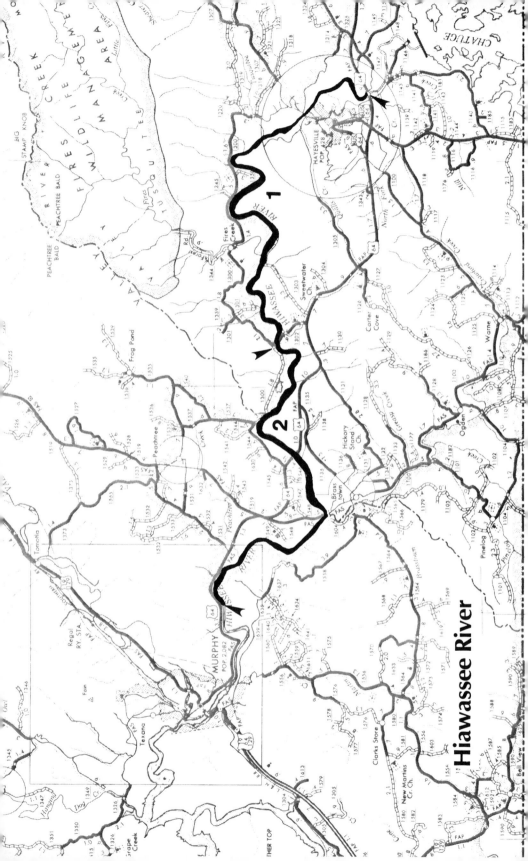

Hiawassee River

Hiawassee River

The Hiawassee heads up in the vicinity of Unicoi Gap in the Chattahoochee National Forest in north Georgia and runs north until the impoundment at Lake Chatuge, where it enters North Carolina. It flows generally west to the backwaters of Hiawassee Lake west of Murphy.

Topo Maps   Hayesville, Peachtree

County   Clay and Cherokee (both North Carolina)

(1)   U.S. 64 in Hayesville to Clay Co. Rt. 1302 bridge

Drop	Difficulty	Distance	Time	Scenery	Water Quality
128′	1-2	11 mi.	2.5 hrs.	A-B	Good

Gage   None. The T.V.A. Plant at Lake Chatuge is generally in operation throughout the week and under certain conditions runs on weekends. This can easily be recognizable if there are no mud flats along the river. The operation schedule is not known until after 8 p.m. the night before. Call (704) 644-5121 after that time to check for the following day.

The paddling times given on both sections are estimates for when power is being generated. When it is not add at least 2.5 hrs. to (1) and 1.5 hrs. to (2).

Difficulties   There is some fairly heavy water at shoals about .5 mi. below the mouth of Fires Creek. This spot can swamp the unwary paddler quite easily. At lower levels there are many rock and boulder gardens throughout the stretch.

(2)   Clay Co. Rt. 1302 (Shallowford) bridge to U.S. 64 west of Peachtree

Drop	Difficulty	Distance	Time	Scenery	Water Quality
137′	1-2	9.5 mi.	3 hrs.	A-B	Good

Gage   See Section (1)

Difficulties   Mission Dam, located about 1.5 mi. below the put in, should be
approached cautiously. There is a log boom below sand flats
on the right, which can be crossed to a fairly easy take out. Portage about 75
yds. down the old road to a well-worn path, and then another 50 yds. below
the fence, to a short path to the race. The dam, operated by Alcoa, only runs
when power is being generated at Lake Chatuge.

The shoals below the dam can best be scouted at this time.

Directions   **Put In**—U.S. 64 bridge in Hayesville.
Take Out—Alongside U.S. 64 2 mi. west of the American Enka
Plant at Peachtree in Cherokee County.

The trip can be extended 2 mi. by taking Rt. 1140 (west of the U.S. 64 bridge)
south to Rt. 1146 and putting in on the Barnard Bridge, below the dam.

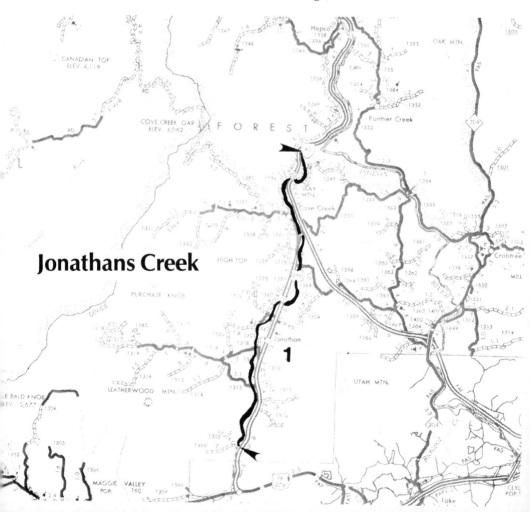

Jonathans Creek

Jonathans Creek

Jonathans Creek heads up at Black Camp Gap (elevation 4,522') just off the Heintooga Overlook Road from the Blue Ridge Parkway at Soco Gap. It plunges down through Maggie Valley before turning north along U.S. 276 and joining the Pigeon below I-40. It is primarily a fast run over gravel bars through farm lands above Cove Creek. Below, it changes to more of a ledge type stream cutting a small gorge as it rushes to the Pigeon.

This is a good trout stream so the paddler should be as considerate of the trout fishermen encountered along the way as possible.

Topo Map   Dellwood

County   Haywood

(1)   Haywood Co. Rt. 1394 bridge to the end of Rt. 1338 just above the confluence with the Pigeon

Drop	Difficulty	Distance	Time	Scenery	Water Quality
355'	2-3	8.8 mi.	4 hrs.	A-B-C	Good to fair

Gage   U.S.G.S. located on Rt. 1338 approximately .5 mi. above the confluence with the Pigeon. Minimum reading for solo is 1.50.

Difficulties   About 1 mi. below the put in there is a chute on the right blocked off by an overhanging tree limb. This is recognizable by a small channel running to the left toward a large silo. This can be carried or lined easily on the small island there.

In the area down from the 276 bridge there is a ledge which presents a fair sized hydraulic at levels above 2.00. This is about .25 mi. below a broken foot bridge and at higher levels should be scouted. Approximately .4 mi. below the I-40 bridge there is a series of ledges where a drop of about 15' occurs within some 100 yds. There is an old automobile in the creek, which marks the beginning of this run. The entire stretch can be easily scouted on the left bank.

Directions   **Put In**—North on U.S. 276 off U.S. 19 at Dellwood for approximately .5 mi., to the Rt. 1394 bridge on the left. The creek runs beside 276 at this point.

    Take Out—North on U.S. 276 to the second bridge across the creek (south of I-40). Go left along the south side of the creek and cross the Rt. 1338 bridge across Cove Creek. Follow Rt. 1338 along Jonathans Creek to its end, and take out about 100 yds. above the old house at the end of the road.

Note: At a water level of 2.50 on the gage a run of about 3 mi., from the Rt. 1306 bridge (off U.S. 19) to the second bridge of Rt. 1307 can be made. However, about .25 mi. of posted property is just downstream from this take out so a run on down to the put in point on Rt. 1394 might present problems. This 3 mi. stretch is quite fast and narrow with a gradient averaging almost 75′ per mi.

■

I am glad I shall never be young without wild country to be young in. Of what avail are forty freedoms without a blank spot on the map?

Aldo Leopold

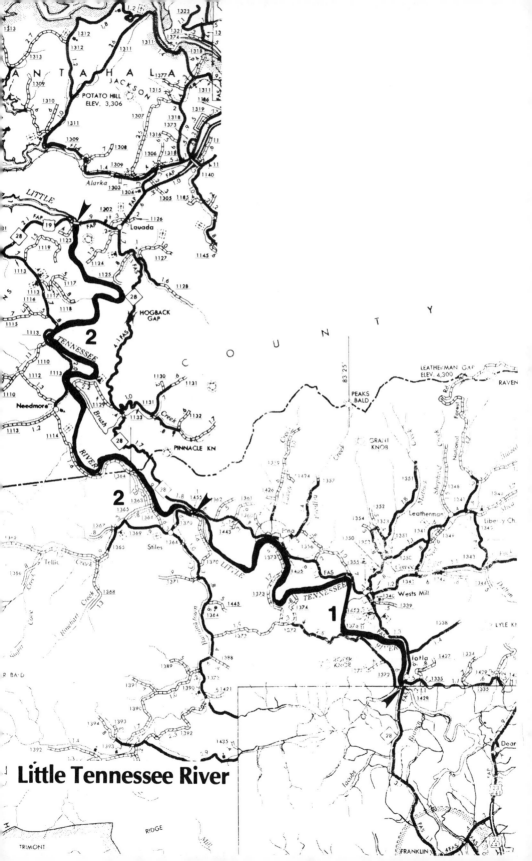

Little Tennessee River

Little Tennessee River

The Little Tennessee first appears to the traveler on U.S. 23-441 south of Franklin as a small creek. One will wonder how such a small stream can grow to a full size river between there and Iotla. It flows generally north between the Nantahala Mountain Range on the west and the Cowee Range to the east before reaching the impoundment at Fontana.

The riverside alternates between farmlands and woodlands in section 1, while below Lost Bridge it becomes heavily forested, except where Rt. 1114 hits it occasionally. The area near Franklin and around much of Macon Co. is widely known for its great mineral deposits and is certainly a rock hound's heaven.

The "Little T" is one of the few rivers in North Carolina that lend themselves to overnight canoe camping. Generally speaking there is enough water to carry gear and at the same time the rapids aren't so formidable that the paddler is likely to finish the day with it wet. Unfortunately there aren't many streams remaining that can claim both these qualities. The good ones have either been "dammed" leaving nothing but flat water, are too shallow to carry the necessary equipment, or are too rough to maneuver through rapids with the extra weight in the boat.

Topo Maps Franklin, Alarka, Wesser

Counties Macon and Swain

(1) N.C. 28 bridge at Iotla to Lost Bridge

Drop	Difficulty	Distance	Time	Scenery	Water Quality
50'	1-2	10 mi.	4.5 hrs.	A-B	Good

Gage U.S.G.S. gage on left bank .8 mi. north of Needmore and approximately 6.8 mi. below Lost Bridge Road bridge. The "Little T" is very seldom too low to run. Only following extreme dry periods would it be so low.

Difficulties None. The first several miles are flat with an occasional riffle. There are a few shallow ledges in the latter part of the section.

(2)   Lost Bridge, off N.C. 28, to U.S. 19 bridge

Drop	Difficulty	Distance	Time	Scenery	Water Quality
182'	2-3	13 mi.	4.5 hrs.	A	Good

Gage   See section (1). The lower section can become dangerous with high water levels when Lake Fontana is low. To check on the streamflow call (615) 632-6065. Minimum reading is about 350 c.f.s., while the maximum will be approximately 2000 c.f.s.

Difficulties   There are several ledges which should be approached cautiously in higher levels.

When Fontana is quite low there is a series of ledges which run for close to 250 yds. At the end of this rapid the entire river, which previously has been up to 300 ft. wide, narrows down to rush through an area no wider than 20 ft. Before Fontana Dam innundated the river, this part was known as "The Narrows."

"The Narrows" should definitely be scouted before attempting to run. In higher waters the entire rapid can be quite formidable and should be scouted. The standing wave created at the bottom of "The Narrows" is as high as 5 ft. at higher levels. At lower levels scout on the left; at higher levels, scout on the right.

The water level of Lake Fontana is generally lowered during the winter in preparation for the spring rains.

Directions   **Put In**—N.C. 28 bridge at Iotla, about 4 mi. north of Franklin.

Take Out—U.S. 19-N.C. 28 bridge southwest of Bryson City.

Paddle beyond the bridge to the right bank, to a small "goat path" which cuts back up under the bridge. This isn't recommended for potential coronary victims. Even if one doesn't fall into this class, there may be some question before reaching the top when the lake is low.

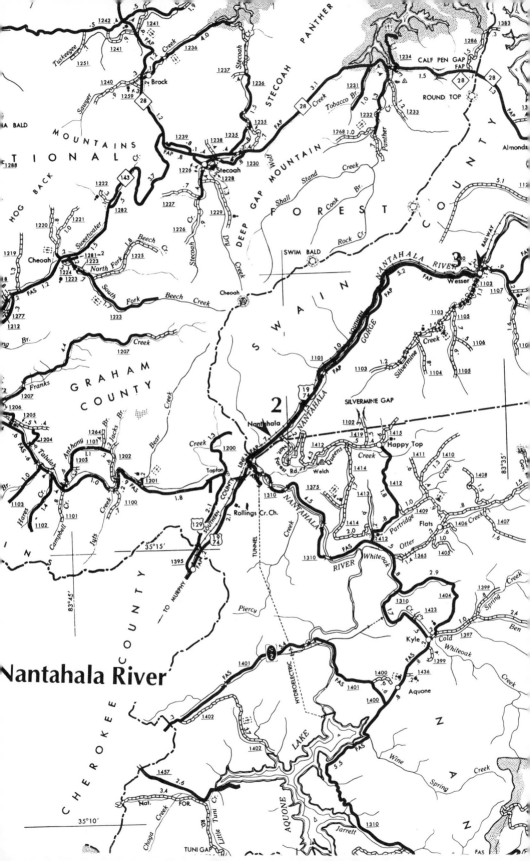

Nantahala River

Nantahala River

The Nantahala heads up in the edge of Nantahala National Forest before entering Nantahala Lake, reportedly the highest lake in North Carolina. From there some water is piped down the mountain to the power plant .25 mi. above the section (3) put in. Sections (1) and (2) only run after heavy, extended rainfall, which results in dam spill-over from Nantahala Lake and heavy feeder stream influence up high. The piped water meets the natural flow just above section (3), one of the most popular whitewater runs in the country. The water temperature on this stretch is generally 45 degrees due to the diverted water being pulled from the bottom of the lake. While section (1) is recommended only for experts, section (2) is challenging for high intermediate/advanced boaters. Section (3) is suitable for intermediate level paddlers and ends just above Class 5 Wesser Falls. Below is Lake Fontana. Nantahala, meaning "land-of-the-noon-day-sun," was the name given by the Cherokee Indians because the deep gorge shuts out the sun for most of each day.

The cold water can create an unusual phenomenon on a very warm day. A fog rises about 3 ft. above the water, sometimes cutting visibility down to a few feet. There is continuous whitewater from Patton's Pool to the take out, below Nantahala Falls. A bailer—make that a big bailer—is a necessity for the canoeist running the Nantahala.

Nantahala Outdoor Center, located at Wesser below Nantahala Falls, is operated by Payson and Aurelia Kennedy. They conduct paddling clinics and raft trips down the river beginning in the spring and continuing on into the fall. This is an excellent way for the uninitiated to try the river for the first time. N.O.C. also has restaurants, stores, and motel accommodations. For those who wish to camp, Lost Mine Campground, which is privately owned, is located on S.R. 1103 only one mi. from Wesser.

Top Maps   Topton, Hewitt, Wesser

Counties   Macon, Swain

(1) S.R. 1310 (gravel rd. turnout 4.2 mi. above Forest Service put in) to first bridge downstream on S.R. 1310.

Drop	Difficulty	Distance	Time	Scenery	Water Quality
210'	4-5/5.1	1 mi.	1.5 hrs.	A	Excellent

Gage   U.S.G.S. gage located just upstream of Ferebee Park on Section (3) should read 4.2 for a minimum level. This assumes a normal release of 3.2 ft. from the power plant. See gage for section (3).

Difficulties   This section, known to the local boaters as the Cascades, is user-friendly only for confident experts. Though not in the top echelon of hard water runs, this 1 mi. stretch will test anyone's skills. After a brief .3 mi. warm-up, you come to the first Class 5 rapid. First Falls is a two-stage drop of 16 ft. The upper drop has one obvious slot while the second ledge has a bit more margin for error. Shortly downstream is the largest, most difficult rapid on this run. Big Kahunah has a total drop of 22 ft. The line is down the right, blasting off the nine-ft. ledge to finish. Almost immediately downstream is Chinese Feet, the last major rapid. Chinese Feet (the name has to be blotter influenced) is best run by hammering into the eddy on the left at the top and then running the eight-ft. slot to the left of the boulder that splits the river. From here to the bridge, there is lots of interesting, though less significant, whitewater. The run can only be done after extended rainfall and generally has a window of two days at best. The road parallels the river on this section allowing for easy scouting, portaging, and aborted trips.

Directions   **Put in**—U.S. 19 south of Wesser to S.R. 1310. Take left onto S.R. 1310 and go 4.2 mi. to small dirt road on right where you can park.
Take out—Take out at the first bridge downstream

(2)   S.R. 1310 bridge to Forest Service put in for standard [section (3)] run.

Drop	Difficulty	Distance	Time	Scenery	Water Quality
320'	3	3.2 mi.	2.5 hrs.	A	Excellent

Gage   See section (1)

Difficulties   This section is solid, continuous, boat-scoutable Class 3 water. There are no major difficulties for the boater who can handle those conditions. The road, as on section (1), follows the river pretty closely.

Directions   **Put in**—see takeout for section (1).
Take out—Forest Service access area [put in for standard run on Section (3)] at intersection of S.R. 1310 and U.S. 19.

(3) Power Plant to Wesser

Drop	Difficulty	Distance	Time	Scenery	Water Quality
265'	1-2/3	8 mi.	2.5 hr.	A-B	Excellent

Gage   Section (3) can be run only when the power plant is operating, which is generally the case during the week and more often than not on weekends. Phone 704-321-4504 or N.O.C. 704-488-2175 to determine whether or not the plant is in operation (also refer to section titled "Explanation").

Difficulties   Below the put in at the forks, Patton's Run begins. It is a long Class 3, requiring the paddler to stay to the inside of the bend. This is heavy fast water. It, as well as most of the river, can be scouted from U.S. 19, which follows the river very closely throughout the run. Scout this one from the pull off on the highway, before launching.

Patton's Pool and Run were dedicated to Charlie Patton of Brevard, N.C., an avid paddler of the Nantahala despite the fact that he had practically no use of one arm. He passed on later in the day following a trip down his beloved river.

The river continues along its fast course with little letup for the next 7.5 mi.

Nantahala Falls, which is about 400 yds. above Nantahala Outdoor Center, is a Class 3, which at higher levels easily becomes a Class 4. There is a short quiet pool above it where one can pull over easily—either to scout the falls or to pull out. It is a small section of flat land on the right with a well marked path. The entrance and approach to the falls is rather difficult and can put a lot of water in the boat before one hits the falls. Be sure to empty the boat before attempting to run. The entrance is generally where the novice or low intermediate skilled paddler gets in trouble, only to be finished off in the falls.

The falls consist of two ledges. The top one doesn't extend all the way across the river, and the passage is just on the left end of it. The paddler then must cut hard back to the right to catch the tongue on the lower drop. With higher water the upper ledge can be run straight through on the right, therefore lining up for the tongue below. This is about 3 ft. off the large boulder on the right.

In the event one swamps or dumps in the falls, get control of the craft immediately. Wesser Falls, which is .25 mi. downstream, will only spew out little pieces.

Directions   **Put In**—North on U.S. 19 from Wesser and N.O.C. to Macon Co. Rt. 1310 on the left and left into NFS access area.
Take Out—Along U.S. 19 just above NOC store.

Oconaluftee River

The Oconaluftee heads up between Indian Gap (elevation 5,286') and Newfound Gap (elevation 5,048') and generally flows beside U.S. 441 through the Great Smoky Mountains National Park, until it confluences with the Tuckaseigee River east of Bryson City. The run above Cherokee is one through many rock gardens in crystal clear water. Below Cherokee the water quality diminishes considerably due to sewage being dumped in. A distinct odor may be noticeable below the 441 bridge, but it doesn't continue for long.

The river enters the Cherokee Indian Reservation .5 mi. below its confluence with the Raven's Fork River, and from this point to the take out is designated as "Enterprise Waters." This stretch can be paddled only on Tuesdays during trout season, when the river is being stocked (first Saturday in April to the last of October).

The approximately 4.5 mi. stretch above the reservation boundary can be paddled at any time. In order to do so one should check in at the ranger station at Park Headquarters, which is located at Pioneer Structures on U.S. 441 north of Cherokee, to inform them of plans to canoe the river. This might save one from being "pulled" off the river by park rangers. This actually happened to Ed Gertler several years ago. It could not only prove embarrassing, but could also lead to a rather long hike.

Topo Maps   Smokemont, Whittier

County   Swain

(1)   Smokemont Campground to Birdtown

Drop	Difficulty	Distance	Time	Scenery	Water Quality
308'	2-3	11.5 mi.	4.5 hrs.	A-B-C	Excellent to Poor

Gage   U.S.G.S. gage is on the south bank 200 ft. upstream from the Rt. 1359 bridge below Birdtown. Minimum for solo run is 1.70. It can be run at 1.32 from Ravensford Bridge (above Pioneer Structures), which cuts about 4. mi. off the total trip. A gage directly across on the opposite bank (along U.S. 19) will read approximately .05 lower than the opposite gage, so estimate accordingly.

Difficulties   There are many tight runs over ledges and through gravel bars that require fast thinking and faster maneuvering.

After entering Cherokee, there are the remains of an old washed-out dam along 441. Iron rods protrude from some of the rocks and it is best to run on the far right directly behind the trailer. This is located about 80 yds. above the Cherokee Information Station and picnic area.

For anyone wishing to extend the trip into the Tuckaseigee, or on to Bryson City, there is a 30 ft. dam 3 mi. below Birdtown. It can be portaged on the right.

Directions   **Put In**—U.S. 441 north of Cherokee, towards Gatlinburg, Tenn. to the entrance to Smokemont Campground; cross bridge.
Take Out—U.S. 19 west of Cherokee to Birdtown; cross the Rt. 1359 bridge (at Cherokee Recreation Park Campground sign), to the gage.

Note: Trout season on the reservation is year-round except for the three weeks preceeding the opening of the state-wide season on the first Saturday in April.

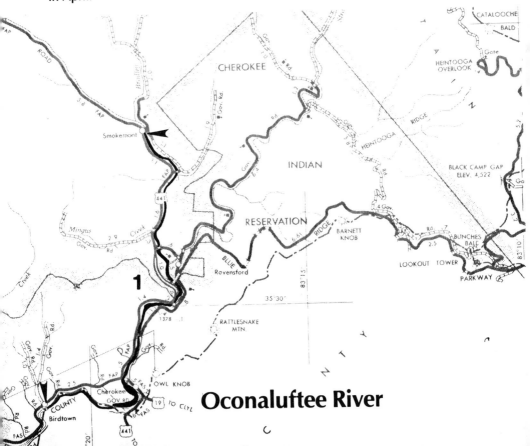

Oconaluftee River

Pigeon River

The Pigeon meanders through farm land above Canton. In Canton it is polluted by the Champion International Plant. Champion, by far the largest employer in Haywood County, has been allowed to dump poorly treated waste products in the area's main waterway for decades. Some progress has been made in cleaning up the water over the past few years, but only after the state of Tennessee brought suit against Champion. The water remains the color of coffee (no cream, please) with a few suds on the sides. As a result of the suit, the plant threatened to close and employees were up-in-arms at the possibility of losing jobs. For a while it was not healthy to be in the area with a canoe on your vehicle because that seemed to equate with the enemy in the minds of many. Here is a prime example of economics taking precedent over any environmental considerations.

Several miles below Canton the river flows through a deep gorge with I-40 running along high above it. The "Dry Gorge" between Waterville Lake and the Walters Plant is just that, except in periods of extremely high water. The distance is approximately 13 mi.

The river below Walters Plant becomes a natural slalom run through a rock-strewn course. This could be made into one of the finest slalom courses in the East except for the amount of pollution.

Topo Maps   Waynesville, Cruso, Canton, Clyde, Fines Creek; Waterville, Hartford, and Newport (Tenn.)

Counties   Haywood (N.C.); Cocke (Tenn.)

(1)   Confluence of East and West Forks of the Pigeon to U.S. 19-23 bridge

Drop	Difficulty	Distance	Time	Scenery	Water Quality
58'	1-2	5 mi.	2 hrs.	B	Fair

Gage   On west side of N.C. 110 bridge at the put in. Minimum for solo 6" below "0." The river can be run from here down most of the year, except during long dry spells.

Difficulties   None.

(2)   U.S. 19-23 bridge in Canton to Ferguson bridge

Drop	Difficulty	Distance	Time	Scenery	Water Quality
158'	1-2	15.6 mi.	6.5 hrs.	B-C	Poor

Gage   Minimum level for solo: 7" below "0."

Difficulties   None. Primarily, the difficulty will be with the olfactory nerves.

(3) Ferguson Bridge (Haywood Co. Rts. 1355 and 1363) to New Hepco Bridge

Drop	Difficulty	Distance	Time	Scenery	Water Quality
157'	2-3-4	6.1 mi.	2.5 hrs.	B	Poor

Gage   Minimum level for solo: 7" below "0."

Difficulties   There is a boulder garden which drops 8 ft. in 20 yds., with standing waves at the bottom (Class 4). This can be recognized by a long stretch of flat water after having paddled along I-40 for some distance. A short rapid just above tends to lead one into the fast water before one recognises the danger. Passage at a normal water level is through the second chute from the right. Scout on the right.

A second long flat stretch precedes the Class 4, which is 600 yds. above the take out. An old dam 4 ft. high, with a heavy hydraulic, is followed by 60 yds. of rather heavy water. The paddler must move from far right to far left through here if attempting to run the dam, or even below it. This hydraulic held a C-1 paddler in for a few anxious moments before he got out. However, his boat remained tumbling for some 30 minutes before a tandem team was able to hook a grab loop and pull it out. One break in the old wall may be run on the far right. *Do not* attempt to run straight down on the right all the way. Cut to the left above the large rock at the bottom of the run.

(4) Below the Walters Plant of Carolina Power and Light to the bridge at Hartford, Tenn.

Drop	Difficulty	Distance	Time	Scenery	Water Quality
78'	3-4	4.5 mi.	2.5 hrs.	A-B	Poor

Gage   None. Call (704) 486-5965 and ask for the water flow from Walters Plant. It is generally in operation. A reading of 50,000 k.w. is maximum for solo open boats.

Difficulties   There are several rapids that should be scouted. Most of these can be seen from the road or highway. The water volume is generally large and presents many large standing waves and souseholes to give any but the most advanced paddlers trouble galore. At a run of 50,000 k.w. one has all the water he'll care to see from an open boat.

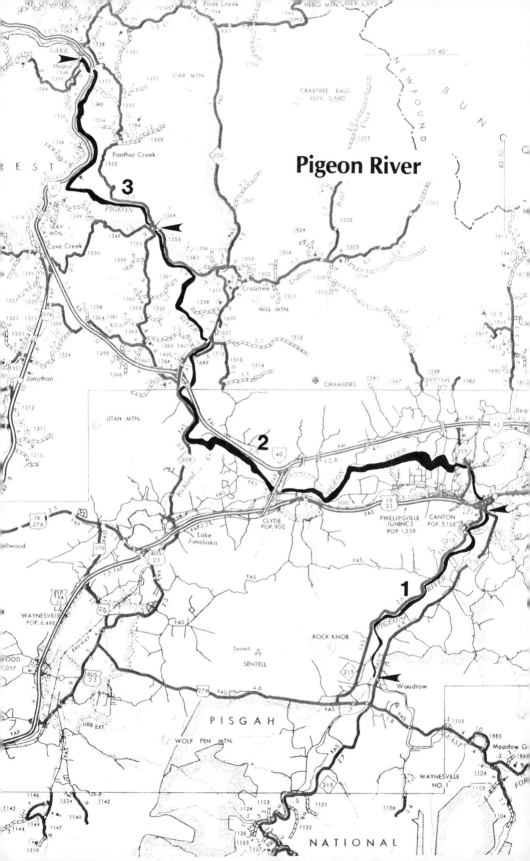

(5) Bridge at Hartford (Tenn.) to Cocke Co. Rt 2484 bridge

Drop	Difficulty	Distance	Time	Scenery	Water Quality
125'	1-2+	8 mi.	3.5 hrs.	A-B-C	Poor

Gage   None. Runnable most of the year, except during dry spells.

Difficulties   None. There are many ledges on the section between the two I-40 bridges. At higher water levels this stretch can be fairly turbulent.

Directions   **Put In**—N.C. 110 and Haywood Co. 1105 at the confluence of the East and West Forks, south of Canton.
Take Out—Section 3. New Hepco bridge off I-40 at Fines Creek Exit, north of Canton.
Section 5. Take I-40 exit 440 and go west to the first right; proceed to Rt. 2484 bridge. An easier takeout may be made along the road on the west side of the river .25 mi. above the bridge.

For those who might like to extend the trip, a run of 7.5 mi. to U.S. 25-70 bridge north of Newport (Tenn.) (an easy take out) can be made. This stretch is fairly flat, but has enough riffles scattered along the way to be interesting, plus some good scenery.

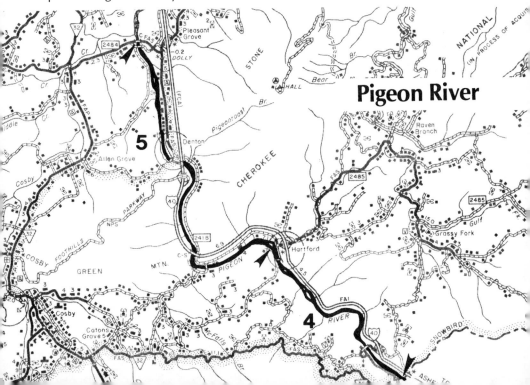

Pigeon River, East Fork

The East Fork of the Pigeon is a shallow low water stream meandering through farm land as it courses back and forth under U.S. 276 before finally joining the West Fork.

Topo Map   Cruso

County   Haywood

(1)   Rt. 1887 bridge (Pisgah Creek Rd.) to N.C. 110 bridge

Drop	Difficulty	Distance	Time	Scenery	Water Quality
258'	2-3	8.7 mi.	4 hrs.	B	Good

Gage   On northwest side of N.C. 110 bridge. Minimum for solo: 6" below "0." You must go down to water level in order to read the gage. Generally runnable during wet seasons, or early spring.

Difficulties   None. The river has a fairly constant gradient with no abrupt drops. At one point the river flows through a gravel pit, which gets rather shallow. This area is evident from the highway. There are 2 or 3 posted signs through this area, which primarily refer to fishing.

Directions   **Put In**—Rt. 1887 bridge east from U.S. 176 (at the community of Caruso), and southeast of the intersection of U.S. 276 and NC. 110.
Take Out—N.C. 110 bridge, 1 mi. north of intersection of U.S. 276 and N.C. 110, at the confluence with the West Fork.

Pigeon River, East Fork **Pigeon River, West Fork**

Pigeon River, West Fork

The West Fork of the Pigeon heads up in the Pisgah National Forest, then flows through Champion Papers' property at Lake Logan before confluencing with the East Fork. The put in is about .25 mi. below the dam at Lake Logan. From there down it is a fast moving low water stream flowing over a series of gravel beds.

Topo Map   Waynesville

County   Haywood

(1) Junction of Rt. N.C. 215 and Rt. 1129 to confluence with East Fork of the Pigeon

Drop	Difficulty	Distance	Time	Scenery	Water Quality
204'	2-3	6.3 mi.	2 hrs.	B	Excellent to Good

Gage   U.S.G.S. gage is on the east bank, downstream at the Rt. 1111 bridge. Minimum for solo: 1.80. Generally runnable during wet seasons, or early spring.

Difficulties   There are several fast runs through long gravel bars. In addition to these, there is one hard "S" turn dropping over two ledges, which is located just beyond a high undercut clay bank as the river bears to the left.

Directions   **Put In**—N.C. 215 bridge at the junction of 215 and 1129 (Little East Fork Rd.), below Champion Papers, Inc. property line. Rt. 1111 is a continuation of N.C. 110, after crossing U.S. 276.

    Take Out—N.C. 110 bridge, 1 mi. north of the intersection of U.S. 276 and N.C. 110, at the confluence with the East Fork.

Raven Fork River

The Raven Fork comes off Breakneck Ridge at what quite often seems to be at just that speed. It flows through the Cherokee Indian Reservation to a point just above the town of Cherokee, where it joins the Oconaluftee River.

It runs through boulder fields and rock gardens, to present one of the most delightful trips the paddler can find anywhere. The Cherokee have designated the river as "Enterprise Waters," (see Oconaluftee), thereby closing the main stretch to paddling, except on Wednesdays. The short stretch running from the National Park Boundary, just above "Crack-in-the-Rock" down to the confluence, is runnable on Tuesdays only, as is the Oconaluftee. Currently the trout season on the reservation begins a week ahead of the season for the rest of the state. Therefore, one may want to check at the Police Station in Cherokee to find out the status of the river before putting in during the normal "off season."

Topo Maps   Bunches Bald, Smokemont

County   Swain

(1)   Confluence with the Straight Fork to the bridge at the Job Corps Center

Drop	Difficulty	Distance	Time	Scenery	Water Quality
408' 1@60'/mi. 1/2@75'/mi.	2-3	8 mi.	4 hrs.	A-B	Excellent

Gage   U.S.G.S. gage is at Sherrills Cove bridge. Minimum for solo: 1.50. Maximum for a safe run through the gorge: 2.50. At a level of 1.50 it would be best to cut the trip shorter and put in at the confluence of Bunches Creek.

Difficulties   There is a rapid with a large hydraulic just below the put in which may encourage one to start below it. It makes for a rather unpleasant trip to take two strokes and find oneself out of the boat. The river drops at a rate of 75'/mi. through the first .5 mi. Fortunately this stretch, as well as much of the rest of the trip, can be scouted from the road, and it will be wise to do so through here.

There are numerous Class 2 rapids before reaching the first Class 4, which cannot be seen completely from the road. This rapid is in the bend of the river behind Smith Memorial Pentecostal Holiness Church. With a higher water level it requires a great deal of difficult maneuvering to prevent swamping the canoe.

After passing Sherrills Cove Creek bridge the river enters a 900 ft. deep gorge and makes a large bend around River Valley Camp, a private campground. There are three Class 3s in the gorge, all of which should be scouted. The gradient increases to over 60'/mi. The approach to the first two rapids will vary somewhat with the water level, but both can be scouted from the right. The third, "Crack-in-the-Rock," can be scouted on the left and run on the left. It is located just beyond the campground and just above the National Park boundary sign. There is fairly heavy water above the rapid, so care should be taken in the approach.

Directions   **Put In**—Take the Government Road east of the U.S. 441 bridge over the Oconaluftee in Cherokee for approximately 10 mi. **Take Out**—Turn west on the first paved road south of Government Road bridge crossing the Raven Fork. This road goes into the Job Corps Center. Take out can be made at this bridge or at the first one (Government Rd.) for a slightly shorter run.

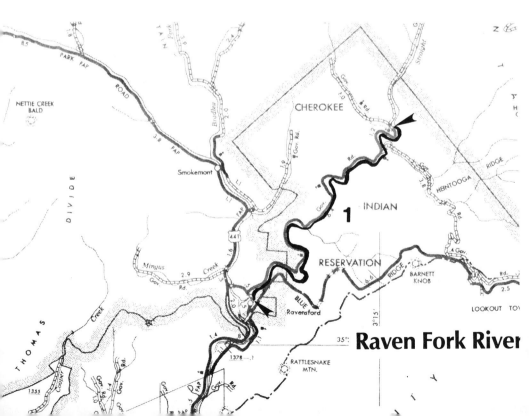

Raven Fork River

Santeetlah Creek

Santeetlah Creek originates in the Nantahala National Forest, just south of the pristine, virgin woods of Joyce Kilmer Memorial Forest. It springs from the Unicoi Mountains a few miles east of the N.C.-Tenn. state line. The upper section of this run is easy Class 2 water with the more interesting stuff towards the end. In 1973, Jim Holcombe and I did this run (maybe the 1st descent), and I remember rolling over and drinking from this fine creek. The water still appears to be drinkable, although we certainly can't advise it! This run is an option only after heavy rainfall and has at best a two-day window of runnability.

Topo Map   Santeetlah Creek

County   Graham

(1)   Government Rd. 81 to Santeetlah Lake

Drop	Difficulty	Distance	Time	Scenery	Water Quality
280'	3-4	4.2 mi.	2 hrs.	A	Excellent

Gage   None. Can be run only after extended rainfall.

Difficulties   This section has lots of fun, boat-scoutable Class 3 and easy Class 4 water. Most of the action is below the S.R. 1127 bridge. There is a five-ft. natural dam that needs to be looked at closely, especially at high water. Shortly before entering the lake there is an eight-ft. low head dam that can be run on the right at moderate levels. Paddle one hundred yds. down the lake to take out.

Directions   **Put in**—Take S.R. 1116 southwest of Robbinsville to S.R. 1127, then go 1.7 mi. and go left on Forest Rd. 81. Follow this to the bridge over the creek.
Take out—Go north of Rattler Ford Campground on S.R. 1127. Take first right onto S.R. 134 and go to the lake.

Slickrock Creek

Slickrock Creek originates in the Unicoi Mountains of southwestern North Carolina and southeastern Tennessee. It forms part of the state line between North Carolina and Tennessee for its entire length. There are 4.8 mi. of paddleable creek above its inundation/confluence with the Little Tennessee River. Slickrock meets the Little Tennessee two mi. below the Cheoah Dam, whereupon one must paddle upstream (uplake) to the take out. The creek flows between Nantahala National Forest (NC) and Cherokee National Forest (TN), where it enjoys a pristine environment and water quality.

Topo Map   Tapoco, NC-TN

County   Graham, NC-Monroe, TN

(1)   Big Fat Gap Trail to access rd. off N.C. 129 (just below Cheoah Dam)

Drop	Difficulty	Distance	Time	Scenery	Water Quality
780'	4-5-5.1	6.5 mi.	4.5 hrs.	AA	Excellent

Gage   None. Can only be run after heavy, extended rainfall. Since the run is unobservable except by hiking (almost two mi. to the put in) or paddling (about 1.7 mi. to the take out) it is advisable to put in at the take out and paddle to the creek's confluence with the Little T (1st left downlake) to check the flow. This bit of trouble will be worth the effort, as too much or too little water will make for an extremely long, hard trip.

Difficulty   With an average gradient of 162 fpm, Slickrock Creek is one of the most demanding runs in the southeast. It is extremely technical, very steep, and next to impossible to catch with enough water to paddle. The run starts off with continuous, steep boulder gardens. Slightly over a mile into the trip is a series of ledge drops of 10, 8, and 22 ft. The big one has a short pool separating drops of 8 and 14 ft. respectively. Water levels will dictate the routes on these falls. Below this section there are alternating stretches of fun and slam dance gradient. About 1.5 mi. above the take out is a 15-ft. ledge best run in the middle or off the far right. Below this ledge the creek continues its quick descent into the Little Tennessee River. Due to the amount of time one will spend out of the boat scouting and carrying deadfalls, it is suggested not to make this run in colder temperatures. A hypothermic paddler would have a long walk to civilization.

Directions   **Put in**—From N.C. 143-129 intersection in Robbinsville go approximately 14.3 mi. north on N.C. 129 to Slickrock Rd. Take left (across Cheoah River) on Slickrock Rd. and go 7.1 mi. to dead-end at Big Fat Gap. Walk 30 minutes down Big Fat Gap trail to the creek.

Take out—Follow N.C. 129 north beyond Slickrock Rd. turnoff, cross bridge over Little Tennessee River (just below Cheoah Dam) and take left on access road to where it dead-ends.

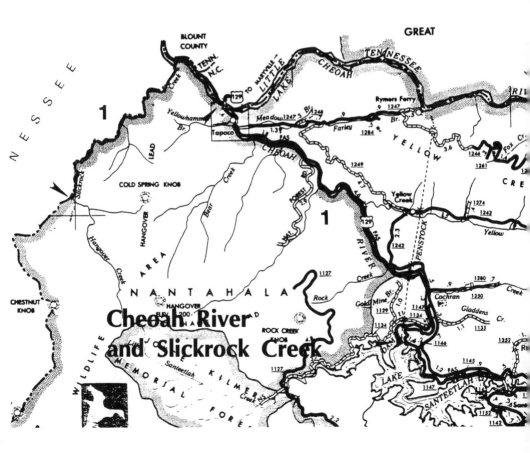

Snowbird Creek

Snowbird Creek has its origin high in the Unicoi Mountains, and within Nantahala National Forest, which ensures excellent water quality. The Snowbird Mountains form the southern rim of the gorge. The upper portion of the creek is very remote and flows through three sections of falls named Upper, Middle, and Big, all of which are well upstream of the sections described. Sections (1) and (2) become less remote as Snowbird winds its way to its inundation at Santeetlah Lake. The creek is only runnable after heavy rainfall and has at best a two-day window.

Topo Maps   Santeetlah Creek, Robbinsville

County   Graham

(1)   Junction to first bridge downstream

Drop	Difficulty	Distance	Time	Scenery	Water Quality
400′	3-4.2	2.8 mi.	1.5 hrs.	A	Excellent

Gage   None. Runnable only after extended rainfall.

Difficulties   This section of Snowbird Creek is extremely tight and technical, but there are no major drops. Extreme hazards exist if the water is very high (read Class 5 screamer) and/or you are any less than an expert boater. This creek has more moves than a 52nd Street lady of the night. Be aware of several boulder and log strainers. Creek meister Jim Holcomb has carried in and run as high as 3 miles above Junction where it is steeper. You may want to consider this ageless Bob Dylan lyric before following suit: "How far do you want to go? Not too far, but just enough so's we can say we have been there."

(2)   First bridge downstream of Junction to S.R. 1127 bridge

Drop	Difficulty	Distance	Time	Scenery	Water Quality
360′	2-3	8.5 mi.	3 hrs.	A-B	Excellent

Gage   None. Runnable only after extended rainfall.

Difficulties   None. Watch out for the three-ft. lowhead dam on the lower part of this section.

Directions   **Put in**—Take S.R. 1116 from Robbinsville to S.R. 1127. Go right on S.R. 1127 to S.R. 1115. Go left on S.R. 1115 to S.R. 1120. Go right on S.R. 1120 to dead end. This is known as Junction.

Take out—First bridge over creek downstream of Junction.

Put in—See section (1) takeout.

Take out—Take S.R. 1116 SW of Robbinsville to S.R. 1127. Take right on S.R. 1127 to first bridge over the creek.

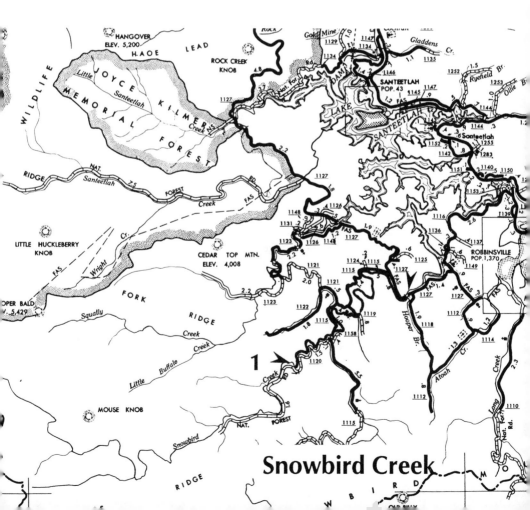

Snowbird Creek

Soco Creek

Soco Creek heads up in Soco Gap (elevation 4,345′), where the Blue Ridge Parkway crosses U.S. 19, east of Cherokee at the Qualla Reservation line. It flows to its confluence with the Oconaluftee River just below the take out. It presents the skilled paddler with a real roller-coaster ride. Although it never strays more than a few yards from U.S. 19, and runs through many backyards, one has little opportunity to view the scenery—good or bad.

Soco is wholly within the reservation and has been designated as "Enterprise Waters." This means that it is open to trout fishermen and is stocked by the tribe. For this reason it can be run only on Tuesdays during trout season, when it is being stocked. At this time, the possibility exists that an extended or "winter" trout season may be established by the Indians. For this reason it might be best to check at the Police Station in Cherokee to learn the status of the stream before putting in during the normal "off season."

Topo Maps Sylva North, Whittier

County Jackson

(1) Soco Creek Rd. and U.S. 19 to U.S. 441 bridge

Drop	Difficulty	Distance	Time	Scenery	Water Quality
566′	2-3-4	8.5 mi.	3 hrs.	B	Excellent
1-3/5 mi. @ 106′/mi.					

Gage U.S. 19 bridge on the southwest side, across from El Camino Restaurant. A reading of 6″ below "0" is minimum for a run from U.S. 19 bridge, while a reading of 2″ below "0" will allow a run from the first put in. Dredging is still being done in some stretches, which will possibly affect the level through those areas.

Difficulties This is a natural slalom course with no big drops, but several rapids might require scouting, especially in the upper 1.75 mi. which drops at the rate of 106′/mi. Much of the run can be scouted from the highway. Below Bluewing Rd. the channel is being changed some due to dredging. Stay to the left here, although this may get into a rather shallow stretch due to rechannelization.

Directions   **Put In**—Soco Creek Rd. where it leaves U.S. 19, going up the creek across from Soco Trail Campground.
Take Out—U.S. 441 bridge, 1 mi. south of Cherokee.

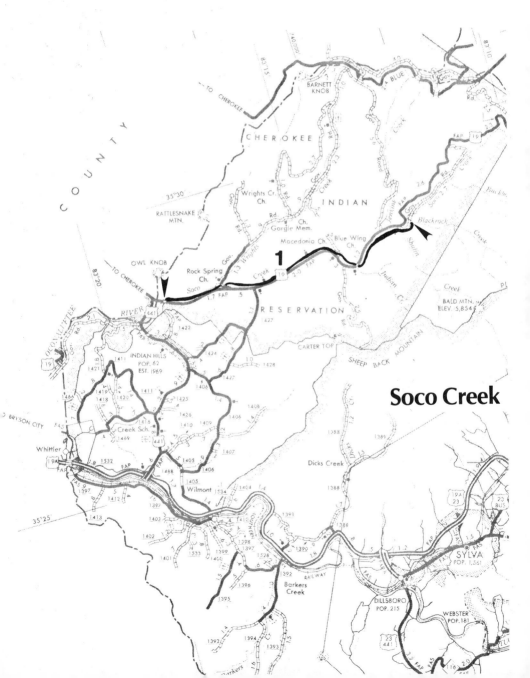

Soco Creek

Straight Fork

The Straight Fork originates between Balsam Mountain and Hyatt Ridge in the Smoky Mountain National Park. The stream is pristine as is the area through which it flows. Although a dirt road parallels the creek, it feels like a wilderness run. The put in is immediately downstream of the Hyatt Creek confluence. With an average drop of 140 ft. per mile, the gradient is deceptively high. It doesn't seem that steep except for one short stretch in the middle portion of the run. This run has a small, densely vegetated watershed and will need considerable rainfall to bring it to runnable level.

Topo Map   Bunches Bald

County   Swain

(1)   Low water bridge on government road to National Park boundary

Drop	Difficulty	Distance	Time	Scenery	Water Quality
310′	2-3-4	2.2 mi.	2 hrs.	A	Excellent

Gage   None. Runnable only after extended, heavy rainfall.

Difficulties   The Straight Fork is an extremely tight, twisty run that will demand your attention from top to bottom. The streambed primarily consists of stubble fields and small boulder gardens. The major danger will be tree strainers that cross the creek in several spots. About a mile into the run the gradient picks up and it becomes a solid, demanding Class 3-4 trip and requires excellent boat control.

Directions   Put in—Take U.S. 441 north of Cherokee to S.R. 1378. Take a right on S.R. 1378 and go to where the two government roads fork. Take the right fork and go to the only low-water bridge (actually under the water).

Take out—Go .6 mi. beyond the fish hatchery on same road as put in. Taking out here will keep the paddler within the National Park and allow for paddling any day of the week. Below the fish hatchery are enterprise waters.

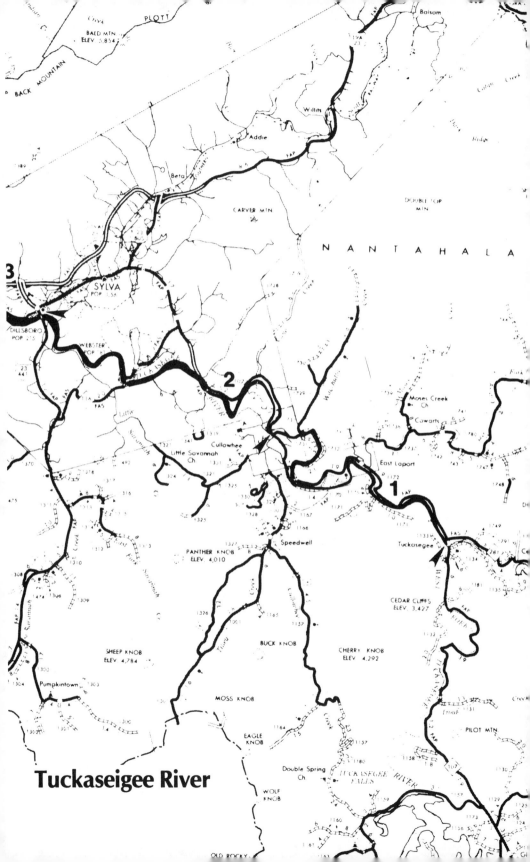

Tuckaseigee River

Tuckaseigee River

The Tuckaseigee begins in the Nantahala National Forest, where the East Fork and the West Fork of the Tuckaseigee confluence. (For information on each of the forks, see directions for the put in.) From there it meanders through a valley with a highway following along its entire length, except for about 4 mi. It flows through Bryson City before entering Lake Fontana.

The river primarily runs over gravel bars until it reaches the gorge below Dillsboro, where it begins to drop over ledges. After leaving the gorge it resumes its original characteristics, with a few ledges and shoals interspersed.

The water quality down from Dillsboro was very poor due to industrial pollution prior to late 1974, when the culprit responsible for it closed down. Since that time the river has steadily improved.

Topo Maps   Tuckasegee, Sylva South, Green's Creek, Whittier, Bryson City

Counties   Jackson, Swain

(1)   N.C. 107 bridge at the community of Tuckaseigee to Lena Davis Landing in Cullowhee

Drop	Difficulty	Distance	Time	Scenery	Water Quality
84'	1-2/3	9.5 mi.	3 hrs.	B	Good

Gage   U.S.G.S. gage is on the left bank at the foot of River St. in Bryson City, or about 150 yds. below the old bridge in the center of town. No reading is available for a minimum level. Generally the river can be run year 'round except during extremely dry spells. A better run is likely if the power plants on the East Fork and West Fork are in operation (see Directions).

Difficulties   There is a low Class 3 rapid beyond East Laport, where the river bends away from the highway. It runs continuously for over 100 yds. Approach it in the center.

The Lena Davis Landing is above a 100-ft. dam. It should be approached cautiously. Take out or carry on river left on the portage trail. To reach the landing take the first road on the southeast side of the Old Cullowhee bridge (down from Hardees).

For those wishing a shorter run, put in at the East Laport Access at the mouth of the Caney Fork. The area, developed by TVA and Jackson County Recreation and Parks Department, has restrooms. The gate is closed at dark. This will make a run of 6.5 mi.

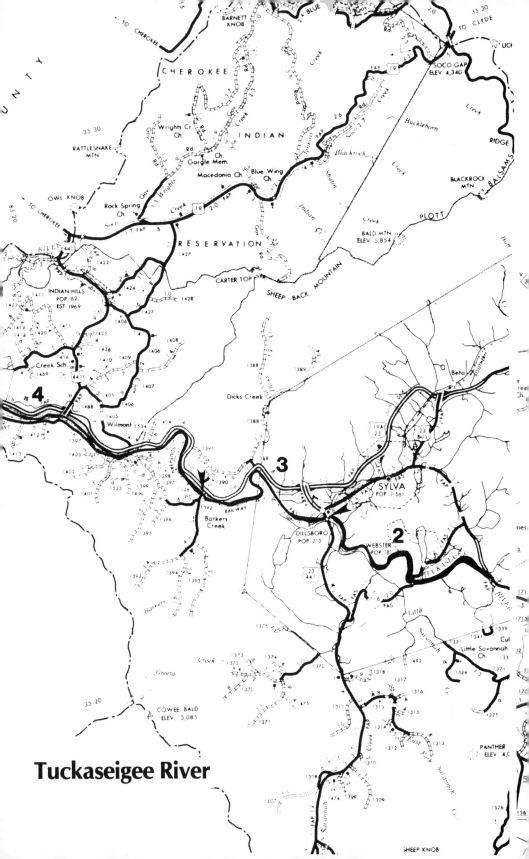

Tuckaseigee River

(2) Dam at Cullowhee to dam at Dillsboro

Drop	Difficulty	Distance	Time	Scenery	Water Quality
88′	1-2	11 mi.	4.5 hrs.	B	Good

Gage   See section (1).

Difficulties   Small riffles and gravel bars, primarily. The take out at Dillsboro is above a 15 ft. dam. An easy take out can be made about 50 yds. above the dam on the right.

For those who wish to continue the trip into section (3), take out should be made on the left in the flats, about 75 yds. above the dam. This will require a portage of about 250 yds. to the road and back down a steep path to a sandy beach below the dam.

(3) Dillsboro River access to Rt. 1392 bridge

Drop	Difficulty	Distance	Time	Scenery	Water Quality
74′	2-3	5 mi.	1.5 hrs.	A-B-C	Poor

Gage   See section (1).

Difficulties   The river drops through a steep gorge while running through rock gardens and over ledges, several of which may require scouting. To put in, cross the first bridge going south on US 441 to the shops on the east side. Turn onto River Street then immediately left onto Webster Street and left again beneath the bridge.

(4) Rt. 1392 bridge at Barkers Creek to the intersection of Shoal Creek Rd. and U.S. 19, west of Whittier

Drop	Difficulty	Distance	Time	Scenery	Water Quality
58′	1-2	8 mi.	3 hrs.	B	Poor

Gage   Can be run all year.

Difficulties   None.

(5) Intersection of Shoal Creek Rd. and U.S. 19 west of Whittier to Bryson City

Drop	Difficulty	Distance	Time	Scenery	Water Quality
108'	2-3	8 mi.	3.5 hrs.	B	Poor

Gage   Runnable all year except during extremely dry periods. A reading of 3.75 on the Bryson City gage would be suggested maximum level for intermediate paddlers. At this level some of the shoals can get quite heavy.

Difficulties   Shortly after leaving the put in, the river runs through an area of shoals which at medium high water can kick up some pretty good waves. This can be best run by staying to the right most of the way. Also, it will keep the paddler from being swept over a double ledge at the bottom. It can be recognized by the first short flat stretch as the river bends right, below the longest continuous shoals. The river drops about 7 ft. in 15 yds. It can be run in several different ways, depending on the water level. Scout from the right bank.

Just after passing under the railroad bridge below Ela, there is a rapid on the right which will have a large hydraulic in medium high water levels.

A series of shoals begin just above the U.S. 19 bridge in Bryson City. These should be approached carefully.

The last rapid above the take out consists of a long run down the left, and ends in a right angle turn. This is known as "Devil's Dip." The right turn should be made soon enough to miss the rather nice souse hole that waits to gobble up the paddler who lets his canoe drift too far to the outside of the turn.

Directions   **Put In**—N.C. 107 bridge, southeast of Cullowhee, at the community of Tuckaseigee.

The trip can be extended 1.5 mi. by putting in on the West Fork, when the Thorpe Power Plant is operating. The put in is found by driving up N.C. 107 along the West Fork, to where the water enters the streambed. This is a very narrow run down very fast water.

If the Main Plant is operating on the East Fork, the run can be extended about 2 mi. by driving up Rt. 1135 to River Park Campground, which is located immediately below the dam on Lake Cedar Cliff.

Information on whether the Main Plant is operating can be obtained by calling Nantahala Power in Sylva, (704) 293-5137.

Take Out—On the left bank downstream from the first bridge in Bryson City. Go north on the road to Deep Creek Campground off Main St. (U.S. 19), and take a left into the parking lot. On Sunday an automobile can be left here, but on weekdays try the Federal Building parking lot, which is west on Main St.

Tuckaseigee River

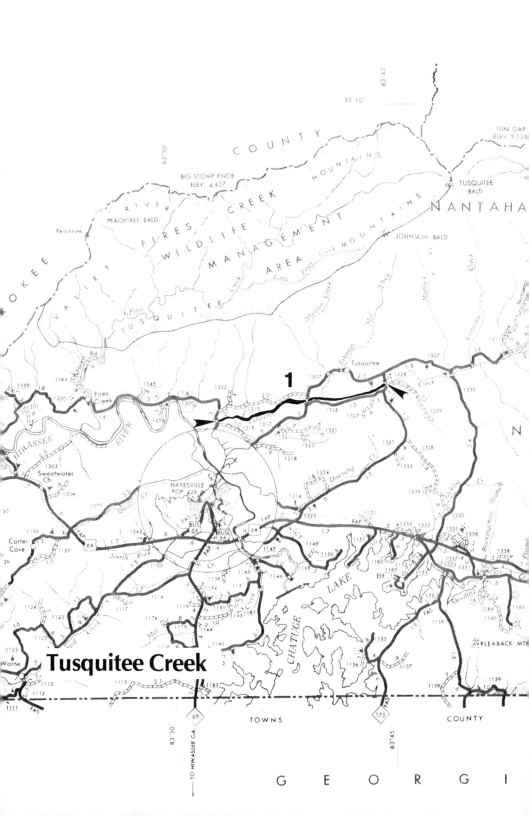

1

Tusquitee Creek

Tusquitee Creek

Tusquitee Creek heads up in Nantahala National Forest and runs along south of the Tusquitee Mountains. It flows primarily through a pastoral region before confluencing with the Hiawassee downstream from Hayesville.

Topo Maps   Shooting Creek, Hayesville

County   Clay

(1)   Rt. 1330 bridge to Rt. 1300 bridge

Drop	Difficulty	Distance	Time	Scenery	Water Quality
140'	1-2	5.2 mi.	2.5 hrs.	A-B	Good

Gage   On the southwest side of R. 1307 bridge at the junction of Rt. 1326. Minimum level for solo: 5'' below the bottom of "0." Can be run most all year except during dry spells.

Difficulties   None. Primarily a series of small rock gardens interspersed with an occasional ledge; however, be on the lookout for downed trees blocking the passage.

Directions   **Put In**—Take Tusquitee St. north out of Hayesville across the Hiawassee and bear northeast on Rt. 1307 to the gage. Go beyond it approximately 3.5 mi. to Rt. 1330 and south to the bridge.

Take Out—Take Tusquitee St. across the Hiawassee and bear northwest on Rt. 1300 approximately 1 mi. to the take out bridge.

The trip can be extended 2.5 mi. by continuing on to the Hiawassee and downstream on it to the second bend, coming close to Rt. 1300. Take out at the junction of Rt. 1345 with Rt. 1300.

Whiteoak Creek

Whiteoak Creek is born high in the Nantahala National Forest between Split Whiteoak Ridge and Rocky Bald Ridge, a few mi. west of Nantahala Lake. From its origin it tumbles steeply for a few mi., slows (somewhat) through a short valley, then picks up steam once more before joining the Nantahala. This last section is described below. Due to its small watershed, this run is available only after long, heavy rainfall.

Topo Maps   Topton, Hewitt

County   Macon

(1)   Whiteoak Dam on S.R. 1310 to just above confluence with Nantahala River

Drop	Difficulty	Distance	Time	Scenery	Water Quality
520'	4.2/5.2/6	2.4 mi.	1.5 hrs.	B	Good

Gage   None. Assuming a normal dam release, a level of 4.5 ft. on the Nantahala River gage may be a good indicator of enough water.

Difficulty   You'd better be strapped in tight and extremely focused before slipping out of the put-in eddy, because you're about to dance a 2.4 mi. waltz with Captain Gravity. With vital statistics of 216 fpm drop, stream width of 30 ft., deadfalls and/or overhanging branches every 50 ft., small to nonexistent eddies, and two huge, kidney-reducing drops, Whiteoak Creek has everything the jaded hairhead could want. Actually, the gradient is very steady and generally unblocked and boat-scoutable, with a few exceptions.

You'll often find yourself going a little faster than your comfort level allows into some semi-blind turn, with little hope of catching an eddy. About two-thirds of the way into the run is a ten-ft. drop best run in the center. Just downstream is a 25-ft., grade 5.2 drop consisting of four ledges practically piling on top of each other. None have particularly clean landings, though a route down the right center is barely feasible. Serious full-contact boating. Hospital air. Scout or carry on the right. Below here the river resumes its steady downhill gradient for about a half mile. The last drop above the confluence with the Nantahala is 28 ft. of mega-gnarl that we'll call Mean Mistreater. Make sure to take out at least 50 yds. above this, as there isn't much of an eddy to depend on any closer. Then tiptoe carefully around and put in for a sane run down the Cascades, if you've got the energy. Mean Mistreater has been run, but not by people who put their skirts on like you and I do.

Directions   **Put in**—U.S. 19 south of Wesser to S.R. 1310. Take left onto S.R. 1310 and go 6.6 mi. to Whiteoak Dam on the right.
Take out—Just above confluence with the Nantahala River on S.R. 1310.

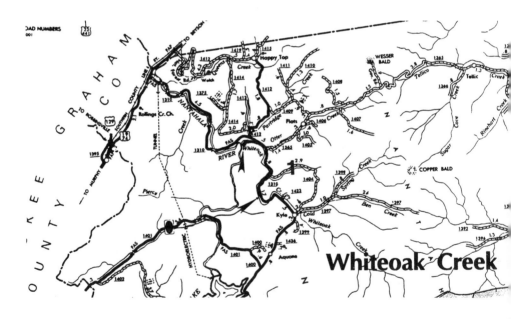

Section 2

Big Creek

Big Creek is born in the Smoky Mountain National Park, which ensures excellent water quality. The creek's origins are northwest of Mt. Sterling and Big Cataloochee Mountain. It confluences with the Pigeon River at Walter's Power Plant. The Big Creek watershed is a very popular hiking and horseback riding area. The stream bed has a constant gradient and is full of medium-sized boulders. When this is combined with adequate water levels, it provides for an exciting, expert-level trip. This section is available only after heavy, extended rainfall and has a small window of runnability.

Topo Maps   Cove Creek Gap, Waterville

County   Haywood

(1)   S.R. 1332 to Walters Plant

Drop	Difficulty	Distance	Time	Scenery	Water Quality
330'	4.2	2 mi.	1 hr.	A-B	Excellent

Gage   None. Runnable only after extended rainfall.

Difficulties   Big, in body building parlance, means extreme muscularity. Big Creek maintains a fully flexed, muscular pose for the duration of the run. Although the authors' view is slightly warped due to having run this at near flood state, the authors' view is clear enough to know that with less water this would still be a bang-up run. At high levels this is hard Class 4 water, typical of steep western rivers. The creek is essentially one long rapid. With 165 fpm gradient, 500-1,000 cfs, and a narrow stream bed, it begets predictably unpredictable results. If the creek is running high, you'll find yourself dodging a myriad of sticky holes, poreovers, and barely submerged boulders, while traveling at speeds that scarcely allow you time to make decent choices on good lines.

S.R. 1332 parallels the river most of the way. The run can be made longer by carrying your boat beyond the S.R. 1332 gate. The road continues to follow the creek for some ways. Be aware of the concrete weir where Big Creek tumbles into Pigeon River. Give yourself plenty of room to take out above it.

This run, at medium and high water, is for confident experts with bulletproof rolls. A failed roll here is probable grounds for permanent paddler-boat separation.

Directions   **Put in**—Take I-40 to Waterville Rd. exit. Follow S.R. 1332 to Walters Plant and continue for two mi. to the gate across the road.

Take out—100 yds. upstream of Walters Plant on S.R. 1332.

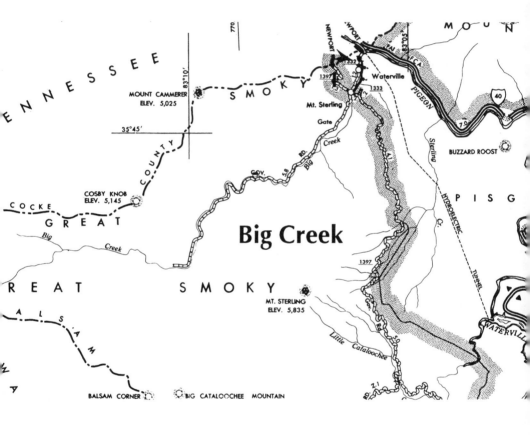

Big Laurel Creek

This is a fast wild water stream cutting a gorge 1,200 ft. deep between Mill Ridge on the north and Walnut Knob on the south. This is truly a most spectacular scenic run. Unfortunately, as with many trips of this type, one isn't able to raise his eyes from the job at hand long enough to be able to enjoy nature's wonders to the fullest.

Big Laurel flows into the French Broad 3.5 mi. above Hot Springs. This section must be run unless the paddler goes upstream 1/4 mi. to the community of Stackhouse (see the French Broad River, section (9)).

Topo Maps   White Rock, Hot Springs

County   Madison

(1)   U.S.25 and 70 bridge to 25-70 bridge over the French Broad in Hot Springs

Drop	Difficulty	Distance	Time	Scenery	Water Quality
200' .5 mi.@80'/mi.	3-4	4 mi.	3 hrs.	AA	Good

Gage   At Rt. 25-70 bridge on the east side. Reading of 6" below "0" is minimum for solo run. At this level two rapids must be carried. A reading of 3" above the bottom of "0" is the maximum level recommended. The great increase in difficulty with the slight increase in level is due to the constricted course. It can be run except in extremely dry seasons.

Difficulties   There are many rapids that should be scouted, the first of which is .25 mi. below the put in. An innocuous looking 2 ft. ledge which is run on the left pushes the bow squarely into a pointed rock at the bottom of the chute. This ledge can be recognized by the cottage just below it on the left bank, which is the last sign of habitation until the railroad bridge 100 yds. above the confluence with the French Broad. This ledge is a warning of bigger and better things to come.

Some other rapids worth mentioning are: The "Stair Steps," a tightly constricted series 3 drops of 3 ft. each, which becomes quite hairy at even 2" below "0" gage. "Suddy Hole," an 8 ft. ledge which can be run on the left at water levels above the bottom of "0," and on the right by those with suicidal tendencies. The "Narrows," easily recognized, certainly should be scouted to determine the best passage. The bed of an old railroad runs on the south side the entire length of the creek, which can help one in scouting.

The previously mentioned railroad bridge marks the end of the Big Laurel run and the beginning of big water on the French Broad (see section (9) of the French Broad River).

Directions **Put In**—On the east side of U.S. 25-70 bridge over the Big Laurel.
Take Out—West side beneath the U.S. 25-70 bridge.

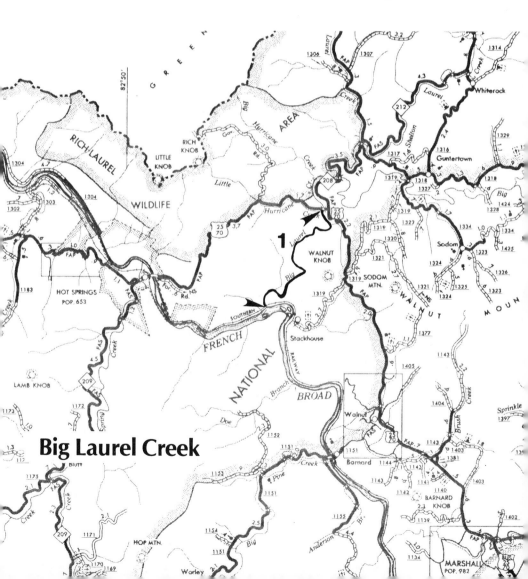

Big Laurel Creek

Broad River

The Broad begins just south of the Tennessee Valley Divide and flows generally southeast above its impoundment at Lake Lure. For the first several miles, it flows through a long, fairly flat valley and can be seen along N.C. 9. The river then tumbles down two steep gorges, most notably Hickory Nut Gorge, and courses by the towns of Bat Cave and Chimney Rock. Downstream of Lake Lure, most of the rapids are found between the dam and the first river bridge at Uree. Beyond Uree the Broad follows U.S. 64-74 closely before cutting away through a heavily wooded and rather remote area to the take out. For those who might want to continue further down the Broad (some additional 113 mi.), see 6.1).

Topo Maps Bat Cave, Lake Lure

Counties Buncombe, Henderson, Rutherford

(1-A) S.R. 2802 (Lower Flat Creek Rd.) to Volunteer Fire Department at Chimney Rock

Drop	Difficulty	Distance	Time	Scenery	Water Quality
910'	3-4-5.1	6.25 mi.	5.5 hrs.	A-B	Good

Gage Located on center piling of S.R. 2802 bridge. Minimum level should be 4" below "0".

Difficulties The Broad starts off with a bang. After a short warm-up of .5 mi. you enter the first gorge with consecutive waterfalls of approximately 10, 16, 8, and 13 ft. None are clean at the bottom, though they all have marginally runnable slots at favorable levels. Though there are some interesting boulder gardens, the first 3 mi. of the run is comprised primarily of ledge drops. The beautiful scenery of this section is compromised somewhat by several cabins along the river.

Once reaching Bat Cave (where the river parallels the road to the take out) the character of the stream bed abruptly changes to boulder-strewn. Large boulders. Strewn everywhere. If you were thinking things were going to ease up because you've hit civilization, think again. The next three mi. are some of the most technically difficult you'll find anywhere. There are two mandatory portages (10 yds. each) in this section where the river is completely choked down by boulders. Everything else is runnable, though at times questionable. One Class 5 drop stands out from the rest. Geek Peek drops 12 ft. through a tight maze with the final drop harboring a strainer tree that is tough to dodge. This stretch that parallels the road has a small allowance for varying water levels. Too little or too much water will either be impossible to get down or impossible to get down and tell about it later.

This is a super, though seldom done, run. Large-volume creek boats are a must. The proximity of the road along the lower part of this run, though comforting, should not encourage any less-than-expert paddlers.

Directions **Put in**—Take N.C. 9 south of Black Mountain to S.R. 2802 (Lower Flat Creek Road).
     Take Out—Take N.C. 9 south of Chimney Rock to the Volunteer Fire Department.

(1-B) Dam at Lake Lure to Rutherford Co. Rt. 1181

Drop	Difficulty	Distance	Time	Scenery	Water Quality
89'	1-2	7.4 mi.	2.75 hrs.	A-B	Good

Gage On U.S. 64-74 bridge at Uree, on southeast pillar. Reading of 6'' below ''0'' minimum for solo run. The entire section can only be run when water is coming through the dam.

Difficulties When the water is coming through the dam, the section between the dam and the bridge at Uree can be run, otherwise the water level will be too low. There are several ledges through here that require some fast maneuvering. Another short set of ledges are located beyond the confluence of Cove Creek. Watch for logs blocking the passages below Uree bridge, wher the river splits into several channels.

Directions **Put In**—North off U.S. 64-74 1 mi. east of the bridge at Uree to dam. You must carry the boat down steps on south end of the dam.
     Take Out—Go 6.8 mi. east on U.S. 64-74 from the bridge at Uree to Rt. 1181, then south to the Rt. 1181 bridge.

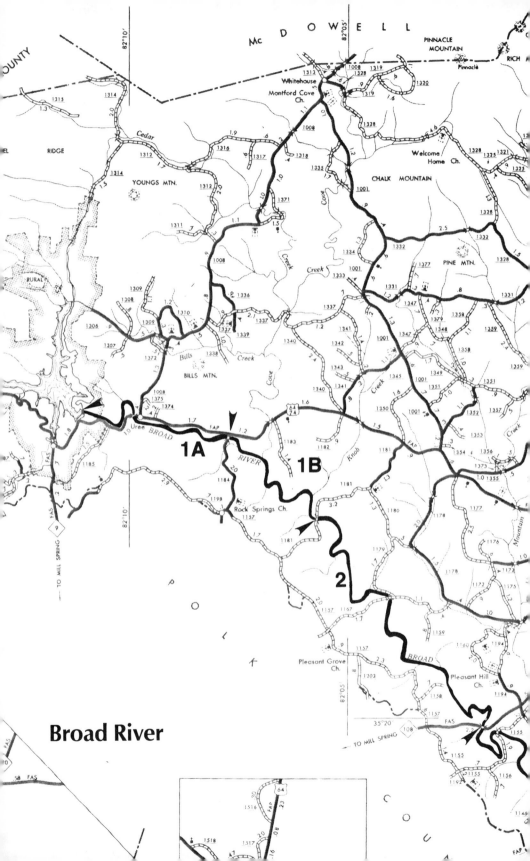

Broad River

Cataloochee Creek

Cataloochee Creek originates on the western slope of the Cataloochee Divide. From there it runs through a beautiful valley for several miles before entering a small gorge below and flowing into Waterville Lake. The entire watershed is within the Great Smoky Mountain National Park. It is one of the most pristine runs in the state. There is a reasonably good watershed that should allow for dependable water levels for much of the wet part of the year.

Topo Map   Cove Creek Gap

County   Haywood

(1)   S.R. 1397 to Waterville Lake Dam

Drop	Difficulty	Distance	Time	Scenery	Water Quality
320'	2-3/4	6.3 mi.	4.5 hrs.	AA-A	Excellent

Gage   U.S.G.S. gage located beside S.R. 1397 bridge. Minimum level is 2.7 ft.

Difficulties   This is a busy, entertaining piece of water. At high water the run can be made by starting at the dead end of the government road. You have to do some quick maneuvering and dodging of occasional strainers and overhanging branches. Things open up considerably one mi. into the run with easy Class 2 rapids down to the S.R. 1397 bridge. From here, both gradient and volume increase as Little Cataloochee Creek joins the fun. The creek maintains a fast Class 2-3 pace for two mi. before reaching a Class 4 drop of ten ft. Scout on the left. Enter the rapid far right with a sharp left angle and finish far left. Immediately downstream is a seven-ft. slide ending just above a 15-ft. unrunnable cascade. The slide can be run far right or far left; just don't miss the eddy at the bottom. Portage the cascade on the left. Paddle another .5 mi.; pristine Cataloochee Creek enters sewage-laden Waterville Lake. The take out is .5 mi. up the lake at the dam. When setting shuttle do not drive to the dam, as the CP&L people don't want congestion on their road. Park up the hill at the gate and carry your boat up so we can maintain good will with these folks.

Directions   **Put in**—Take the Maggy Valley-U.S. 276 exit off I-40. Take S.R. 1395 (Cove Creek Rd.) to Cataloochee. Take S.R. 1397 approximately .5 mi. above ranger station.

        Take out—Traveling west on I-40, look for the 11-mi. marker and turn right through an opening in the fence. You can only get on or off this road traveling west. Drive under the interstate to the gate at the top of the hill and park. To get back on I-40 east you must drive to the next exit (Harmon Den).

Davidson River

The Davidson is formed in northern Transylvania County by Shuck Ridge, Daniel Ridge, and Right Fork Creeks. Its headwaters are in the Nantahala National Forest assuring the paddler of clean, clear water. The upper Davidson must be caught at the crest of high water to ensure a decent run. An outstanding point of interest in the area is Looking Glass Mountain, a large granite dome that presents many challenging routes for the rock climber.

Topo Maps   Shining Rock, Pisgah Forest

County   Transylvania

(1)   Forest Service Rd. 475-A to confluence of Davidson River and Looking Glass Creek at U.S. 276 bridge

Drop	Difficulty	Distance	Time	Scenery	Water Quality
230'	2-3	3.5 mi.	2.5 hrs.	A	Excellent

Gage   U.S.G.S. Gage is located 50 yds. above 276-64 bridge on the west bank. Minimum reading should be "2.0".

Difficulties   Approximately .5 mi. below the put in is an easy Class 3 drop of 7 ft. Scout on the left and run on the right. Less than .25 mi. below this drop is another long Class 3 rapid dropping 10 ft. The run here is obvious because there is only one clear channel. Scout on the left. If you make it through these two in good shape, you'll do fine on the remainder of the run. This is a very busy and technical piece of water and everything below the second Class 3 can be boat-scouted. The scenery is great although you

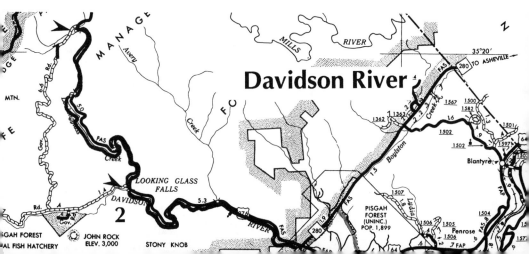

won't have much time to notice. Be aware of the 3.5 ft. fish weir adjacent to the fish hatchery.

Directions   **Put in**—Take U.S. 276 north out of Brevard to Looking Glass Creek bridge and take left onto Forest Service Rd. 475-A and go 3.6 mi. to put in on side of road.

Take out—Looking Glass Creek bridge on U.S. 276.

(2)   Confluence of Davidson and Looking Glass Creek to U.S. 276 bridge

Drop	Difficulty	Distance	Time	Scenery	Water Quality
132′	1-2	6.1 mi.	2 hrs.	A	Excellent

Gage   U.S.G.S. gage is located 50 yds. above the 276-64 bridge, on the west bank. Minimum reading for solo run is 1.0.

Directions   **Put In**—Northwest of Brevard on U.S. 276 to Looking Glass Creek bridge. Pull off to the left on the forest road.

Take Out—U.S. 276-64 bridge northeast of Brevard.

First Broad River

The First Broad rises on the slopes of South Mountain and flows easterly through Golden Valley below the South Mountain range before cutting south through central Cleveland County and joining the Broad River below Shelby.

The upper stretches meander through the foothills, many of which are filled with mountain laurel and rhododendron.

Topo Maps   Benn Knob, Shelby

Counties   Rutherford, Cleveland

(1)   Rutherford Co. Rt. 1726 bridge to Rt. 1737 bridge.

Drop	Difficulty	Distance	Time	Scenery	Water Quality
114'	1-2	8.8 mi.	3 hrs.	A	Good

Gage   U.S.G.S. gage is located 75 yds. above Cleveland Co. Rt. 1530 bridge on the south bank. Minimum level for solo run is 1.52.

Difficulties   None. Primarily pebble fields with occasional ledges. The stretch below Rt. 1734, which is filled with laurel and rhododendron, is particularly scenic.

(2)   Rutherford Co. Rt. 1737 bridge to Cleveland Co. Rt. 1529 bridge

Drop	Difficulty	Distance	Time	Scenery	Water Quality
64'	1-2	6.1 mi.	2.5 hrs.	A-B	Good

Gage   U.S.G.S. minimum is 1.47.

Difficulties   None, other than many small pebble fields. The lower half of the run has many trees down, presenting a natural slalom for the paddler.

Directions   **Put In**—Southeast on N.C. 226 from U.S. 64 to Rutherford Rt. 1726 (50 yds. west of the river bridge), then southwest for 1.1. mi. to the put in bridge.

Take Out—N.C. 226 south of the Rutherford-Cleveland Co. line to Cleveland Rt. 1529, then northeast .5 mi. to the take out bridge.

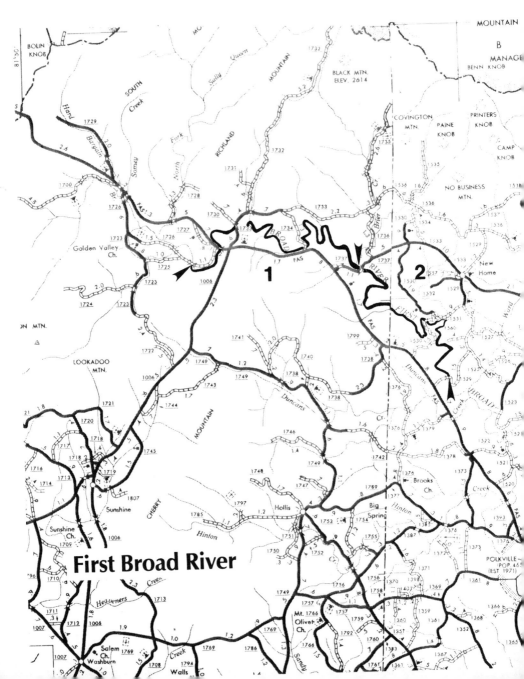

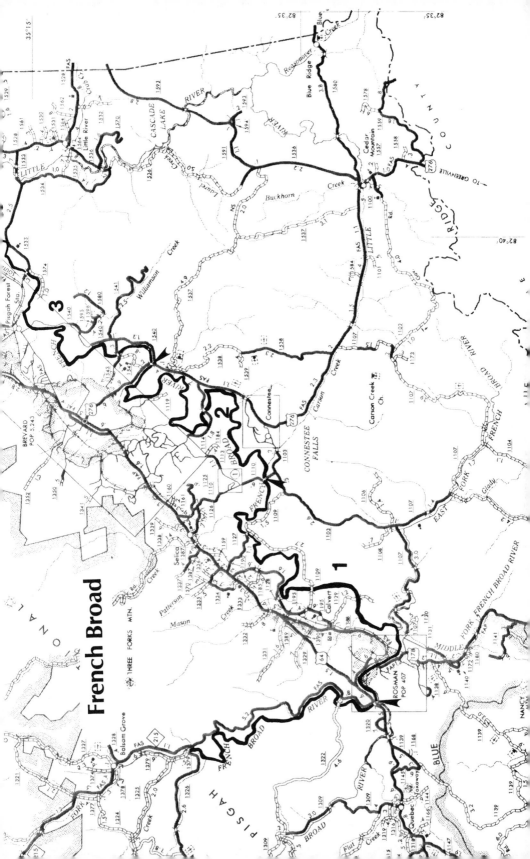

French Broad

French Broad

The French Broad is formed in the vicinity of Rosman, N.C., where the North Fork, West Fork, Middle Fork, and East Fork join together. The upper reaches of the river are primarily flat, flowing over shallow shoals alternating between farm lands and wooded areas. It is ideal for quiet float trips.

From Asheville down to Hot Springs the river cuts through a more mountainous area and changes complexion greatly as the volume and gradient increase. It becomes a wide powerful force, flowing through scenic gorges, over series of ledges, and through large boulders. The river here requires a much higher level of skill from the paddler.

Below Hot Springs the river slows down to flat stretches interspersed with rapids, along with some outstanding rock formations, such as Paint Rock and Chimney Rock.

Topo Maps   Rosman, Brevard, Pisgah Forest, Horseshoe, Skyland, Asheville, Weaverville, Leicester, Marshall, Spring Creek, Hot Springs (N.C.); Paint Rock and Needy Mountain (Tenn.)

Counties   Transylvania, Henderson, Buncombe, Madison (N.C.); Cocke (Tenn.)

(1)   Rosman Public Access in Champion Park on U.S. 64 to Transylvania Rt. 1110 bridge (Island Ford Road)

Drop	Difficulty	Distance	Time	Scenery	Water Quality
54'	1-2	10.5 mi.	4.5 hrs.	A-B-C	Good

Gage   None. The river is runnable all year, except during periods of extreme dryness and even then the lower section can be run. See section (9) for maximum safe level.

Difficulties   None. Primarily flat running over shallows and shoals.

(2)   Rt. 1110 bridge (Island Ford Road) to Public Access at Hap Simpson Riverfront Park on U.S. 276

Drop	Difficulty	Distance	Time	Scenery	Water Quality
32'	1	9.7 mi.	4 hrs.	A-B-C	Good

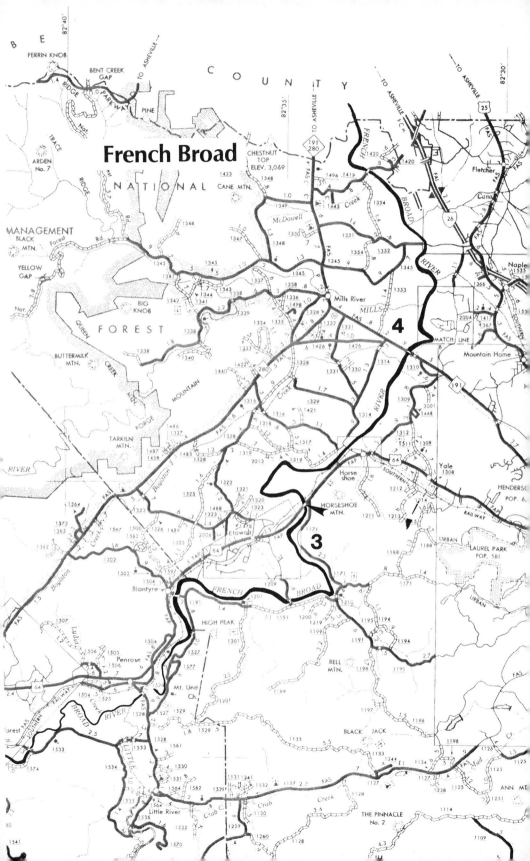

Difficulties   None. Same as (1).

(3-A)   Public Access at Hap Simpson Riverfront Park on U.S. 276 to Public Access at Blantyre Park on Henderson Rt. 1202

Drop	Difficulty	Distance	Time	Scenery	Water Quality
23'	C-1	13.3 mi.	5.5 hrs.	A-B-C	Fair

(3-B)   Public Access at Blantyre Park on Rt. 1202 to U.S. 64 (McLean Bridge)

Drop	Difficulty	Distance	Time	Scenery	Water Quality
16'	C-1	6.5 mi.	3 hrs.	A-B	Fair

(4-A)   U.S. 64 (McLean) bridge to Rt. 1419 (Fanning Bridge)

Drop	Difficulty	Distance	Time	Scenery	Water Quality
23'	1	11.8 mi.	5 hrs.	A-B	Fair

Difficulties   None. Same as (1). It was in the area of Johnson Bridge, next bridge below 64, that the "Mountain Lily" (hailed as "the highest steamboat in the world") was constructed to run between Asheville and Brevard (circa. 1878). It had a short life due to floodwaters that destroyed the channel, as well as the "planting" of the "Lily."

(4-B)   Rt. 1419 (Fanning Bridge) to Sandy Bottoms Park Access off N.C. 80

Drop	Difficulty	Distance	Time	Scenery	Water Quality
24'	1-2	7.1 mi.	3 hrs.	A-B	Fair

Difficulties   None.

(5-A)   Sandy Bottoms Park Access off N.C. 80 to Riverbend Park Access on Amboy Road in west Asheville.

Drop	Difficulty	Distance	Time	Scenery	Water Quality
41'	1-2	8.8 mi.	3.5 hrs.	A-B	Fair

Difficulties   None except shoals. (During the fall there are outstanding views of the Biltmore Estates through this section.)

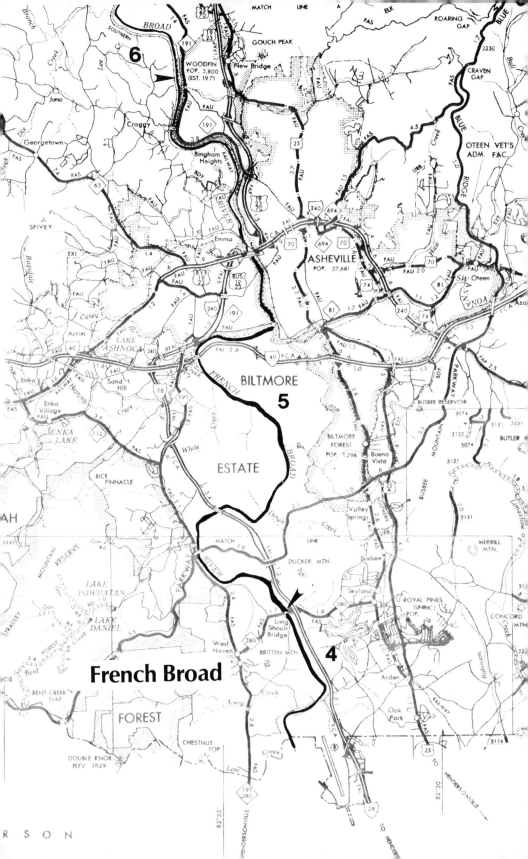

(5-B) **Riverbend Park Access on Amboy Road in west Asheville to North Carolina Electric Power dam on N.C. 191**

Drop	Difficulty	Distance	Time	Scenery	Water Quality
35'	102	7.3 mi.	3 hrs.	A-B-C	Fair

Difficulties There is a 10' dam at the end of this section. Take out on left and carry around, then ferry across to the right bank if taking out.

(6) **North Carolina Electric Power dam at N.C. 191 north of Asheville at Woodfin to Buncombe Co. Rt. 1634 bridge**

Drop	Difficulty	Distance	Time	Scenery	Water Quality
130'	2-3	6.5 mi.	2 hrs.	A-B	Fair to Poor

Difficulties Below the dam the current picks up speed as the river begins to drop over a series of ledges and heavier shoals. On the far right about 1 mi. below the dam, a Class 3 chute with heavy water presents the experienced paddler with an exciting run. This can be by-passed by working through the rock gardens in the center. With the increased gradient and widening of the river, this section can become quite difficult in higher water. The Metro. Sewage Treatment Plant empties just below the put in, which might give one added incentive to stay upright.

(7) **Buncombe Co. Rt. 1643 bridge at Alexander to dam at Marshall in Madison Co.**

Drop	Difficulty	Distance	Time	Scenery	Water Quality
140'	1-2	11.5 mi.	4.5 hrs.	A-B	Fair to Poor

Difficulties The 8' dam at the end of this section can present problems, so if taking out it would be best to pull out on the right bank in the vicinity of the intersection of N.C. 213 and U.S. Business 25-70, which will cut about .5 mi. off the trip. If continuing, a carry of some 400 yds. to below Rt. 1001 bridge will be necessary due to the bulkhead built along the banks below the dam.

(8) **Madison Co. Rt. 1001 bridge in Marshall to Madison Co. Rt. 1151 bridge**

Drop	Difficulty	Distance	Time	Scenery	Water Quality
100'	2	6.5 mi.	3 hrs.	A	Fair

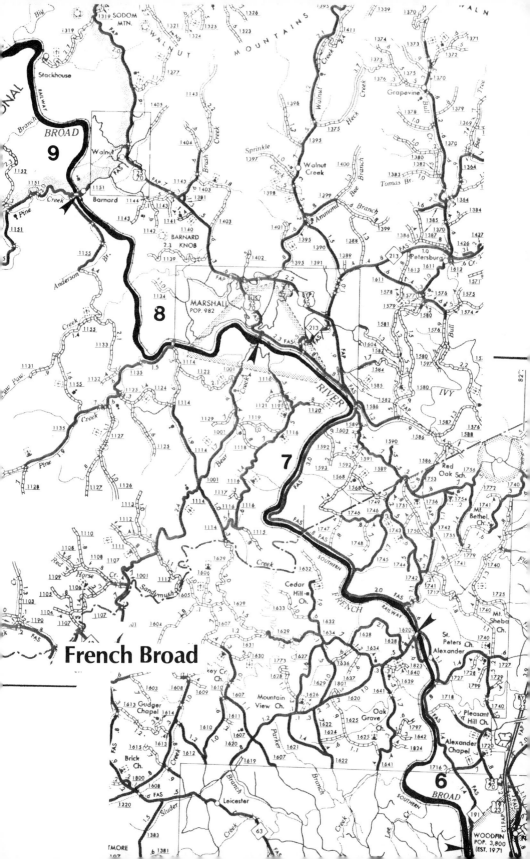

French Broad

Difficulties   About 1.5 mi. below Marshall, a 25 ft. dam should be ap-
          proached quite cautiously. A carry of some 200 yds. on the
right side is necessary. Beyond the dam the river continues with a constant
gradient presenting the paddler with steady Class 2 water and practically no
flat water. Those running this section only who don't wish to portage the dam
can put in below the dam and above Rt. 1135 bridge, at Redmond Park, on
the right bank. This leaves a trip of some 5 mi.

(9)   Madison Co. Rt. 1151 bridge at Barnard to U.S. 70-25 bridge in Hot Springs

Drop	Difficulty	Distance	Time	Scenery	Water Quality
210′	3-4/5	7.5 mi.	3 hrs.	A	Fair

Gage   Call (615) 632-6065 (TVA). A reading of 4,000 c.f.s. is maximum
       for open boats.

Difficulties   The increased gradient combined with greater width and heav-
          ier water makes for an exciting trip through this section. Scout-
ing becomes very difficuilt but quite necessary. For those who don't have a
very dependable eddy turn in their repertoire, this simply "ain't the place to
be." Generally the rule to follow is to stay to the left of all islands of any size.

There are seven major rapids in this section, all of which should be
approached cautiously. The third of these rapids, "Big Pillow," will be found
on the left side. The main flow of the river runs left, as the right side is clogged
with boulders. The entrance rapid, a fast chute, flows diagonally left and
requires the boater to fight to get back to the right in order to get by the large
pillow and souse hole below it. There is, however, a narrow chute on the
immediate left of the pillow, which can be negotiated in the event one ends
up too far to the right. Both the entrance and the pillow should be scouted
carefully. "Big Pillow" is located approximately 1.5 mi. below the put in. The
next two rapids should be scouted on the left and right, respectively.

The community of Stackhouse, located approximately halfway through the
section, can be recognized by the second island on the right. From this island
a row of iron rods extends diagonally upstream about 2/3 of the way across
the river. Move to the far left as soon as the island is observed. These rods can
be seen at levels below 4,000 c.f.s.

Big Laurel Creek joins the French Broad about .25 mi. downstream from
Stackhouse. Another .75 mi. downstream is Needle Rock, a sliver of shining
rock located on the left bank high above the island separating the main
channel. The main channel, which is on the left, has big standing waves which

can easily swamp an open boat. It can be best scouted from the island. A small protected chute just left of the island drops rather quickly but can be run without too much danger. To the right of the island is "Kayak's Ledge," a six-ft. vertical drop that dumps into a pool. Scout on river right.

The next large island in the middle of the river below Needle Rock will indicate the Class 5 and the last rapid of any consequence on the section. The rapid on the right has become known as "Frank Bell's Rapid" by canoeists in the area.* It consists of 3 concentric ledges which funnel the river into a giant whirlpool at the bottom. The passage to the left of the island is safest but certainly not unexciting. Both sides can be best scouted from the island.

(10)   U.S. 70-25 bridge to U.S. 70-25 bridge in Tennessee

Drop	Difficulty	Distance	Time	Scenery	Water Quality
150'	2-3	13 mi.	4.5 hrs.	A-AA	Fair

Difficulties   At normal water levels there are several rapids where standing waves build up enough to give tandem paddlers problems. All can be "sneaked" by scouting carefully and generally staying to the inside on the bends. Below the second railroad bridge there is a 4' ledge that can be best run on the far left. Around the next bend there is a rapid, running some 75 yds., which one should approach cautiously on the right, and run on the right. At medium to high levels a giant eddy is formed between this rapid and the next ledge downstream, which is a natural dam. It should be scouted— left or right—and be given the same respect one should any dam. There are breaks that can be run, but hydraulics are formed at higher levels.

Directions   Practically all put ins and take outs are located on main arteries or in towns included on state maps, so no further explanations will be given here.

Take Out—On the east bank beneath U.S. 70-25 bridge, in Cocke Co., Tenn.

For those wishing to continue farther down, a run of 11.4 mi. can be made to U.S. 25-70 (Bridgeport Bridge). Take out on river left. About 3 mi. below Del Rio Bridge (TN 107), the river begins dropping again, presenting some 3 mi. of rapids ending in a 4' ledge called the Falls. Scout on the right and run on the right.

---

* Frank Bell, owner of Camp Mondamin in Tuxedo, N.C., was fortunate enough to be around at a time before dams were the answer to all problems. He ran the French Broad from its headwaters to the Gulf of Mexico. An attempt to run down the right side ended with his canoe remaining in the whirlpool for some 10 minutes, with him getting out after great difficulty.

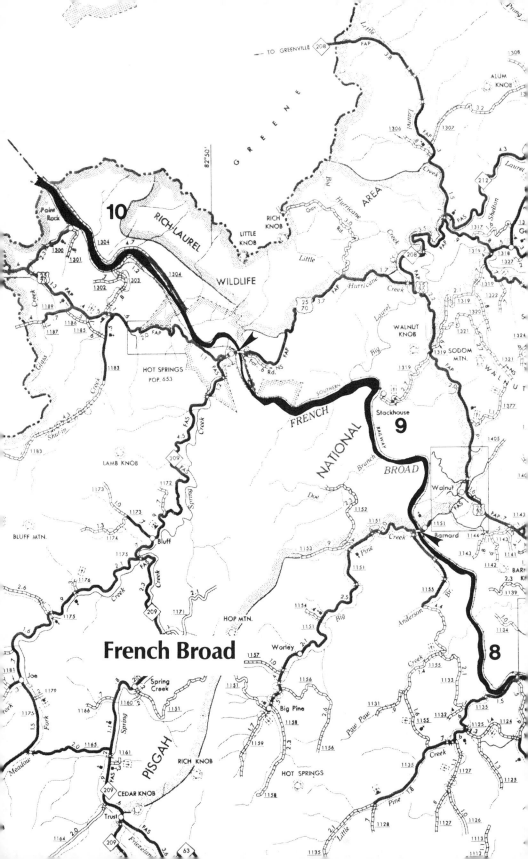

French Broad

To GREENVILLE 208

GREENE AREA

ALUM KNOB

10

Point Rock

RICH LAUREL

LITTLE KNOB

RICH KNOB

WILDLIFE

Shelton

Laurel

HOT SPRINGS
POP. 653

FRENCH

WALNUT KNOB

SODOM MTN.

WALNUT

NATIONAL

9

Stackhouse

BROAD

LAMB KNOB

Walnut

BLUFF MTN.

Bluff

Barnard

Doe

Branch

BARN KN

HOP MTN.

Worley

8

Joe

Spring Creek

Big Pine

HOT SPRINGS

Anderson Br.

Paw Paw

PISGAH

RICH KNOB

CEDAR KNOB

Trust

Pine

Little

63

A fine detailed map of the river from Rosman, N.C. to Newport, TN, has been prepared by the Land-of-Sky Regional Council. It is available from the French Broad River Foundation, 70 Woodfin 19., Suite 327, Asheville, N.C. 28801 (phone 704-252-1097).

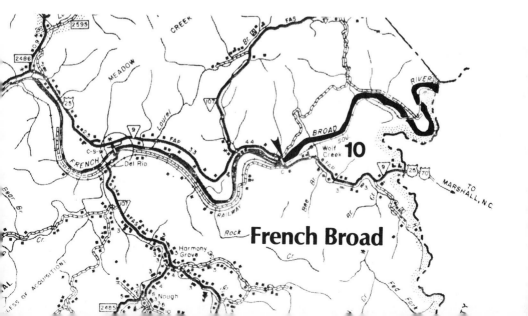

French Broad

French Broad, North Fork

The North fork of the French Broad heads up on the eastern edge of the Nantahala National Forest. The stream originates in the vicinity of Devil's Courthouse, off the Blue Ridge Parkway. Its protected watershed ensures excellent water quality. High in the mountains it tumbles over Courthouse Falls, a stunning 50-ft. drop. Below the falls it remains a steep mountain rivulet for some miles before entering the flat valley at Balsam Grove. Downstream of Balsam Grove there are several beautiful falls—most notably Birdtown Falls, a runnable 20-footer. Flatwater follows Birdtown Falls down to the section described. The North Fork drains a small area, so extended rainfall is necessary to be able to paddle it.

Also worth mentioning here is the current interest Rosman farmers have for a dam in the Balsam Grove area, which would essentially inundate the North Fork gorge. Their interest is in flood control; Rosman is on the French Broad flood plain. Things are only in the talking stage at this point, but this is something paddlers need to be aware of and respond to if it goes any further.

Topo Map   Rosman

County   Transylvania

(1)   S.R. 1326 bridge to U.S. 64 bridge

Drop	Difficulty	Distance	Time	Scenery	Water Quality
390' (1 mi. at 145')	4.2/5/5.2	7 mi.	3.5 hrs.	AA-A	Excellent

Gage   Located on center piling of U.S. 64 bridge. 6" below bottom of "0" is a minimum level.

Difficulties   At the end of the first mile, there is a slide dropping 12 ft. followed by a Class 3. Scout on the left. The next rapid of consequence, Boxcar Falls, is so named because of a mishap which occurred when the narrow gauge railroad was in operation. Legend has it a boxcar fell in the narrow, deep sluice at the base of the falls. Boxcar Falls drops about 22 ft. into a narrow rock trough. There are two obvious routes over the drop, neither pleasant, both with a reasonable degree of potential for injury. Scout or portage on the old railroad bed on the right. Below here is good Class 4 gradient for several hundred yds. Razorback comes at the end of this stretch. Below Razorback is the Clog, a steep Class 5 boulder garden of a hundred yds. Scout or carry on the left. More interesting Class 4 rapids follow, leading into Submarine, a nine-ft. slide on the far left. The gradient starts to slow progressively from Submarine to the take out. For those interested in cutting some flatwater out of the run, take out at Alligator Rock. Alligator Rock (so named because of a jaws-like formation above the road on the right) pull-off is 1.7 mi. north on N.C. 215 from the intersection at U.S. 64.

Directions   **Put in**—North on N.C. 215 off U.S. 64, 1 mi. west of Rosman. Go west on S.R. 1326.
Take out—U.S. 64 bridge, .1 mi. west of Rosman.

∎

A man's life should be constantly fresh as this river. It should be the same channel, but a new water instant. Most men have no inclination, no rapids, no cascades, but marshes, and alligators, and miasma instead.
                    Thoreau, *A Week on the Concord and Merrimac Rivers*

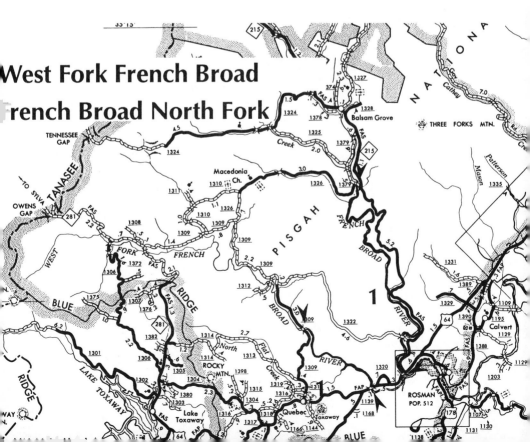

West Fork French Broad

The West Fork of the French Broad forms as drainage between Round Mountain and Big Pisgah Mountain in Pisgah National Forest. It runs quietly through a valley for several miles before entering a short, steep gorge below where it confluences with the North, East, and Middle Forks to form the French Broad. This run starts off with a bang—the three largest rapids come in the first mi. of the run. Below the first mile, the river settles into a fun Class 2-3 pace. This section is only runnable after extended rainfall.

Topo Maps   Lake Toxaway, Rosman

County   Transylvania

(1)   S.R. 1309 bridge to U.S. 64 bridge

Drop	Difficulty	Distance	Time	Scenery	Water Quality
340'	3-4/5/5.1	3.4 mi.	2.5 hrs.	A-B	Good

Gage   Located on river left piling of S.R. 1309 bridge. Minimum is 4" below bottom of "0."

Difficulties   Approximately .25 mi. below the put in is a 13-ft. Class 4-5 (depending on the water level). Bow pin potential looms large at the base of this drop. The only route is obvious. Scout or carry on the left. Around the bend is another rapid dropping 14 ft. in a cascading slide. During a solo exploratory run, a bow pin did occur in the middle of this drop causing the C-1 to fill instantly and ripping both thigh straps out. It was just a split second pin, but the potential for worse is there. Scout or carry on the left. Two hundred yds. downstream is a cascading Class 5.1 with a total drop of 22 ft. Scouting this drop is tough because the rhododendron is very thick. Last seen, this rapid had a large tree in the middle bottom. Scout or carry on right. After these three major drops the river can be boat-scouted down to the confluence.

Directions   Put in—Take U.S. 64 west of Brevard to S.R. 1309. Take a right and go 2.4 mi. to the bridge.
Take out—Take U.S. 64 west of Brevard to bridge at N.C. 215 intersection.

Green River

The Green River has its origins southwest of Tuxedo where it runs quietly for several miles before its inundation at Lake Summit. The Saluda mountains are the southern border of this upper section. Below the dam at Lake Summit the river drops through a short gorge, flattens out for a few miles, and then enters the Narrows, a world-class stretch of whitewater. Downstream of the Narrows, it levels out into a delightful fast-flowing stream cutting between Cove and Chimney Top mountains to the south and McCraw Mountain to the north. Through this area is a fairly small stream dropping over easy ledges and flowing through mild rock gardens. The area is sparsely settled, but evidence of encroaching civilization is growing fast.

Next to the Nantahala, section (4) of the Green is paddled more than any river in North Carolina. During the summer months, hardly a day passes without two or three groups of canoeists from various summer camps holding classes there. It is an excellent stretch for teaching the basics of river canoeing.

This popularity has created problems for people who live in the Cove. On summer weekends dust hangs in the air as shuttles race up and down the river road, litter is strewn about, and nudity is flaunted. This is a nice place to visit, but not as nice to live. At this time there is limited parking on the side of the road through the Cove. It is patrolled regularly—especially on weekends.

Please note the overlapping of sections (2) and (3). They are presented in this manner because this is the way they are paddled. The expert-level paddlers running the Narrows generally put in at the hydro plant because of the good, long warm-up it provides.

Topo Maps   Zirconia, Hendersonville, Cliffield, Lake Lure, Rutherfordton South

Counties   Henderson, Polk, Rutherford (Broad)

(1)   Lake Summitt dam to Tuxedo Hydro Plant

Drop	Difficulty	Distance	Time	Scenery	Water Quality
160'	3-4.2/5	1.3 mi.	1.5 hrs.	A	Good

Gage   None. This is a dam-controlled stream and is runnable only when the plant in Tuxedo, N.C. is operating. Generally under normal conditions the plant operates during the week. The water normally takes 3-4 hours to reach section (4). Call (704)594-0681 to check the sched-

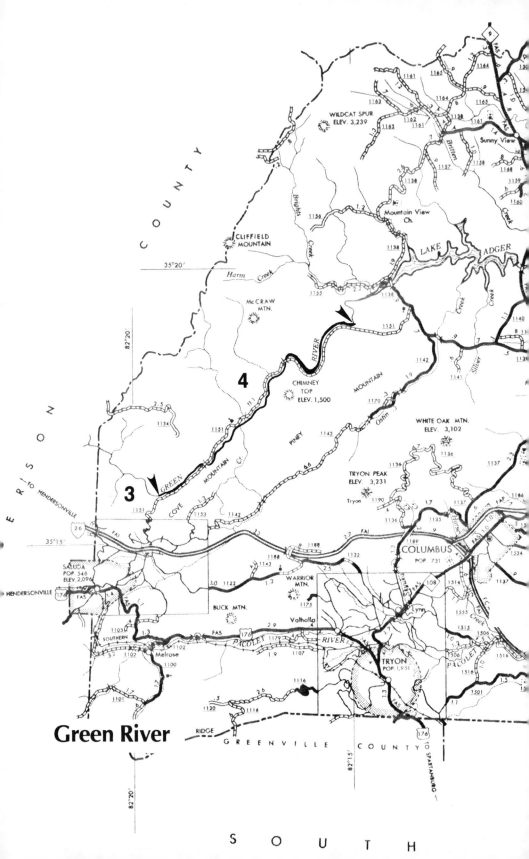

Green River

ule of operations on weekends, holidays, or during extreme dry spells. All sections can run with 2 or 3 valves operating. Section (3) should be approached with extreme caution if Hungry River is thought to be dumping in above-average quantities of water from run-off.

Difficulties   As of the printing of this edition, this section will not be available to paddle except (and we are told this will rarely happen) during extreme flood conditions when the water may spill over the top of Lake Summitt Dam. This section has been bypassed due to Duke Power diverting the water from Lake Summitt to the Tuxedo Hydro Plant. If paddleable conditions occur, carry up the river left side .4 mi. to the dam. Class 2 water will be encountered until you reach the 2 large slides that can be seen from the U.S. 176 bridge. Run generally left center on the first and right center on the second. Downstream of the bridge is the meat of the run, with .25 mi. of steep, boulder-strewn drops. Below here is easy Class 2 water to just above the hydro plant. The last rapid on this section, Powerhouse Falls, is a 12-ft. vertical fall best run left of center off a slight roostertail at the lip of the drop.

(2)   Tuxedo Hydro Plant to Big Hungry Road trail

Drop	Difficulty	Distance	Time	Scenery	Water Quality
180'	2-3/4	3.6 mi.	1.5 hrs.	A	Good

Gage   See Section (1)

Difficulties   With the exception of two drops, this section has no real difficulties, just pleasant, semi-continuous Class 2 water. The first large rapid, Bayless' Boof, comes about a mi. into the run and consists of a slide into a vertical ledge with about ten ft. total drop. The run is generally far left (about 8 ft. off the left bank), angling left off the ledge. There is a rock just underwater at the bottom to the right of the preferred line, where boats have been known to front ender. Downstream of the 1-26 bridge is the second large rapid, Pinball. It consists of consecutive drops of 4 and 6 ft. Enter about 20 ft. off the left bank and angle left across the first drop, which generally puts you on line for the next ledge.

Approximately .6 mi. downstream of this rapid is the take out trail. Look for an easy Class 2 sluice with a fun play wave at the top. The trail is on the left at the bottom of this rapid. If you see the Hungry River confluencing on the left, you've gone too far. The hike out is .6 mi. up to Gallimore Road. One note of caution about the take out: this is private property with "No Trespassing" signs posted where paddlers park. Apparently there have been some problems with drunks and litter bugs. The landowner has given paddlers permission to

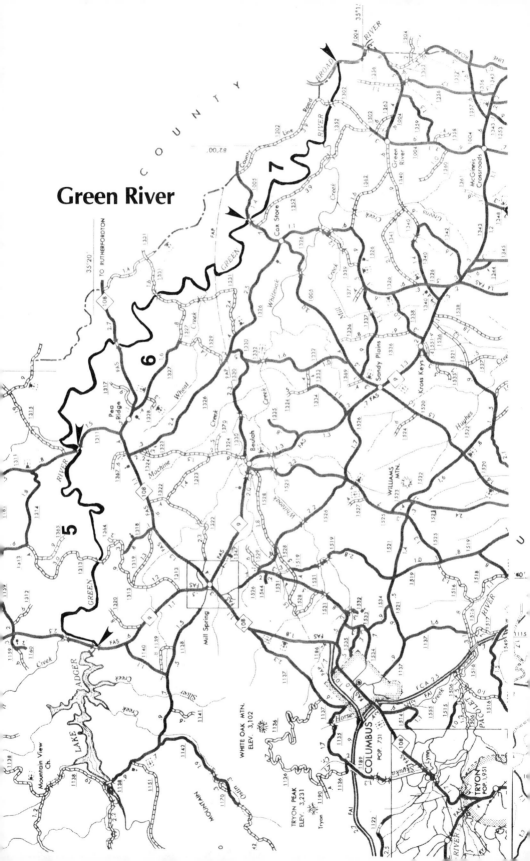

Green River

park here and haul boats out. Try to keep shuttle vehicles to a minimum on this end. Pick up any litter lying around. This is a tenuous situation that needs to be approached with respect and care by the paddling community or we may lose it.

(3) Tuxedo Hydro Plant to Green Cove Road

Drop	Difficulty	Distance	Time	Scenery	Water Quality
700' (1 mi. @ 350')	4-5.2/6	6.6 mi.	4 hrs.	AA-A	Good

Gage   See section (1)

Difficulties   There is a somewhat contorted adage which applies here: "the bigger they fall, the harder they are." The Narrows of the Green begin approximately .25 mi. downstream of the Hungry River confluence. The entrance to the Narrows is quite evident as the river constricts to half its former width and crashes off a complex 8-ft. ledge. The next 5,280 ft., known as the Monster Mile, drops 350 ft. Though everything on this stretch has been run numerous times by many paddlers, there is a sense of ominous possibility on many of these rapids. The Narrows generally has a zero tolerance policy on missed lines. The list of major and minor mishaps and injuries incurred by the best paddlers in the country is growing month by month. The outstanding rapids (in the order met as one descends) include Frankenstein, Boof or Consequence, The Slot, Zwink's Backend, Chief, Gorilla, Power Slide, Rapid Transit, Nutcracker, Sunshine, and Fishtop Falls (a.k.a. Hammer Factor). At this point, Gorilla is generally considered the most bodacious rapid ever run by the elite eastern hairheads. It is a runnable, legitimate Class 6 rapid. Sunshine Falls, the second most feared drop, marks the end of the Narrows.

If problems arise in the Narrows and an evacuation or aborted trip is in order, one can walk out a trail that originates in the vicinity of Nutcracker (the next to last major drop in the Narrows). This trail is steep and will take an unhindered person at least 45 minutes to walk out. The trailhead is 4.8 mi. down Big Hungry Road from the Upward Road intersection. Below Sunshine the river eases up to hard Class 4 for 1.3 mi. Fishtop Falls comes at the end of this stretch and brooks no relaxation. The take out is just downstream.

Due to the Green being a dam-controlled stream, paddlers in the east will enjoy a certain familiarity with it as they have no other extreme run. (It is indeed the hardest dam controlled stream in the east, if not the country.) Hopefully this familiarity will not breed contempt, either with the truly exceptional hardboater who handles this water with relative ease or with the hair boating wanna bes who have little business being there. Be extremely confident on every other high-caliber run around before attempting this—your reputation might not be the only thing you make or break, or you may end up walking through a lot of impossible to avoid poison ivy on the way "down the river."

Directions **Put In—Section (1)** Take U.S. 176 west of Saluda to bridge over Green River. Carry up river left side .4 mi. to base of Lake Summitt dam.

Take Out—Take 176 west of Saluda 300 yds. beyond bridge over river. Take right onto S.R. 1836 and go approximately 1 mi. to the river.

Put In—Section (2) Take 1-26 to Upward Road exit. Go Northeast on Upward Road (S.R. 1722) to Big Hungry road (S.R. 1802) and take a right. Once on S.R. 1802 take left-fork at first intersection and right fork at second intersection, then take right onto S.R. 1956 (this road is numbered 1154 on the Polk County map) and go .8 mi. to pull off on left. River is .6 mi. down a jeep track.

Put In—Section (3) See section (2) put in.

Take Out—Off I-26 at Saluda exit, go east approximately 300 yds. to Green Cove Road (S.R. 1151) and left down a series of hairpin turns to where the road straightens. Turn into the first pull-off on the left.

(4) Rt. 1151 (Green Cove Rd.) to where the river leaves the road

Drop	Difficulty	Distance	Time	Scenery	Water Quality
126′	1-2	6 mi.	2.5 hrs.	A-B	Good

Gage None. This is a dam-controlled stream and is runnable only when the plant in Tuxedo, N.C. is operating. Generally under normal conditions the plant operates during the week, in which case water arrives at the put in each day about 1 p.m. Call (803) 585-4419 to check out the schedule of operation on weekends, holidays, or during extreme dry spells.

Difficulties Green Cove Rd. follows along the river the entire distance, making scouting rather easy. The first rapid of any consequence is "Big Corky" (1.3 rd. mi. below the first bridge) which can be recognized by the quiet pool above it and the sandy beach on the left below it. When both turbines are running it presents a nice standing wave to douse the bowman in.

A second rapid about .25 mi. below "Big Corky" can present problems to the unwary paddler. It bears to the left and drops over a rock bed for about 75 yds. Farther downstream a series of ledges running for some 200 yds. should be approached cautiously. The road is high above the river at this point.

The approach to "Little Corky," a low Class 2, occurs just beyond a point where the road has dropped down to the river and a sizeable island separates the main stream. The more difficult run is on the left of the island. It drops fast with an apparent straight chute off the right bank. One rock barely under water is the grabber awaiting the straight shooter. A slight movement to the left will shoot the canoe between it and a similar rock on the left. They are little more than a canoe width apart. Scout on the left.

Below "Little Corky" the river continues to drop fast for .5 mi., then it slows down somewhat. Primarily fun water following the last "Corky."

Directions   **Put In**—Off I-26 at Saluda Exit, go east approximately 300 yds. to Green Cove Rd. (Rt. 1151), and left down a series of hairpin curves to where the road straightens. The river is on the left. Turn into the first pull-off on the left. This puts one above a fast water rapid, requiring some quick maneuvering.

Put In—From Mill Spring (N.C.) take N.C. 9 north about 100 yds., then go west on Rt. 1138 to Silver Creek Baptist Church. Turn left on Rt. 1151 to the river. Proceed to the point where the road starts up the mountain and turn right into the parking lot.

Take Out—6.3 rd. mi. from the put in parking area to the second parking area, located just beyond a point where one loses sight of the river.

The following sections have been included for those who might like to take a more leisurely float trip, or who might be looking for quieter waters for overnighters. If one wishes an extended trip beyond the reaches of the Green, see sections (4) through (10) on the Broad.

(5)   N.C. 9 below Lake Adger Dam to Polk Co. Rt. 1311

Drop	Difficulty	Distance	Time	Scenery	Water Quality
52'	1-2	7 mi.	2.5 hrs.	A-B	Good

Gage   None. When the upper Green is running, generally the dam at Adger will be generating, thus giving a very nice water level.

Difficulties   None, but beware of downed trees.

(6) Polk Co. Rt. 1311 to N.C. 1005

Drop	Difficulty	Distance	Time	Scenery	Water Quality
38′	1-2	10.2 mi.	4.5 hrs.	A-B	Good

Gage   See Section (5).

Difficulties   None.

(7) N.C. 1005 to N.C. 1004 on the Broad River

Drop	Difficulty	Distance	Time	Scenery	Water Quality
26′	1	6.7 mi.	3 hrs.	A-B	Good

Gage   See Section (5).

Difficulties   None.

Take Out—Southeast approximately 11.5 mi. from Mill Spring to N.C. 1004, then north to the river.

We used to joke occasionally about setting the shuttle on the wrong river—always considering such below our level of intelligence. In this area the impossible can happen. On the first trip by the author on section (1) of the Broad we arrived at the take out only to find no vehicle. Same story at the next bridge. Here we were, mid March and cold, and getting more so with the sun setting and no transportation. Well, logic finally prevailed and we found our shuttle after a 5 mi. walk in the dark—not on the Broad, but on the Green.

Spring Creek

Spring Creek cuts a deep, scenic gorge between Long and Deer Park Mountains on the west and Spring Creek Mountain on the east. Its drainage lies within Pisgah National Forest. The put in is just downstream of the confluence of the Meadow Fork of Spring Creek and Spring Creek. Rarely would there be adequate water to run above the confluence, because the creek itself is only runnable after fairly extensive rainfall.

Topo Maps Spring Creek, Hot Springs

County Madison

(1) N.C. 209 to town of Hot Springs

Drop	Difficulty	Distance	Time	Scenery	Water Quality
520'	3-4/5	6.8 mi.	3 hrs.	A-B	Good

Gage Located on river right bridge piling of U.S. 25-70 bridge in downtown Hot Springs. Minimum level is 9" above "0."

Difficulties Spring Creek introduces itself in a brisk manner. With the exception of one drop, the toughest water comes in the first mile. The run starts off with several interesting boulder gardens. Two of the three Class 4 drops on the trip come within the first .5 mi. After the first mile the run eases up just a bit, though it remains very busy down to the take out. The creek primarily intersperses ledge drops with small boulder gardens. In the second mile there is a six-ft. drop that can be run left center or far right (the more interesting line) at higher water. The steepness of the gorge that Spring Creek cuts can't be as fully appreciated from the water as it can from the road to the put in. As the river starts paralleling the road, you will soon come under the first N.C. 209 bridge. Approximately .5 mi. downstream of the bridge is a nasty 10-ft., Class 5 drop. Scout and/or carry on the right. The main chute is inundated with rock and leads into a rock wall. At higher levels this rapid can be cheated on the left, which is the only advisable place to run at any level. Be aware of the occasional well-placed log or tree sweeper throughout the trip. This is a suitable trip for the high intermediate/advanced boater.

Directions Put in—Take N.C. 209 south of Hot Springs to the intersection with S.R. 1173. Continue on 209 for 50 yds. and take another left onto the dirt road, which leads to the river.
Take out—U.S. 25-70 bridge in downtown Hot Springs.

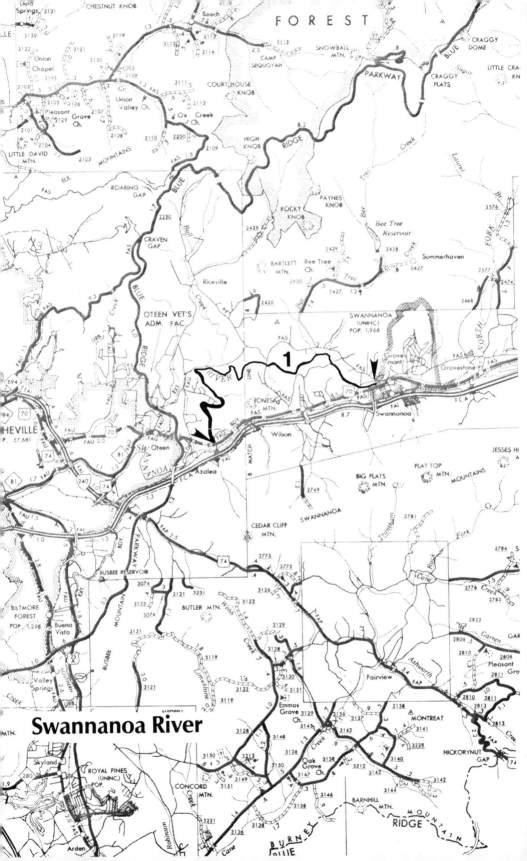

Swannanoa River

Swannanoa River

The Swannonoa drops off the western slopes of the Blue Ridge at Swannanoa Gap, just east of the town of Black Mountain. It remains fairly small and narrow until joined by the North Fork, east of Swannanoa.

It flows through wooded areas and farmland, much of which is owned by Warren Wilson College, before passing under U.S. 70 and through an industrial area in Asheville. It joins the French Broad in the city limits.

Bob Watts, of Black Mountain, has been a one man "Save the Swannanoa" gang in trying to clean up the river and keep it clear for canoeing. Every stream needs a friend like Bob.

Topo Map   Oteen

County   Buncombe

(1)   Main bridge in Swannanoa (above Mr. Zip) to the U.S. 70 bridge at Azalea

Drop	Difficulty	Distance	Time	Scenery	Water Quality
135'	1-2	8.6 mi.	4 hrs.	A-B-C	Good

Gage   On the southwest side of the bridge by Mr. Zip. Minimum for solo is 4" below "0." Can be run at 6" below "0" from Charles D. Owen Park. Generally there is adequate water to run during the spring through mid June and during wet seasons.

Difficulties   Always be on the lookout for downed trees.

There is a sewer pipe across the river at the upper end of Charles D. Owen Park. At water levels at the bottom of "0" and above, the paddler won't be able to run under it. Move right quickly and portage.

Just below the park there are several small islands with narrow channels. The one main channel can easily be blocked by downed trees. Proceed carefully.

Directions   **Put In**—On the north side of the river about 50 yds. below the bridge. There is adequate parking along the shoulder here. Please don't use the lot at Mr. Zip for parking.

To Charles D. Owen Park (Buncombe Co. Parks and Recreation Dept.) bear right on Farm School Rd. off old 70 from the main bridge in Swannanoa. Put in at the lower end of the park. A small road runs to within a few yards of the river. It would probably be best to park cars at the main lot after unloading. Putting in here will shorten the trip by about 2 mi.

Take Out—On the southeast side of U.S. 70 bridge at Azalea. Opposite Azalea Methodist Church.

Dave McPherson at Second Falls, Broad River. A Cathy Kuyper photo.

Section 3

Boone Fork

The Boone Fork arises as a tiny tributary falling off the eastern flank of Grandfather Mountain and then flowing a few miles before being backed up by Price Lake. Price Lake is small and man-made with a spill-over dam. This run is available only during, or immediately after, serious rainfall because of its tiny watershed.

Topo Map   Boone

County   Watauga

(1)   Julian Price Memorial Park to S.R. 1557 bridge

Drop	Difficulty	Distance	Time	Scenery	Water Quality
460'	3-4	4.5 mi.	2.5 hrs.	AA	Excellent

Gage   Check small foot bridge at Julian Price Memorial Park. White paint slash on river left concrete piling should be underwater for a minimum level.

Difficulties   The first 1.5 mi. of the run is easy Class 1 and 2. After coming to the old washed-out timber bridge you'll go two hundred yds. to the first portage. This section drops 100 ft. in less than 100 yds. Portage on a small trail that appears at the top of this section on river left. After putting back in you'll paddle perhaps .4 miles before coming to the second portage. Take out on the left and carry along the Boone Fork Trail for 60 yds. and put in below the second boulder clog. For the next mile there is continuous Class 3/4 water and everything is runnable at favorable water levels. The total length of the gorge is about 1.75 mi. Then the rapids slack off to Class 2/3 down to the confluence with the Watauga River. Paddle .5 mi. down the Watauga to the take out. This is gorgeous country and a highly recommended trip if there is adequate water.

Directions   **Put in**—Take the Blue Ridge Parkway south out of Blowing Rock to Julian Price Memorial Park. Put in at small footbridge. **Take out**—Take N.C. 105 south of Boone to S.R. 1568 (Old Shulls Mill Rd.). Follow S.R. 1568 .8 mi. to S.R. 1557. Go left to bridge.

Buck Creek

Buck Creek has its headwaters in the Mt. Mitchell Wildlife Management Area below the Blue Ridge Parkway. It flows along N.C. 80 into Lake Tahoma. Above the lake it is a small, fast dropping stream while below it flattens out somewhat, flowing over small ledges and rocks. Property above the lake is posted as well as patrolled. Don't be tempted.

Topo Map   Marion

County   McDowell

(1)   Lake Tahoma Dam to U.S. 70

Drop	Difficulty	Distance	Time	Scenery	Water Quality
72'	1-2	3.2 mi.	1.5 hrs.	A-B	Good

Gage   U.S. 70 on northeast side of bridge. Minimum for solo run is reading of 6" below "0." Buck Creek drains a small area and can be run in later winter, spring, and following rain.

Difficulties   None, but fast maneuvering will be required in several tight passages.

Directions   **Put In**—Turn off Rt. 80 on the first road below the dam. There is little space for turning around at the end of this road.
Take Out—East side of U.S. 70 bridge just east of the community of Pleasant Gardens.

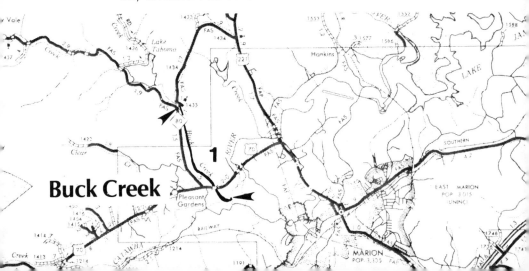

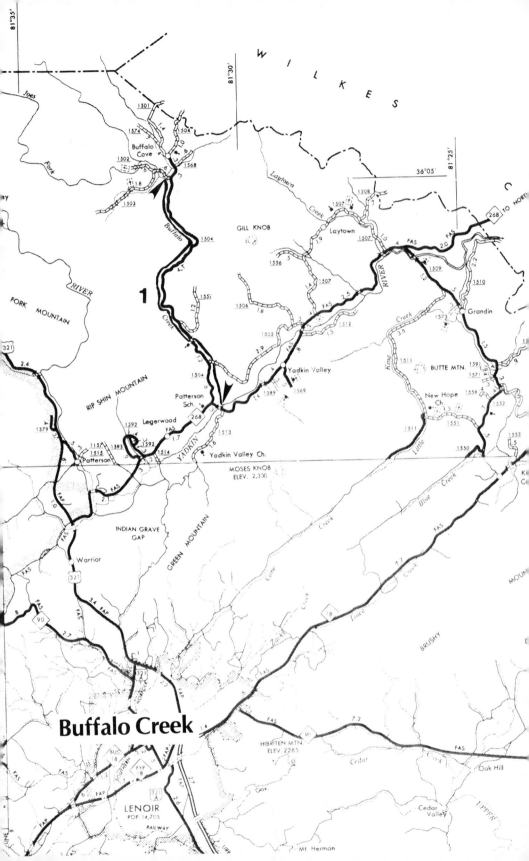

Buffalo Creek

The Buffalo flows from the junction of several small streams in Buffalo Cove. It courses through a small valley until it cuts through a deep remote gorge. After leaving the gorge it comes back along the highway before leveling out slightly as it confluences with the Yadkin. The Buffalo throughout its course is a small low water stream flowing over gravel bars with a few small ledges.

Topo Map   Bufaflo Cove

County   Caldwell

(1)   Rt. 1503 bridge to N.C. 268 bridge

Drop	Difficulty	Distance	Time	Scenery	Water Quality
180'	2/3	6 mi.	3 hrs.	A-B	Good-Fair

Gage   On Rt. 1505 low water bridge on the northwest side. Go to water level on the northeast side to read. A minimum level of 6" below "0" is required for solo. Rt. 1505 is the first road on the right off Rt. 1504 after leaving N.C. 268. The best water level will be obtained during the spring and following runoffs from rain.

Difficulties   There are two broken dams on this section, the first of which is located in the first gorge the stream enters below the put in. The chute appears open but a large rock and an iron bar which are barely under the surface can easily damage a boat attempting to pass through.

    The second dam, about 10 ft. high, can be seen from Rt. 1505 bridge where the gage is located. It should be approached very carefully when the water is high enough to be flowing over the top. It can be portaged on the left bank.

Directions   **Put In**—Northeast of Patterson on N.C. 268, north of Rt. 1504 to Rt. 1503.
    Take Out—The junction of Buffalo Creek with the Yadkin River about 50 yds. from N.C. 168 bridge over the Yadkin.

Cane River

The Cane forms between Big Pine Mountain and Bearwallow Stand Ridge on the western slope of Mt. Mitchell. It flows north then west from the Burnsville area before turning north again to join the Toe River where the Nolichucky is born.

Below Section (1) highways run alongside the river for most of the way. Generally the course is well below the level of traffic.

Topo Maps Burnsville, Bald Creek, Chestoa, Huntsdale

County Yancey

(1) U.S. 19E bridge to Yancey Co. Rt. 1381 bridge

Drop	Difficulty	Distance	Time	Scenery	Water Quality
78'	1	5.4 mi.	2.15 hrs.	A	Good to Fair

Gage Located on Rt. 1381 bridge on river left downstream. Minimum for solo is 6" below "0."

Difficulties Only possible strainers and one low footbridge located about .5 mi. below the first bridge.

(2) Route 1381 bridge to U.S. 19W bridge at Lewisburg

Drop	Difficulty	Distance	Time	Scenery	Water Quality
198'	1-2	6.2 mi.	3.5 hrs.	B	Good to Fair

Gage Minimum for solo is 7" below "0."

Difficulties There is a double ledge upstream from the second bridge and it can be scouted from river left. Below the second bridge a boulder clog in a bend to the left makes it difficult to determine the best passage. Scout on the left. There are three low water bridges that have to be portaged.

(3)   U.S. 19W bridge at Louisburg to Rt. 1354 bridge at Ramseytown

Drop	Difficulty	Distance	Time	Scenery	Water Quality
128'	1-2	5.1 mi.	2.5 hrs.	B-C	Good to Fair

Gage   Minimum for solo is 9" below "0."

Difficulties   Gradient increases for some 400 yds. downstream from the second bridge. Two low water bridges have to be portaged.

(4)   Rt. 1354 bridge at Ramseytown to Rt. 1354 (.3 mi. above the Toe River)

Drop	Difficulty	Distance	Time	Scenery	Water Quality
86'	1-2	5.0 mi.	2.5 hrs.	B-C	Good to Fair

Gage   Minimum for solo is 8" below "0."

Difficulties   None.

Directions   **Put in**—U.S. 19E bridge west of Burnsville.
Take out—Continue northeast of Rt. 1417 where 19W cuts west toward Erwin, Tennessee to Rt. 1343 bridge.

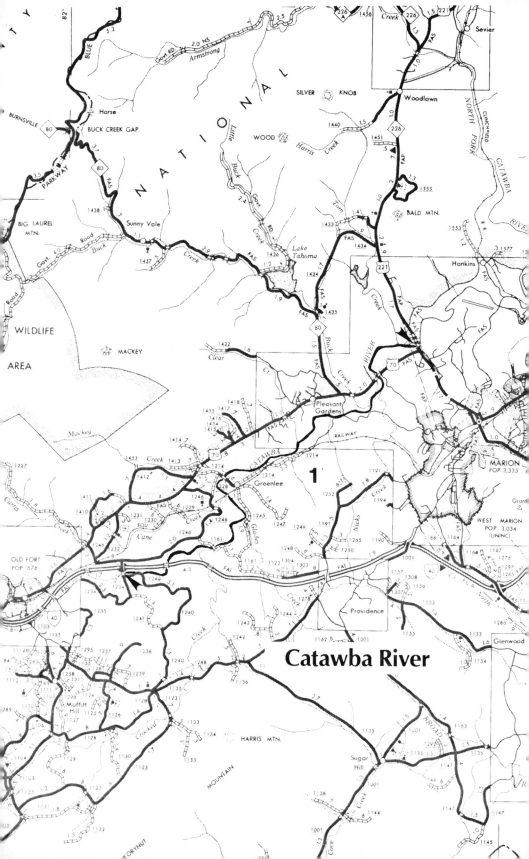

Catawba River

The Catawba heads up above Catawba Falls in the extreme western portion of McDowell County and flows into Lake James north of Marion. Below Linville Dam on Lake James, it continues until it reaches the backwaters of Lake Rhodhiss. After Lake Rhodhiss the river is impounded several times with little fast free flowing water, therefore the reason for no further description.

The river is small and fast in section (1), but carries industrial pollution east of Old Fort. Except for this it could be a very pretty run. However, there are several areas where gravel operations are evident.

Below Lake James the river flows primarily through woodlands until it reaches Morganton. **The Catawba is currently being studied for inclusion as a state water trail.**

Topo Maps   Marion, Glen Alpine, Morganton South, Morganton North

Counties   McDowell, Burke

(1)   McDowell Co. Rt. 1234 bridge to U.S. 221 bridge

Drop	Difficulty	Distance	Time	Scenery	Water Quality
85'	1-2	12 mi.	6 hrs.	B-C	Poor

Gage   Southside of Rt. 1234 bridge. Minimum level for solo paddling is 6" below "0." Can be run year round except during extreme dry seasons.

Difficulties   There are several series of ledges, the first of which is below the confluence of Crooked Creek on the right. This one in particular should be scouted. An earlier take out can be made along McDowell Rt. 1214 for those who desire a shorter run.

Directions   **Put In**—Catawba Rt. 1234 off I-40 east of Old Fort (at the Parker Padgett Rd. exit).
Take Out—U.S. 221 bridge north of Marion.

(2)   Burke Co. Rt. 1223 bridge to Rt. 1147 bridge

Drop	Difficulty	District	Time	Scenery	Water Quality
41'	1-2	8.5 mi.	3 hrs.	B	Good

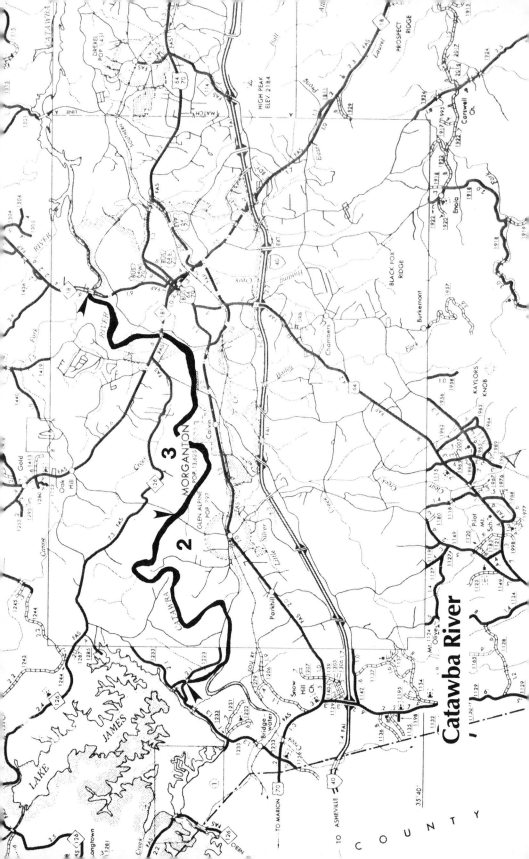

Catawba River

Gage   None. The power plant is operating if there are no significant mud flats along the banks. This will provide plenty of water. When it is not in operation the first two gravel bars in section (2) probably will need to be walked. Afte these two the remainder can be negotiated.

Difficulties   The volume of water coming from the Bridgewater Plant of Duke Power Company is completely unpredictable. This presents a situation where the water level increases approximately two feet within a matter of seconds and can be rather dangerous in the first 200 yds. below the put in, particularly so 50 yds. downstream, where a large tree blocks most of the channel on the right. Put in on the left of the bridge to be safe. The stretch above the second bridge has several islands that should be approached carefully when the water is up.

(3)   Burke Co. Rt. 1147 bridge (Watermill Rd.) to N.C. 18 bridge

Drop	Difficulty	Distance	Time	Scenery	Water Quality
17′	1	7.5 mi.	3 hrs.	A-B	Good

Gage   See section (2).

Difficulties   A low head dam located just around the bend above Independence Boulevard in Morganton. It is well marked. Carry on the posted trail on the left. For those wishing to shorten the trip, an access area has been constructed as part of Morganton's new greenway at Judges Riverside Restaurant off Airpark Road.

Directions   **Put In—(Section 2)** Burke Co. Rt. 1223 bridge west of Glen Alpine and 400 yds. east of Bridgewater Power Plant at Lake James.
Take Out—(Section 3) N.C. 18 bridge north of Morganton on south bank at gravel pit.

■

The movement of a canoe is like a reed in the wind. Silence is part of it, and the sounds of lapping water, bird songs, and wind in the trees. It is part of the medium through which it floats, the sky, the water, and the shores. A man is part of his canoe and therefore part of all it knows. The instant he dips his paddle, he flows as it flows, the canoe yielding to his slightest touch and responsive to his every whim and thought. . . .

Sigurd F. Olson

Catawba River, North Fork

━━

The North Fork has its headwaters on Humpback Mountain below the Blue Ridge Parkway. It is a small shallow stream which U.S. 221 follows down the mountain, until Armstrong Creek comes in and it picks up considerably. Also, in the Sevier area it receives some degree of industrial pollution. Below Sevier it enters a small gorge and continues on its way to Lake James. The river runs parallel to and below the western ridge of the Linville Gorge Wilderness Area. With the exception of the Clinchfield Railroad running along the east bank for about half way down, this is an uninhabited area. It remains fairly narrow as it courses over ledges and through small boulder gardens.

Topo Maps   Little Switzerland, Marion East

County   McDowell

(1)   On McDowell Co. Rt. 1559 to Rt. 1552 bridge

Drop	Difficulty	Distance	Time	Scenery	Water Quality
160′	2-3	5.6 mi.	3.5 hrs.	A	Good

Gage   On northwest side of railroad bridge at put in; minimum level for solo is 2″ below "0."
Can generally be run during wet seasons or immediately after a rain. Run off will be fast.

Difficulties   600 yds. below the put in a boulder garden runs about 100 yds. This will require a great deal of maneuvering. It would be best to scout on the right bank.
There are several interesting rapids before arriving at the railroad bridge, but below it an 8 ft. slanting falls should be approached with caution. Three 2 to 3 ft. ledges follow it closely. Run on the right. The river drops about 16′ within 150 yds. through this area. Scout on the right bank again.
With a reading of approximately 4″ above the bottom of "0" on the gage, several of the rapids will require scouting.

Directions   **Put In**—North of Marion on U.S. 221 to Woodlawn, then east on Rt. 1556 to Rt. 1559 and 100 yds. to put in on river's edge, between the creek bridge and railroad bridge.

Take Out—North of Marion on U.S. 221. East on Rt. 1501 (Hankins Rd.) to Burnett's Landing. Turn left on Rt. 1552 to the bridge. A slightly easier take out can be made at the Wildlife Access Area .5 mi. downstream from Rt. 1552 bridge. Look for the sign on the right, after passing Burnett's Landing.

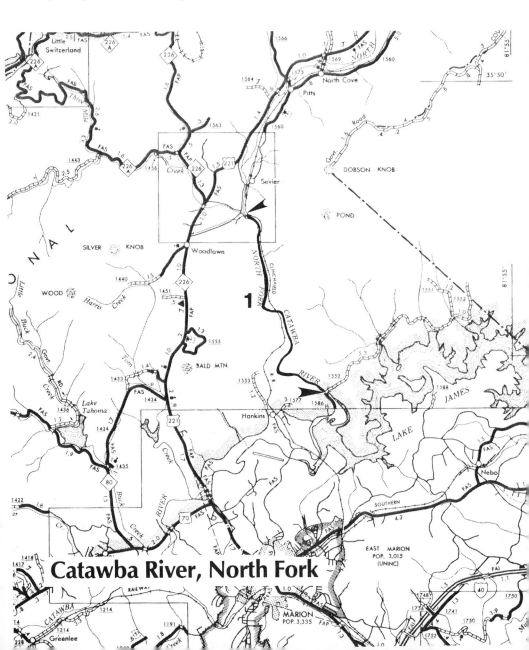

Catawba River, North Fork

Big Crabtree Creek

Big Crabtree Creek originates up in Sugar Cove Gap and then flows through the Crabtree Meadow area along the Blue Ridge Parkway. It drops quickly off the Blue Ridge quickly and runs northerly before confluencing with the North Toe.

Topo Map   Micaville

Counties   Mitchell, Yancey

(1)   Old 19 bridge to N.C. 80 bridge over the North Toe at Booneford

Drop	Difficulty	Distance	Time	Scenery	Water Quality
151'	1-2	6.2 mi.	2.45 hrs.	A	Good to Fair

Gage   On northeast side of S.R. 1102 bridge (first bridge south of U.S. 19E bridge). Minimum for solo is 6" below "0."

Difficulties   About one mi. into the run a downed tree will require a carry on river left. The last two mi. of the creek drop at a rate of some 40 ft. per mi., so action will pick up somewhat.

Directions   **Put in**—Old 19 bridge is the old bridge located just downstream from 19E.
Take out—Yancey County Rt. 1300 to N.C. 80 and right to bridge.

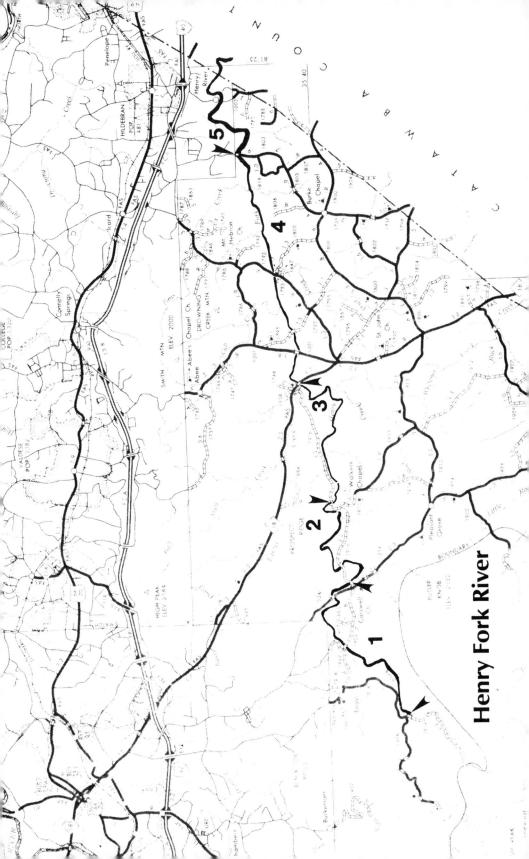

Henry Fork River

Henry Fork River

The Henry Fork heads up in the South Mountains and flows east out of Burke County into Catawba County, where it meets the Jacob Fork and forms the South Fork Catawba River. The first 15 mi. flow through an area abounding in laurel and rhododendron, making a very scenic run. The stretches below are generally flat and include two dams. Also, sewage is pumped into the river below the dam at Brookford.

Topo Maps   Morganton South, Valdese, Longview, Hickory

Counties   Burke, Catawba

(1)   Burke Rt. 1919 bridge south of Enola to Rt. 1916 bridge

Drop	Difficulty	Distance	Time	Scenery	Water Quality
160'	2-3	4.4 mi.	2 hrs.	A-B	Good

Gage   On the south side of N.C. 18 bridge. Reading at the bottom of 1 for solo run through first 2.3 mi. to Rt. 1922 bridge; 4" below "0" from 1922 to 1916 is a minimum. Run only after rain.

Difficulties   None that are dangerous, but a constant gradient of 48'/mi. through the first 2.5 mi. will demand great caution through here. This section consists of many small ledges which are generally followed by pools.

(2)   Burke Rt. 1916 bridge, just off Rt. 1924 (old N.C. 18), to Rt. 1916 bridge

Drop	Difficulty	Distance	Time	Scenery	Water Quality
74'	1-2	5 mi.	2.5 hrs.	A	Good

Gage   4" below "0" minimum for solo. Run most of the year except dry seasons.

Difficulties   None. Primarily shallows and small shoals.

(3)   Burke Rt. 1916 bridge (second bridge below the put in on section (2)) to N.C. 18 bridge

Drop	Difficulty	Distance	Time	Scenery	Water Quality
92'	1-2/3	5.2 mi.	2.5 hrs.	A-B	Good

Gage   2" below top of "0" minimum for solo. Run late winter, spring or after rain.

Difficulties   There are several shoals which drop quickly. The Class 3 consists of a series of staircase ledges which continue for 125 yds. and necessitate a lot of maneuvering.

(4)   N.C. 18 bridge to Rt. 1803 bridge

Drop	Difficulty	Distance	Time	Scenery	Water Quality
43'	1-2	4.9 mi.	2 hrs.	B-C	Good to Fair

Gage   6" below "0" minimum for solo run. Run year round except during extremely dry spells.

Difficulties   One small rock garden.

(5)   Burke Rt. 1803 bridge to N.C. 127 bridge

Drop	Difficulty	Distance	Time	Scenery	Water Quality
70'	1-2	7.6 mi.	3 hrs.	B	Fair

Gage   6" below "0." Run year round.

Difficulties   A 20 ft. dam at the Henry River Mills, just below Catawba Rt. 1002 bridge, requires a portage of 150 yds. on the left side around the mill.

(6)   N.C. 127 bridge at Brookford to Catawba Rt. 1143 bridge

Drop	Difficulty	Distance	Time	Scenery	Water Quality
38'	1	6 mi.	2.5 hrs.	B	Fair to Poor

Gage

Difficulties   A 30 ft. dam in the town of Brookford can be portaged on the right bank. Approach with caution.

Directions   **Put In**—Take the Enola Rd. south off I-40 at the Western Carolina exit in Morganton. Proceed to Rt. 1918, the first paved road to the right beyond the community of Enola, and continue to end of pavement.

Take Out—N.C. 127 south, off U.S. 64-70, to Brookford; south on Catawba Rt. 1008 to Rt. 1144, then east to the bridge.

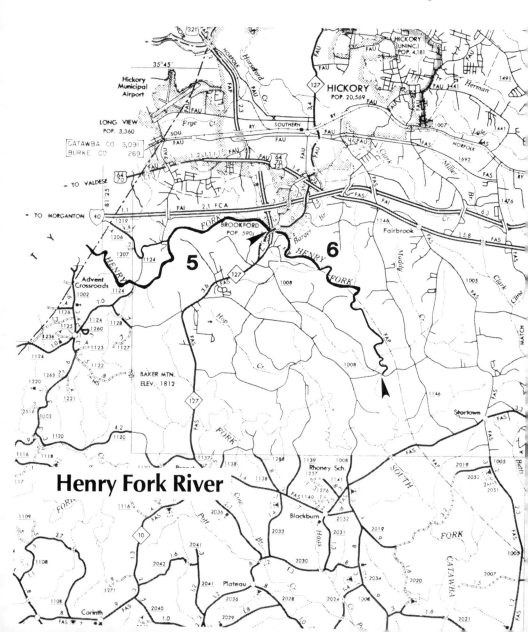

Henry Fork River

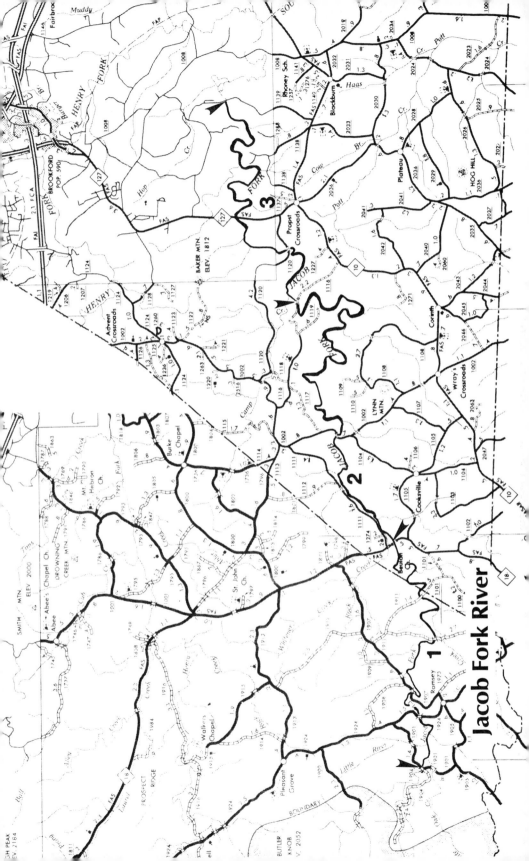

Jacob Fork River

Jacob Fork River

The Jacob Fork flows out of the South Mountains through an area of rolling hills, until it confluences with the Henry Fork. Most of the sections listed are closed in, with little signs of habitation except in the immediate areas around the bridges. The banks generally abound in laurel and rhododendron.

Topo Maps   Casar, Banoak, Longview, Hickory

Counties   Burke, Catawba

(1)   Burke Co. Rt. 1901 bridge to N.C. 18 bridge

Drop	Difficulty	Distance	Time	Scenery	Water Quality
136'	1-2	9.2 mi.	3 hrs.	B	Good

Gage   U.S.G.S. gage at Burke Co. Rt. 1924 bridge (old N.C. 18). Minimum for solo is 2.75. Can be run most of the year except during dry spells.

Difficulties   In the horseshoe bend between Burke Co. Rt. 1907 bridge and 1910 bridge there are remains of a 10 ft. dam. Approach very cautiously in higher water levels. Portage on the left.

(2)   N.C. 18 bridge to Catawba Co. Rt. 1116 bridge

Drop	Difficulty	Distance	Time	Scenery	Water Quality
145'	1-2	12.2 mi.	4.5 hrs.	A-B	Fair

Gage   U.S.G.S. gage. Minimum for solo is 2.0. Gage also on N.C. 127 bridge on northwest side. Minimum for solo is 4'' below "0."

Difficulties   None

(3)   Catawba Co. Rt. 1116 bridge to Rt. 1139 bridge

Drop	Difficulty	Distance	Time	Scenery	Water Quality
82'	1-2	7.4 mi.	2.5 hrs.	A-B	Good to Fair

Gage   N.C. 127 bridge. Minimum for solo is 4'' below "0."

Difficulties   None

Directions   **Put In**—Burke Co. Rt. 1924 (old N.C. 18) south of Morganton
approximately 12 mi., then west on Rt. 1901 to bridge.
Take Out—Catawba Rt. 1139 bridge, then 3.1 mi. north of
N.C. 10 (south of Hickory).

■

*There is magic in the feel of a paddle and the movement of a canoe, a magic
compounded of distance, adventure, solitude and peace. The way of a canoe is
the way of the wilderness and of a freedom almost forgotten, the open door to
waterways of ages past and a way of life with profound and abiding satisfactions.*
Sigurd F. Olson

Johns River

The Johns heads up in the Globe area of the Pisgah National Forest. It wanders through farm land and wooded areas until it reaches the backwaters of Duke Power Company's Lake Rhodhiss, north of Morganton. A gap, between sections (1) and (2), has been left due to the many low water bridges located through that stretch.

Topo Maps   Globe, Collettsville, Morganton North

Counties   Burke, Caldwell

(1)   Johns River Camp Bridge to second low water bridge after leaving N.C. 90.

Drop	Difficulty	Distance	Time	Scenery	Water Quality
115'	1-2	4.5 mi.	2.5 hrs.	B	Excellent

Gage   East side of Caldwell Co. Rt. 1337 bridge in Collettsville. Minimum for solo is 4" below "0." There is also a corresponding gage on the east side of Burke Co. Rt. 1438 bridge. With a level of 2" above the bottom of "0" the trip can be extended 3.5 mi. by putting in at Caldwell Co. Rt. 1367 low water bridge.

Difficulties   None, other than a couple of very tight passages which might be blocked by downed trees. Do not trespass on private property through here, which can prove rather difficult with some 7 low water bridges.

(2)   Caldwell Co. Rt. 1337 bridge in Collettsville to Rt. 1328 bridge

Drop	Difficulty	Distance	Time	Scenery	Water Quality
43'	1-2	6 mi.	2.5 hrs.	B	Good

Gage   Minimum for solo is 6" below "0."

Difficulties   One area below the old sand and gravel pit, which may be clogged with debris after high water.

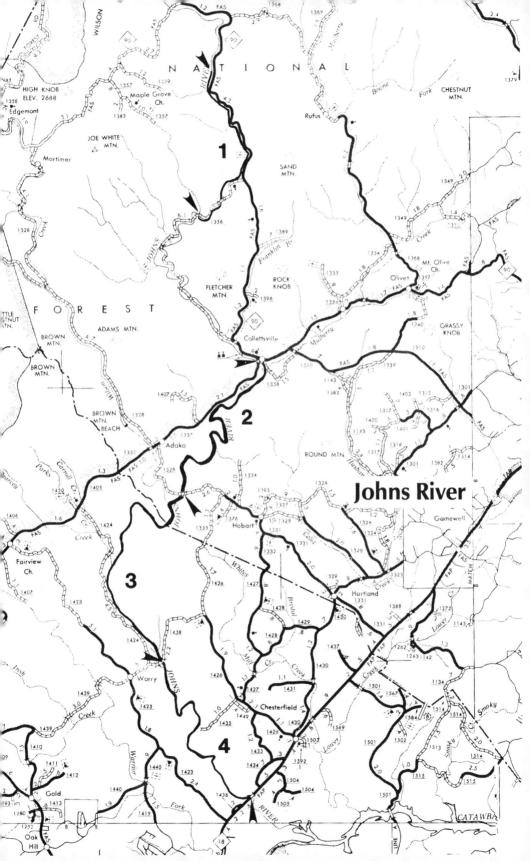

(3)   Rt. 1328 low water bridge to Burke Co. Rt. 1438

Drop	Difficulty	Distance	Time	Scenery	Water Quality
38'	1-2	6.5 mi.	2.5 hrs.	B	Good

Gage   Minimum level for solo is 6" below "0."

Difficulties   None.

(4)   Burke Co. Rt. 1438 bridge (30 yds. upstream on east bank) to N.C. Wildlife Access Area at N.C. 18 bridge

Drop	Difficulty	Distance	Time	Scenery	Water Quality
12'	1	5.5 mi.	2.5 hrs.	B	Good

Gage   Minimum level for solo is 6" below "0."

Difficulties   None.

Directions   **Put In—Section (1)** N.C. 90 north of Collettsville at Johns River United Church of Christ Camp bridge. Ask permission if the campground is open.

Take Out—Second low water bridge on Rt. 1356 southwest off N.C. 90.

Put In—Section (1) Rt. 1337 bridge at N.C. 90 in Collettsville.

Take Out—N.C. 18 bridge northwest of Morganton.

Linville River

The Linville River originates approximately one mi. east and down slope of Sugar Mountain, just across the valley from Grandfather Mountain. From its origin the river flows quietly for several miles before reaching Linville Falls, a drop of some 85 ft. Below this point the Linville Gorge proper begins, and the river and its immediate environs are protected by the Linville Gorge Wilderness Area, an 11,000-acre tract that is part of Pisgah National Forest. This remote, rugged, beautiful country lends itself to hiking, rock-climbing, and fishing, pursuits much saner than attempting to paddle this river.

Due to its length, inaccessibility, and gradient, Linville River Gorge is arguably the most difficult stretch of whitewater in the eastern U.S. The gorge is 17 mi. long and drops 1,880 ft. The first 14 mi. are Class 4, 5, and 6 water, and the lower three mi. slow down to Class 2 and 3. The entire Gorge is seldom run due to the following:

1. The river runs infrequently, generally only after extended rainfall, and has a small window of runnability.

2. The remoteness makes for difficult put ins and take outs. Evacuations would be extremely strenuous and time-consuming.

3. Scouting and portaging are hard and sometimes dangerous.

4. The rapids are long, complex, unforgiving and have several undercuts. In short, unless you're quite comfortable on every other high caliber hair run in the East, you're about to get in over your head if considering a run down the Gorge. This is full contact boating at its finest.

Although the Gorge has been run in a single-bone-jarring, glycogen-depleting day by one group, it should be considered a two-day trip. The break point between Linville Falls and N.C. 126, Sandy Flats trail, is the most logical place to split the trip due to similar time requirements for the section above and below. This also divides the hardest section of the river (the middle ten mi.). The most popular section for a single day of paddling is from Conley Cove trail to N.C. 126, which has about 3.5 mi. of hard water and 3.5 mi. of easy rapids.

Topo Maps   Linville Falls, Ashford

County   Burke

(1)   Linville Falls to Sandy Flats Trail

Drop	Difficulty	Distance	Time	Scenery	Water Quality
880'	4-5.2-6	7 mi.	8 hrs.	AA	Good

Gage   U.S.G.S. gage located 100 yds. upstream of N.C. 126 bridge on river right. Minimum level is 1.8 ft.

Difficulties   The first 2.5-3 mi. below Linville Falls are a natural slalom course of primarily Class 3 rapids. The first big drop of 14 ft. lets you know you're about to enter more serious water. The next several miles do not let up. It gets generally harder and harder. The scouting is strenuous and the portages even more so. Some of the rapids encountered are First Falls, Harvey's Folly, Group Grope, and Map Falls. It is advisable to know something of the trail system in case of evacuations or aborted trips.

(2)   Sandy Flats Trail to N.C. 126 bridge

Drop	Difficulty	Distance	Time	Scenery	Water Quality
1,000'	4-5.2	10 mi.	8 hrs.	AA	Good

Gage   See section (1). Minimum level is 1.7 ft.

Dawn Benner at Twiggy's Revenge, Linville River. A D. Benner photo.

R.B. Binegar at Cathedral Falls, Linville River. A D. Benner photo.

Difficulties   The rapids and their complexities are numerous. There will be about 6.5-7 mi. of hard water before the gradient starts to slow down. This section has been done in two portages, both mandatory. One is a ten-yard walk and the other is a forty-yard walk (longest portage on the river) ending above Cathedral Falls. Cathedral Falls will come about two mi. into this section. The rapid is composed of a 6-ft. horseshoe-shaped ledge feeding a fast runout to a 16-ft. vertical drop where one must be on line. Other significant drops include The Narrows, Kidney Reducer, The Slot, Slam Dance, Twist and Shout, and The Wall.

Directions   **Put in**—Take N.C. 181 north of Morganton to left on N.C. 183. Follow N.C. 183 to left on N.C. 1238 (Old Hwy. 105). Go to Linville Falls parking lot. Hike in below Linville Falls on river right side.

Take out—Take N.C. 126 west of Morganton bridge over Linville river. Take out 100 yds. upstream of bridge.

Lost Cove Creek

Lost Cove Creek is born deep in the mountains between Lost Cove Cliffs and Sassafrass Knob. A beautiful, sparkling stream, its entire drainage is within Pisgah National Forest. It is the major tributary of Wilson Creek. There is current legislation pending in the state to consider designating this a Wilderness Area. Here's hoping. This is strictly a high-water run with a window of two days at best. A good flow is probably 150 cfs. Make sure you're well warmed up before putting in. There is continuous Class 3 water for two mi. after pulling out of the first eddy, with more interesting stuff below. This is a true wilderness run and you must hike 2.2 mi. to get to the put in. The run is well worth the walk.

Topo Map   Grandfather Mtn.

Counties   Avery, Caldwell

(1)   Forest Rd. 464-A to Edgemont Church Rd. at N.C. 90 bridge

Drop	Difficulty	Distance	Time	Scenery	Water Quality
520'	3-4/5	5.0 mi.	4 hrs.	AA	Excellent

Gage   Wilson Creek gage should read a minimum of 2 ft.

Difficulties   The creek forks in several spots making for very tight maneuvering. After 2.5 mi. of continuous boulder gardens, the stream enters a 3/4 mi. gorge and changes character with several ledge drops. The first and most difficult, Hunt Fish Falls, is a low Class 5 rapid consisting of two drops of seven and ten ft. in close succession. Scout or carry on the right. The rapid has been run by staying far right on both drops. Note the beautiful waterfall tumbling down the mountain on the right. Below Hunt Fish Falls is a 12-ft. slide best run right center. The next rapid should be entered far right with a cut to the left down the runout trough. A tight boulder garden is below here. This is followed by Air Baker, the last large drop on the run, which should be entered far left and finished with a traverse to the right. Below Air Baker the gradient subsides somewhat but continues with entertaining Class 2 and 3 rapids for the next two mi. to the take out.

Directions   **Put in**—Take N.C. 90 west out of Mortimer. Take left onto Forest Service Rd. 464 and go 4.75 mi. to Forest Service rd. 464-A. Walk 464-A the 2.2 mi. to the creek because the road is not in good shape.
Take out—Take N.C. 90 to Edgemont Church Rd. and park. This is right above the confluence with Wilson Creek.

Muddy Creek

North Muddy Creek heads up in the hills south of Marion and wanders east and north before meeting the South Muddy downstream of I-40 and the put in. It then flows northerly entering the Catawba River about one mi. down from the Bridgewater Power Plant at Lake James.

Topo Map   Glen Alpine

Counties   Burke, McDowell

(1)   **McDowell Rt. 1763 beneath I-40 to Burke Rt. 1223 (100 yds. above bridge) along the Catawba River**

Drop	Difficulty	Distance	Time	Scenery	Water Quality
47'	1	5.1 mi.	2.5 hrs.	A-B	Fair

Gage   I-40 bridge piling. Minimum for solo is 6" below "0."

Difficulties   None.

Directions   **Put in**—From U.S. 70 west of Glen Alpine go south on Burke Rt. 1156 which becomes McDowell Rt. 1763.
Take out—Take U.S. 70 north on Burke Rt. 1233 (opposite Burke Rt. 1156) to Rt. 1223 and east to old road bed about 100 yds. upstream from the bridge on river left of the Catawba. The old bridge abutment is evident here.

North Fork of the Catawba River. Photo by Bob Benner.

New River

The New begins with the confluence of the North and South Forks. At this point it has already become a fairly wide river although still primarily shallow (see section (6), South Fork, New River). From Mouth of Wilson to Stuart Dam the New is mostly flat, therefore the reason for omitting these 2.5 mi.

The river flows through forested rolling hills and pastoral lands and in general is a very scenic stream. We recommend Randy Carter's *Canoeing White Water* to those who wish to paddle further sections of the New to the north and into West Virginia.

Topo Maps   Mouth of Wilson (Va.); Sparta West and Sparta East (N.C.-Va); Briarpatch Mtn. and Galax (Va.)

Counties   Grayson (Va.); Alleghany (N.C.)

(1) Stuart Dam to State Access area on river left below U.S. 221-21 bridge (located on S.R. 700)

Drop	Difficulty	Distance	Time	Scenery	Water Quality
72′	1-2/3	11.3 mi.	4 hrs.	B	Good

Gage   None, however the river can be run all year. The river has widened considerably and care should be taken if conditions are such that there might be high water.

Difficulties   Downstream one mile from Grayson Co. 601 bridge in the community of Cox Chapel as the river bends to the right there are two rapids. The first, a long class 2, should be scouted from the left in higher water. The second, a couple of hundred yards beyond the first, is a class 3 where most of the water flows hard left by a large boulder on the bank. Watch for the drop just beyond the boulder. Attempt to scout on the right. At higher water levels this can be run in the center.

This area of the rapids is where Appalachian Power Company proposed to construct their dam (see South Fork, New River).

(2) State Access area below 221-21 bridge to Access area on Grayson County Rt. 641

Drop	Difficulty	Distance	Time	Scenery	Water Quality
125′	1-2	26.2 mi.	10 hrs.	A-B	Good

Gage   None. Can be run year round.

Difficulties   None. This is primarily flat with occasional riffles and a few shoals. This is a favorite float trip for canoe camping.

Directions   **Put In**—At Stuart Dam alongside U.S. 58 east of Mouth of Wilson.
        Take Out—North on Rt. 634 from U.S. 58-221, then left on Rt. 641. For overnighters one may feel safer about leaving a vehicle at Carl Chapman's Riverwind Outfitters located at VA 94 bridge (old 58). This cuts some three mi. off the trip. A nominal fee is charged.

New River

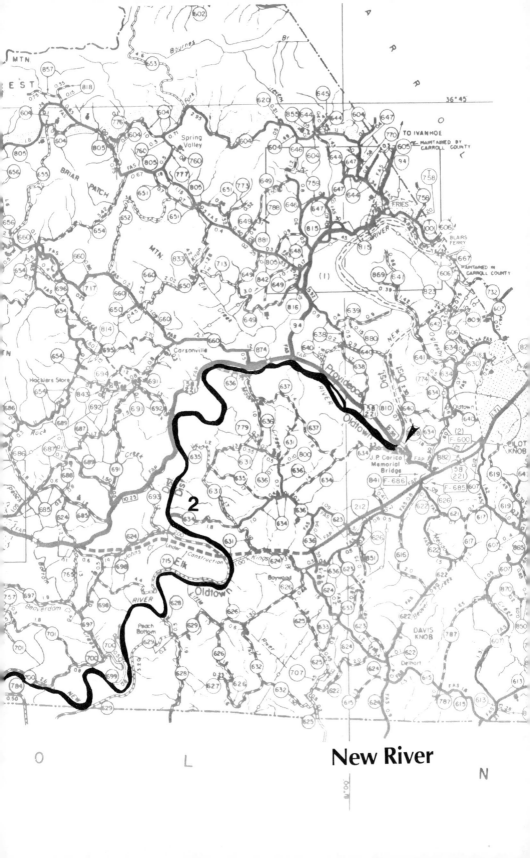

New River

North Fork, New River

The North Fork heads up in the extreme western end of Ashe County just over the Tennessee line. It flows northeast in the shadows of The Peak, Three Top Mountain, and Phoenix Mountain on the south before confluencing with the South Fork and forming the New River.

It is primarily a stream of shallow ledges with an occasional gravel bar through its upper reaches. Then it flattens out to where it presents a few riffles and a ledge now and then. River access is quite easy with roads following alongside most of the entire distance. This also gives it a pastoral setting through most of the sections.

Topo Maps   Baldwin Gap, Warrensville, Jefferson, Grassy Creek, Mouth of Wilson (Va.)

County   Ashe

(1)   Ashe Co. Rt. 1119 bridge at community of Maxwell to Rt. 1100 bridge

Drop	Difficulty	Distance	Time	Scenery	Water Quality
76′	1-2	6.8 mi.	3 hrs.	B	Excellent

Gage   On northeast piling of Rt. 1644 bridge at Sprague Electric (Rowie McNeil Rd.). Minimum for solo is 4″ below "0." Can be run from Clifton down most of the year except during extremely dry seasons.

Difficulties   A series of gravel bars in the first 1.5 mi. which drop at a rate of about 25 ft./mi.

(2)   Rt. 1100 bridge at Creston to N.C. 88 bridge

Drop	Difficulty	Distance	Time	Scenery	Water Quality
85′	1	7.2 mi.	3 hrs.	B	Good

Gage   Minimum for solo is 6″ below "0."

Difficulties   None, but watch for low water bridges.

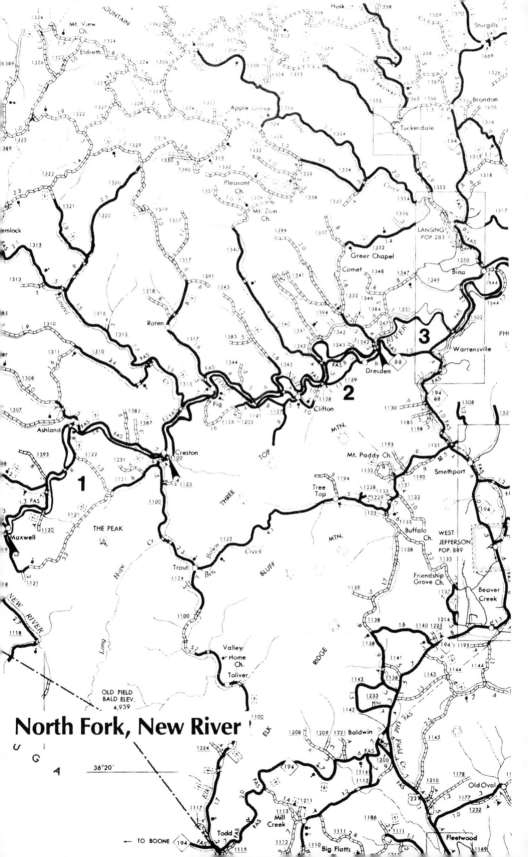

North Fork, New River

(3)   N.C. 88 bridge west of Clifton to Rt. 1644 bridge

Drop	Difficulty	Distance	Time	Scenery	Water Quality
89'	1-2	11 mi.	4.5 hrs.	A-B	Good

Gage   Minimum for solo is 6" below "0."

Difficulties   Below Clifton where the river bends sharply away from N.C. 88 and then back, there is a 12 ft. dam which can be seen from the highway. Carry on the left. There is a 4 ft. slanting ledge immediately below the dam which can be run with a couple of inches above the minimum. Watch for low water bridges.

(4)   Rt. 1644 low water bridge (Bernard Miller Rd.) to N.C. 16 bridge

Drop	Difficulty	Distance	Time	Scenery	Water Quality
101'	1	10 mi.	4 hrs.	A-B	Good

Gage   Minimum for solo is 6" below "0."

Difficulties   None other than a few gravel bars.

(5)   N.C. 16 bridge to Ashe Co. Rt. 1549 and Alleghany Rt. 1311 below the confluence with the South Fork.

Drop	Difficulty	Distance	Time	Scenery	Water Quality
126'	1-2	8 mi.	3.5 hrs.	A-B	Fair

Gage   Minimum for solo is 7" below "0."

Difficulties   Below the first bridge after the put in there are the remains of a washed out low water bridge that will require portaging at normal water levels. Carry or scout on the left.

One low water bridge farther downstream should be approached with caution at higher levels.

Directions   **Put In**—West on N.C. 88 to Ashe Co. Rt. 1119, and south to the bridge.

Take Out—East on Ashe Co. Rt. 1535 off N.C. 16 (just south of Va. state line) to Rt. 1549 along the New River.

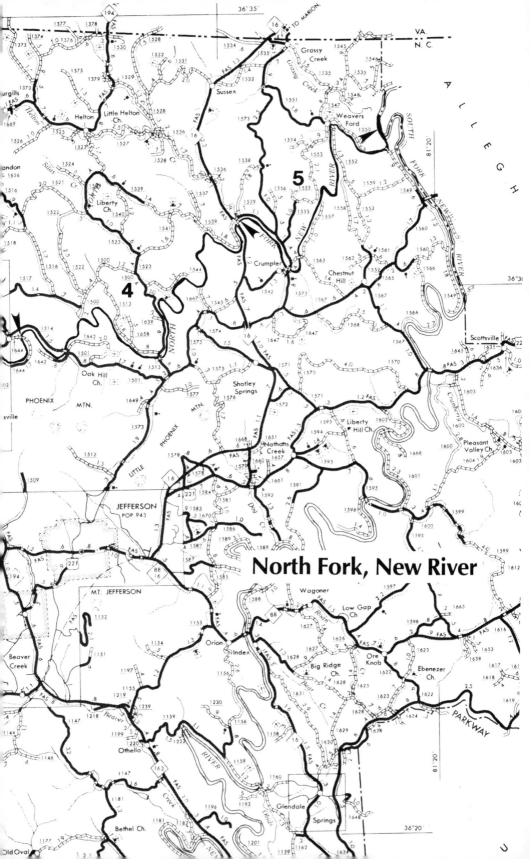

North Fork, New River

South Fork, New River

The South Fork begins at the confluence of several small streams southeast of Boone, meanders across the three most northwesterly counties in North Carolina before joining the North Fork and forming the New just south of the Virginia line. It is primarily an easy flowing stream over rocky beds, with occasional riffles as it threads its way between mountains on one side and fields on the other. The South Fork is an excellent stream for canoe camping, even though there are low water bridges on practically every section that will generally require carrying.

The South Fork is by far the more popular canoe stream of the two forks of the New River. Its popularity is due primarily to its greater length of canoeable water and its easier accessibility. Trips ranging in length from an hour or so up to several days are possible on the South Fork, all in water with only Class I rapids suitable for novice canoeists and canoe camping. There are many open areas and pastures along the South Fork that make beautiful spots to stop for lunch or to camp. There are also four public campgrounds along the South Fork with facilities for camping; all charge a small fee.

The forks, as well as the New itself, were known as the Teays River on maps showing ancient rivers, and at one time was the master water system of North America. The New cuts north and west across Virginia into West Virginia, where it is joined by the Gauley and becomes the Kanawha.

The river, perhaps the oldest in the country, appeared to be short lived when plans for a giant hydroelectric plant were firming up in the early seventies. Two dams were planned which would have flooded some 42,000 acres, mostly in North Carolina. After a long hard battle which gathered national support, the river was saved when President Ford signed a bill on September 11, 1976 establishing a 26.5 mile section as a National Wild and Scenic River. This section consists of 22 miles of the South Fork plus the first 4.5 miles of the main stem (most of sections 7 and 8).

Naturally this has brought an influx of paddlers to the river—especially on the Wild and Scenic section, which quite often has resulted in property damage and hard feelings by residents. Perhaps we can keep this in mind when floating here.

Topo Maps   Deep Gap, Todd, Glendale Springs, Jefferson, Laurel Springs, Mouth of Wilson

Counties   Watauga, Ashe, Allegheny (N.C.); Grayson (Va.)

(1) U.S. 421 bridge to Watauga Rt. 1347

Drop	Difficulty	Distance	Time	Scenery	Water Quality
110'	1	18 mi.	6 hrs.	A-B	Fair

Gage   U.S.G.S. gage is on the right bank 200 yards upstream of N.C. 16 and 88. Minimum for solo is 2.50. Gage on U.S. 221-441 on southwest side. Minimum for solo is 5" below "0." The river below Todd can be run year round. It would be wise to check the gage during spells of extreme dryness to determine the advisability of running the upper section in particular.

Difficulties   None, other than low-water bridges and shallow gravel bars at lower water levels. There are, however, many low overhanging branches.

(2) Todd to Fleetwood

Drop	Difficulty	Distance	Time	Scenery	Water Quality
85'	1-2	12 mi.	4.5 hrs.	A-B	Good

Gage   U.S.G.S. minimum for solo is 2.40. Gage on U.S. 221-441. Minimum is 6" below "0."

Difficulties   None, other than low-water bridges. One set of shoals about two miles above the take-out.

S.R. 1347 runs along the South Fork in the small town of Todd N.C. Although the section of the river upstream between Boone and Todd is passable in the spring, for most of the year Todd is as far upstream as paddling is practical. Railroad Grade Road (S.R. 1100), the pathway of the old railroad bed to Todd, runs alongside the river for this whole section, making it somewhat more populated and less scenic that other sections of the river. There are also many low-water bridges that require portaging. For this reason, this section is not as popular as those further downstream.

The take-out for this section is a low-water bridge just off Railroad Grade Road upstream from Fleetwood. This is a private property, so permission should be sought before using it or leaving a car there.

(3) Fleetwood to Windy Hill Road (S.R. 1169) Length approximately 4 miles. Paddling time about 1-1.5 hours.

The short section of the South Fork between Fleetwood and Windy Hill

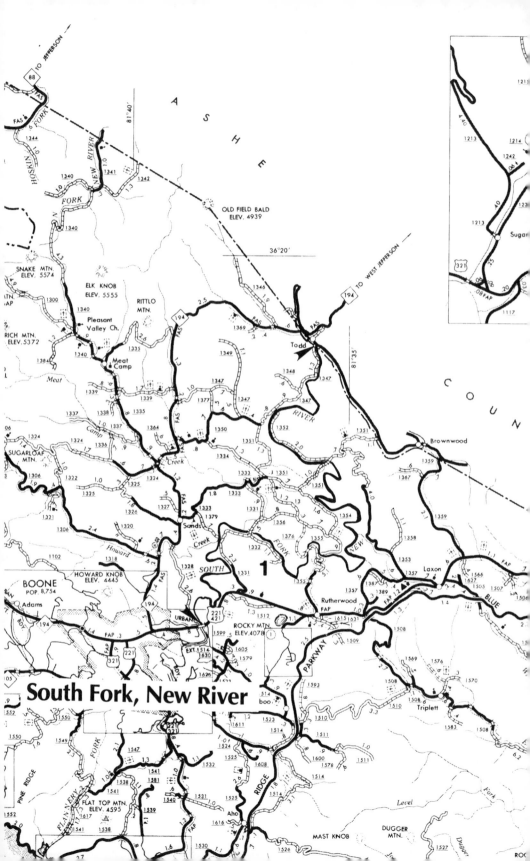

South Fork, New River

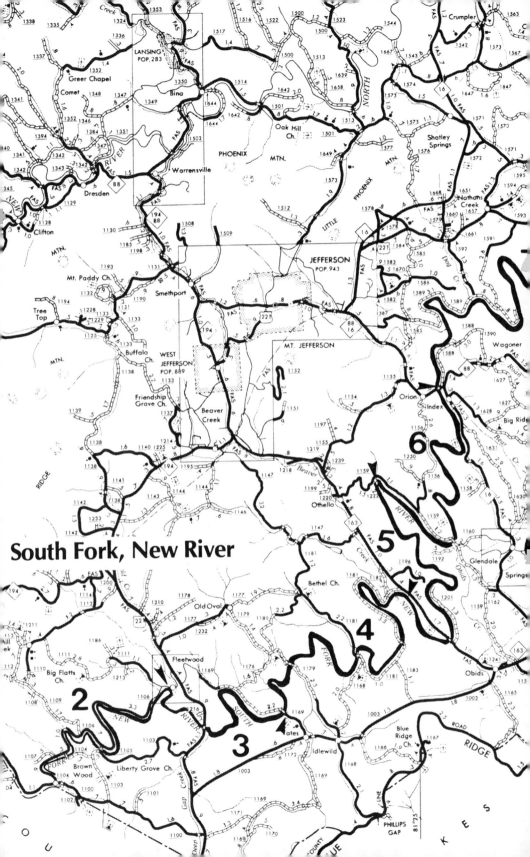

South Fork, New River

Road is a pretty section that flows under the U.S. 221 bridge along the way. Put-in is at the first low-water bridge along Railroad Grade Road above Fleetwood. The U.S. 221 bridge is not a practical put-in point because the bridge is so high off the water, necessitating a long carry from the road to the river. There is one low-water bridge downstream from U.S. 221. Because of its short length, this section of the river is seldom paddled except as part of a longer trip.

The take-out is at the low-water bridge on Windy Hill Road (S.R. 1169).

(4) Windy Hill Road (S.R. 1169) to Daniel's Daughter (N.C. 163). Length approximately 10 mi. Paddling time about 4.5 hrs.

Gage   U.S.G.S. minimum is 2.40. Gage on U.S. 221-441. Minimum is 6' below "0."

Put-in is at the low-water bridge where Windy Hill Road (S.R. 1169) crosses the river. Windy Hill Road runs between U.S. 221 just south of Fleetwood and Idlewild Road (S.R. 1003). This section of the river is one of the prettiest and most popular for day trips, although there are three low-water bridges to portage along the way. The scenery is spectacular, and the fishing is often quite good in this part of the river. The shuttle to the take-out point is also easy by following Idlewild Road to Highway 163 and then toward West Jefferson to Daniel's Daughter.

The take-out is at a low-water bridge alongside Highway 163 where it runs next to the river. There is a sign on Highway 163 for Daniel's Daughter, a small development on the opposite side of the river. Please be careful not to block the road or bridge at this take-out point. The low-water bridge just upstream would be a more convenient take-out, but the land is privately owned, and canoeists are not allowed. The Highway 163 bridge just downstream is not practical, since it is high above the river with only a barely passable road going down to the water.

(5) Daniel's Daughter to Elk Shoals Length approximately 7 miles. Paddling time about 2.5 hours.

Put-in is at the low-water bridge at Daniel's Daughter as described above. This is probably the most popular short (half-day) trip on the south Fork. It is a very scenic section of the river, there are no low-water bridges, and the shuttle is very convenient.

Take-out is at the beach at the Elk Shoals Methodist Campground along Bogg's Road (S.R. 1159). Take Bogg's Road off Highway 163 and cross the river on a low-water bridge at the sign to the Elk Shoals Campground. Elk Shoals is open to the public, but since it is a church camp, no drinking is allowed and canoeist should respect the rights of others using the beach.

(6) Elk Shoals to Highway 16 and 88 bridge Length approximately 10 miles. Paddling time about 3.5 hours.

Put-in is possible at the low-water bridge going into the Elk Shoals Campground, but this necessitates portaging two low-water bridges just downstream. A better put-in is at the bridge where Bogg's Road crosses the river about two miles further downstream. The section between Elk Shoals and the Bogg's Road bridge is seldom paddled except on longer trips that pass through this section. The six-mile section below the Bogg's Road bridge is very pretty until the last mile where it runs along Highway 16.

Take-out is at the bridge where Highways 16 and 88 cross the river. This is shown as Index on USGS maps and is known as Sheet's Store locally. Please do not leave cars along the small road next to the river. There is plenty of room for parking along Highway 16.

(7) Highways 16-88 to Gentry Road bridge Length approximately 10 miles. Paddling time about 3.5 hours.

Put-in is at the bridge where highways 16 and 88 cross the river. This is the most heavily used section of the South Fork due to its accessibility and a livery located just upstream. If you want solitude, this is not a part of the river to paddle! About four miles downstream is the old Cockerham Mill, a grist mill used from the late 1800s until the early 1950s. The land is privately owned, and canoeists should not stop. Just downstream on the right bank opposite a large island is the Wagoner Road Access Area of the New River State Park. Trips can be started or ended here, and the state park makes a nice stop-over point for lunch or camping. Canoe-in camping only is allowed, and a small fee is charged.

Take-out is at the bridge on Gentry Road (S.R. 1595). Take S.R. 1593 off U.S. 221 at Nathan's Creek north of Jefferson. Both the put-in and take-out for this run are heavily used, and canoeists should take care in parking to avoid blocking access by other canoeists and the two liveries that service the river in this area.

(8) Gentry Road to Piney Creek bridge Length approximately 15 miles. Paddling time about 5 to 6 hours.

Put-in at the bridge on S.R. 1595 as described above. About three miles downstream is a low-water bridge at Fulton Reeves Road (S.R. 1602). This can be used as an alternative take-out to lengthen the trip above or as a put-in to shorten this trip. Another four miles downstream U.S. 221 crosses the river. This is not a practical put-in or take-out because the bridge is very high over the river, and all the land is privately owned.

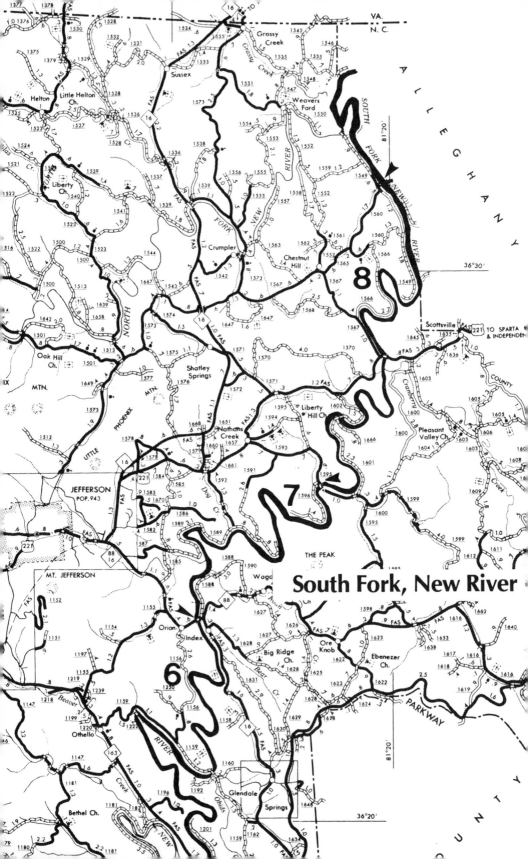

South Fork, New River

Take-out is at the low-water bridge where the old Sparta Road (S.R. 1560) crosses the river. Just downstream from here is the Twin Rivers Campground, a popular camping spot for canoeists. Don't, however, use the campground as a take-out unless you are camping there.

(9) Piney Creek Bridge to mouth of Wilson Creek Length approx. 8 miles. Paddling time about 3 hours.

Put-in is at the bridge on S.R. 1560. Just downstream is the Twin Rivers Campground, just below which is the only rapid approaching Class II on the whole South Fork. Around the bend from the campground the North Fork joins the South Fork to form the New River itself. From this point on the river is much larger, and offers some beautiful scenic vistas. About three miles below the confluence is the Allegheny County Access Area of the New River State Park. This can be used as a camping or picnic area but does not currently have road access to use as a take-out point.

Take-out is at a river access site built by the State of Virginia just off Highway 58 under the bridge where Highway 93 crosses the river just east of Mouth of Wilson, VA. Shortly downstream from here is a dam that backs up almost to the bridge, so there is little reason to go further.

South Fork, New River

Nolichucky River

Below the confluence of the Toe and Cane Rivers the Nolichucky is born—not as a small, gurgling trickle but as a full grown, boisterous, fast flowing river. Down from Poplar the river enters Cherokee National Forest while cutting a gorge 800-1,000 ft. deep between the Bald Mountains on the south and the Unaka Mountains on the north. The Clinchfield Railroad follows the river through the entire gorge. For those who would like to enjoy the rugged grandeur of the gorge and the river to the fullest, hiking is the way. The paddler can only enjoy the river, for it gives one little opportunity to view the magnificent scenery above. The river has many long rapids with heavy water, which offer little opportunity for rescue. This is a river for the advanced canoeist.

Section (2), although not as spectacular, offers the paddler outstanding scenery with such rock formations as Devil's Looking Glass.

Topo Maps   Huntdale (N.C.); Unicoi, Erwin (Tenn.)

Counties   Mitchell (N.C.); Unicoi, Washington (Tenn.)

(1)   National Forest Service put in at Poplar, N.C. to Ervin, Tenn.

Drop	Difficulty	Distance	Time	Scenery	Water Quality
338'	3-4	11.5 mi.	7 hrs.	A-A	Fair
.5 mi. @ 66'/mi.					

Gage   Call T.V.A. (615) 632-6065 for a 24 hr. recorded message on stream flow. A flow of 500 c.f.s. is a minimum, while 2,000 c.f.s. can be considered a maximum.

Difficulties   The first rapid below the railroad bridge is about 75 yds. long, over a series of ledges. There is an open passage to right of center, but two large standing waves tend to swamp open boats in higher water. The next rapid, "On the Rocks," can be easily recognized. An attempt at running it may well prove why it's so named. A line of boulders on the right forces the main current through a narrow chute in the center. A hidden rock left of center blocks what normally appears as an open run through here. At about 1,200 c.f.s. the 4' vertical drop to the immediate left of the chute is runnable. Both of these rapids can be best scouted by pulling in at the railroad bridge and walking down the tracks. The time spent walking here can save a considerable amount that would be required to free a boat.

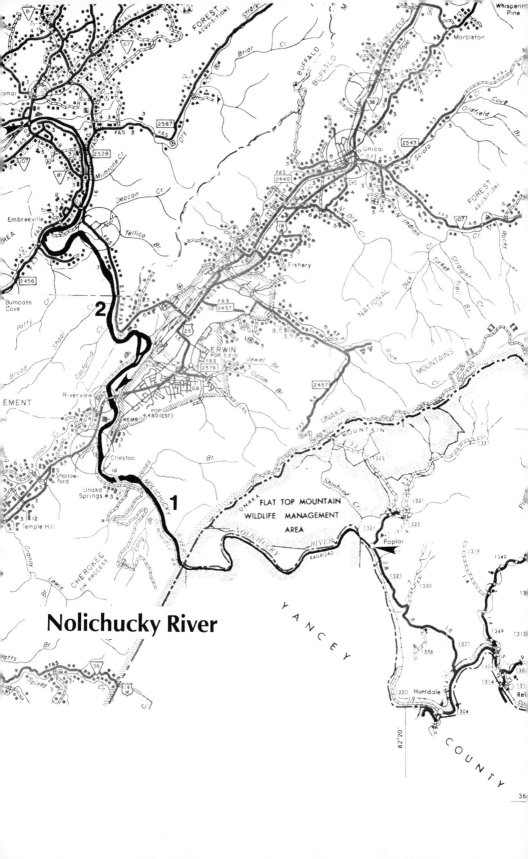

Nolichucky River

If the passage on each of the rapids which follow isn't immediately apparent, scout! Generally most of them can be run on the right side.

The third and fourth are series of ledges interspersed with boulders. The fourth, some 250 yds. long, ends up with a 4 ft. ledge. Run the chute on the far right at medium levels. Scout on the left.

The third rapid, "Quarter Mile," contains a series of ledges interspersed with boulders that ends with a four-ft. ledge. Not a good place to swim, but many do. (If you want to try your time for 440 yds., do it in a pool.) Run the chute on the far right at medium levels. Scout on the left.

There is still plenty of action beyond here, but if the paddler has made it this far without major mishaps he can breathe a little easier. Most of the remaining rapids have passages that are easily recognized.

There is one, however, "The Sousehole," that should be approached very carefully. A creek enters the river through a culvert 10 ft. above the river on the left. Below it the river bears hard right by an island and then back to the left. Stay close to the left bank all the way around these two bends. At the bottom of the left bend one will find "The Sousehole." It's a nice place to pass and look in on but certainly not to visit.

Downstream the river continues to drop over a few ledges and through some stubble fields until it reaches the take out.

Directions   **Put In**—From Spruce Pine, N.C., take N.C. 226 to .1 mi. north of Red Hill; go west on Mitchell Co. 1304 to the river, then continue along it to Mitchell Co. 1321, then north and west approximately 5 mi. to Poplar.

Take Out—West from Poplar on 1321, to 1323 (Forest Rd. 230) over Indian Grave Gap to state line and Tenn. Rt. 30, into Erwin. Go south on U.S. 19-W and 23 to Nolichucky bridge.

(2)   U.S. 19W and 23 bridge south of Erwin to Tenn. Rt. 67 bridge

Drop	Difficulty	Distance	Time	Scenery	Water Quality
185'	2-3	11.8 mi.	5.5 hrs.	A	Fair

Gage   U.S.G.S. gage is located on west side, 100 yds. upstream of Tenn. 81 bridge at Embreeville. A medium level would be a reading of about 2.40. See section (1).

Difficulties   There are several long rapids in this section which require scouting, particularly at levels even slightly above normal, especially in the area of Devil's Looking Glass, about 3.5 mi. below the put in.

High standing waves will be found on most of these, so following the rule of staying toward the inside of the bend will generally give the safer passage.

Scout the first rapid, located .5 mi. downstream from Tenn. 81 bridge at Embreeville, on the left bank. The main chute is obvious but difficult.

Directions   **Take Out**—Tenn. 67 and 81 bridge. The trip can be shortened some 2 mi. by taking out on the river, left just off Dr. A. J. Willis Rd. The sandy area at this take out is slightly over .5 mi. below the old bridge abutments. Take the first right going west on 81 in Embreeville and proceed approximately 1.4 mi. to this spot.

Upper Oconaluftee River. Photo of Bob Benner.

North Harper Creek

North Harper Creek is born high in Pisgah National Forest between Head-quarters Mountain and Big Lost Cove Ridge. It is a beautifully scenic run alternating between fast current through steep gorges and quiet water through the valley floor. A large portion of the gradient is comprised of unrunnable falls and very congested (read unrunnable) boulder chokedowns. Indeed, the creek has been run/walked by walking in the Little Lost Cove trail. This tacks an additional 1.6 mi. of distance and 480 ft. of drop to the run, most of which is unrunnable.

Topo Maps   Grandfather Mtn., Chestnut Mtn.

Counties   Avery, Caldwell

(1)   Forest Rd. 464 to S.R. 1328 bridge over Harper Creek

Drop	Difficulty	Distance	Time	Scenery	Water Quality
760'	3-4.1	5.4 mi.	5 hrs.	AA	Excellent

Gage   Located on river left piling of S.R. 1328 bridge over Harper Creek. Minimum level is bottom of "0."

Difficulties   From the 266A trailhead put in, there is .5 mi. of easy water and then the gradient increases for .3 mi. and culminates in a 50-ft. waterfall. Carry on the right. From here everything is doable down to Harper Falls, a triple stage drop of 100 ft. Carry on left. Approximately 1.5 mi. above Harper Falls, the creek confluences with Hull Branch Creek, doubling the volume and forming Harper Creek. The run is primarily easy Class 3 water, though quite technical. This is a true wilderness run; you're guaranteed to see none but the occasional, hard-core fisherman. North Harper Creek is only runnable after heavy, extended rainfall and has a window of one to two days at best.

Directions   **Put in**—Take N.C. 90 west out of Mortimer. Go left on Forest Rd. 464 to Harper Creek trailhead sign. Walk one mi. to the creek.
Take out—Take S.R. 1328 to bridge over Harper Creek, just above confluence with Wilson Creek.

North Toe River and Toe River

The North Toe heads up east of Minneapolis in the vicinity of Newland. It moves south through a mountainous area until it turns west entering the Toe Valley, which is widely known for its mineral deposits. Below the junction with the South Toe, the river gets considerably wider and becomes known as the Toe. From the Toe's confluence with the Cane the Nolichucky is born.

There are several areas of outstanding scenic beauty, in particular the rock formations of section (3). Unfortunately much of the natural beauty is marred by the grayish color of the water from Spruce Pine down the rest of the river. This is the result of many mica mines and feldspar plants in the area. Although the quality of the water is rather poor, it has improved considerably.

Topo Maps   Newland, Carvers Gap, Spruce Pine, Linville Falls, Micaville, Bakersville, Burnsville, Huntdale

Counties   Avery, Mitchell, Yancey

(1)   Avery Co. Rt. 1164 bridge at Minneapolis to dam at Plumtree

Drop	Difficulty	Distance	Time	Scenery	Water Quality
302'	2-3	8.5 mi.	4 hrs.	B	Good

Gage   U.S. 19E bridge on the southwest side (north of Spruce Pine). Minimum level for solo is the bottom of "1." The upper section can be run only following rain. Sections (2) and (3) can be run year round except following long dry seasons, while the remainder can be run year round.

Difficulties   This section, runnable only with a good runoff, drops continuously over many small stubble fields. Watch for low water bridges and logs. Take out and carry on the left of the dam at Plumtree (15 ft. high), which is located just below the bridge.

(2)   Rt. 1123 south of Spear to U.S. 19E bridge

Drop	Difficulty	Distance	Time	Scenery	Water Quality
102'	1-2	4.5 mi.	2 hrs.	A-B	Good

Gage   3" below "0."

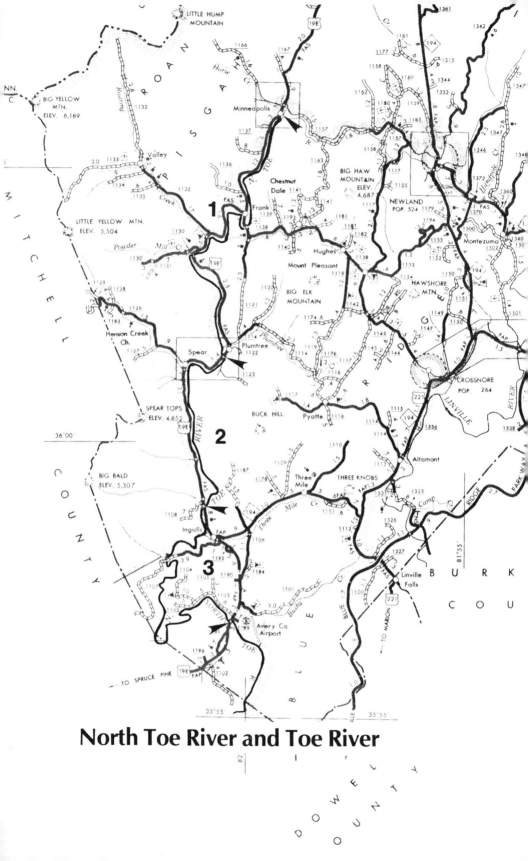

North Toe River and Toe River

Difficulties If starting here, put in about 400 yds. below the dam on Rt. 1123. There is one broken dam a little over halfway down that should be approached and scouted very carefully. This can be run on the left at a good water level. Difficulty class 3 + .

(3)   U.S. 19E bridge north of Ingalls to U.S. 19E bridge south of Ingalls

Drop	Difficulty	Distance	Time	Scenery	Water Quality
123'	1-2	7.5 mi.	4 hrs.	AA-A	Good to Fair

Gage   6" below "0."

Difficulties Many gravel bars and one ledge that will require some tight turning in approaching it. Can be scouted on the left, run on the right. This is a most scenic area with many overhanging rocks.

(4)   U.S. 19E bridge south of Ingalls in Avery Co. to Stroupe Rd.

Drop	Difficulty	Distance	Time	Scenery	Water Quality
123'	1-2	11 mi.	4.5 hrs.	A-B-C	Fair

Gage   6" below "0."

Difficulties Watch closely for a broken dam (10 ft. high) approaching the outskirts of Spruce Pine. The river bends to the left and the paddler should stay to the left, inside the bend, where the carry should be made. This can be a very dangerous area with high water, so proceed with caution. This is a scenic run with many high bluffs over the river.

(5)   Stroupe Rd., above the sewage treatment plant in Spruce Pine, to N.C. 80 bridge

Drop	Difficulty	Distance	Time	Scenery	Water Quality
68'	1-2/3	7.5 mi.	3.5 hrs.	B	Fair

Gage   6" below "0."

Difficulties A broken dam about 3 ft. high should be scouted on the right. This may be run on the far left depending on the water level. If doubtful about making it, don't try it! This is located about a mile below the put in. There are two other low washed dams that can be easily scouted.

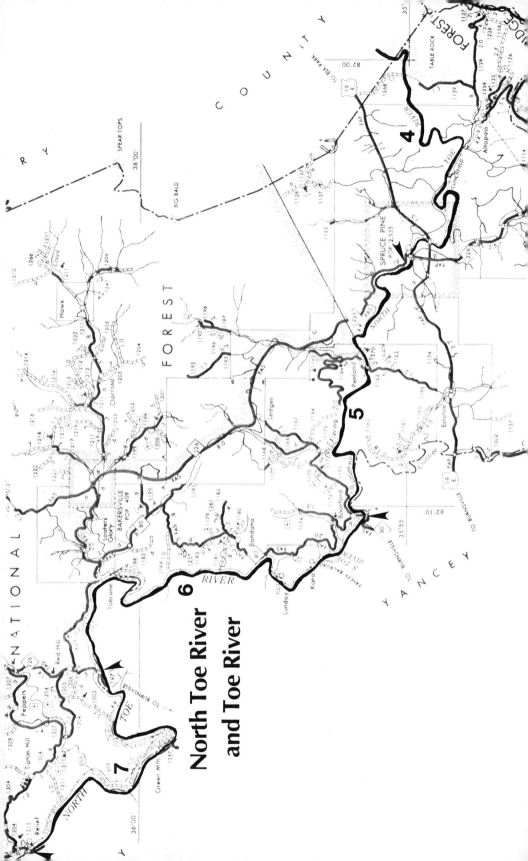

**North Toe River
and Toe River**

(6) N.C. 80 bridge at Boonfield in Mitchell Co. to N.C. 197 bridge

Drop	Difficulty	Distance	Time	Scenery	Water Quality
202'	2-3	11.5 mi.	5.5. hrs.	A-B-C	Fair

Gage   N.C. 197 bridge, on the southwest side. Minimum level for solo is 5" below "0."

Difficulties   1.5 mi. below the confluence of the South Toe, a class 3, consisting of a boulder garden, should be scouted on the left. Enter on the right. Several canoes have broken up here. Below the bridge at Toecane the river begins dropping faster, at the rate of 30 ft./mi., through a gorge that presents constant white water for close to two miles. The first ledge below the bridge should be scouted.

(7) N.C. 197 bridge south of Red Hill in Mitchell Co. to intersection of Yancey Co. Rts. 1304 and 1349.

Drop	Difficulty	Distance	Time	Scenery	Water Quality
102'	1-2	7.7 mi.	3.5 hrs.	B	Fair

Gage   6" below "0."

Difficulties   None; fairly flat, but wider and fast moving.

(8) Intersection of Yancey Co. Rts. 1304 and 1349 to NFS put in at Poplar

Drop	Difficulty	Distance	Time	Scenery	Water Quality
100'	1-2	7.6 mi.	3 hrs.	A-B	Fair

Gage   6" below "0."

Difficulties   None. A series of shoals occur in the latter portion of this section, beginning 1.5 mi. above Poplar.

Directions   **Put In**—Avery Co. Rt. 1164, off U.S. 19E south of Minneapolis. **Take Out**—From N.C. 197 and 226 at Red Hill, go west on Mitchell Co. Rt. 1304 to Rt. 1321, then north to the community of Poplar.

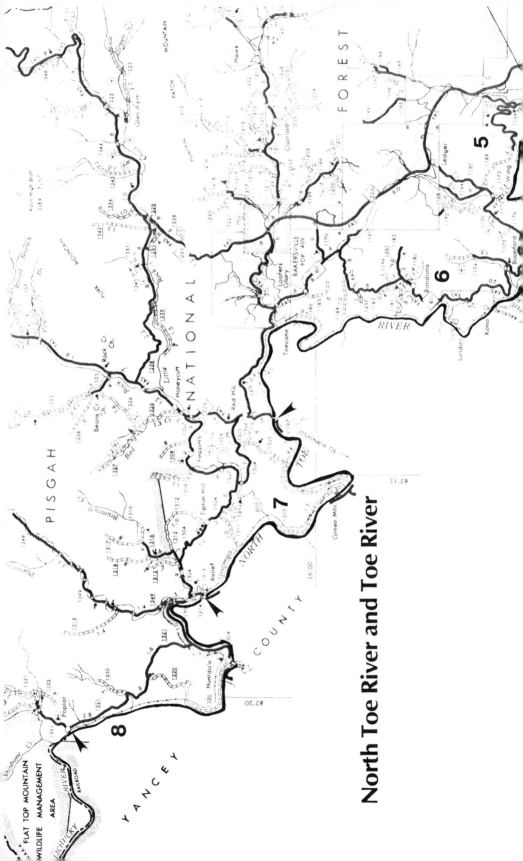

North Toe River and Toe River

South Toe River

The South Toe has its headwaters on Mt. Mitchell, the highest peak east of the Rockies (elevation 6,684 ft.), which is south from the put in. It is a delightful stream winding through the mountains over gravel bars and through boulder gardens. Section (2) flows through a particularly scenic area. The water quality drops considerably around Newdale, due to silt from mica mines in the area. It confluences with the North Toe below Newdale to form the Toe River.

Topo Maps   Celo, Micaville

County   Yancey

(1)   Carolina Hemlocks Campground or N.C. 80 bridge north of the campground to Rt. 1152 bridge

Drop	Difficulty	Distance	Time	Scenery	Water Quality
130'	1-2	8 mi.	3.5 hrs.	A-B	Excellent

Gage: U.S.G.S. located above Rt. 1167 bridge alongside Rt. 1168. Minimum level for solo is 1.09. Can generally be run following periods of wet weather.

Difficulties   Requires a good bit of maneuvering through the gravel bars and over small shoals.

(2)   Rt. 1152 bridge (Bluerock Rd) to N.C. 80 bridge in Newdale

Drop	Difficulty	Distance	Time	Scenery	Water Quality
108'	1-2-3	6.5 mi.	3.5 hrs.	A	Excellent

Gage   Minimum level for solo is 1.10.

Difficulties   This section cuts through a narrow rocky gorge that has some ledges which will require scouting. The first one has a large flat rock on the left. The second and largest entering the gorge has a series of three drops totaling some 10 ft. in 40 yds. Scout it on the left.

South Toe River

(3) N.C. 80 bridge in Newdale to Yancey Co. Rt. 1311 on the Toe

Drop	Difficulty	Distance	Time	Scenery	Water Quality
120'	1-2	8 mi.	3.5 hrs.	B	Fair to Poor

Gage   Minimum level for solo is .80.

Difficulties None. A lot of maneuvering will be required at low water levels.

Directions   **Put In**—N.C. 80 south of U.S. 19E to U.S. Forest Service campground at Carolina Hemlocks.
Take Out—Yancey Co. Rt. 1308 (.5 mi. east of Micaville) north from U.S. 19E for approximately 5.4 mi., then east on Rt. 1311 until reaching the river opposite Lunday. You must ford the creek three times before reaching the river. The take out can be recognized from the river by the footbridge just upstream.

■

Perhaps our grandsons, having never seen a wild river, will never miss the chance to set a canoe in singing water.   *Aldo Leopold*

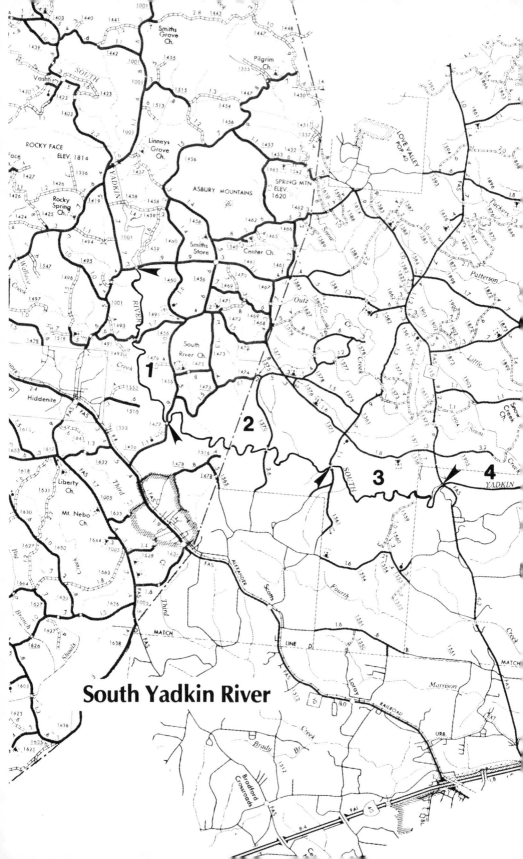

South Yadkin River

South Yadkin River

The South Yadkin heads up on the southern slopes of the Brushy Mountains. It flows by Rocky Face (elevation 1,814 ft.), the last prominent peak of the Brushy chain, and heads south and east across the Piedmont to join the Yadkin. We pick it up, just southeast of Rocky Face, as it makes its last drop into the more gently rolling hills of the upper plateau.

Sections (6)-(9) provide some 42 miles of waters suitable for canoe camping.

Note: As streams cut their way through the softer hills of the Piedmont, one will encounter more downed trees, a result of the eroding banks. This becomes the most common difficulty encountered below section (1) and should not be taken lightly—especially at the higher water levels.

Topo Maps   Hiddenite, Central, Harmony, Calahaln, Cool Springs, Coolemee, Churchland

Counties   Alexander, Iredell, Davie, Rowan

(1) Alexander Co. Rt. 1461 bridge to Alexander Co. Rt. 1456 bridge

Drop	Difficulty	Distance	Time	Scenery	Water Quality
118'	1-2	5 mi.	3.5 hrs.	A	Good

Gage   On Rt. 1461 bridge on the southeast corner. Reading of 6'' below "0" is the minimum for a solo run.

Difficulties   A 12 ft. combination dam and ledge is located about 50 yds. down from the put in. Carry on the right. About 1 mi. down, a large tree blocks the only chute. Approach it carefully. About .5 mile beyond the culvert under Rt. 1491, there is an 8 ft. ledge, which possibly could be run off center, angling to the right. Further down, there is a 3 ft. ledge. Carry on the left.

(2) Alexander Co. Rt. 1456 bridge to Iredell Co. Rt. 1561 bridge

Drop	Difficulty	Distance	Time	Scenery	Water Quality
53'	1	6.8 mi.	2.75 hrs.	A	Good to Fair

Gage   On Iredell Co. Rt. 1570 on the southeast corner. Reading of 6'' below "0" is minimum for solo.

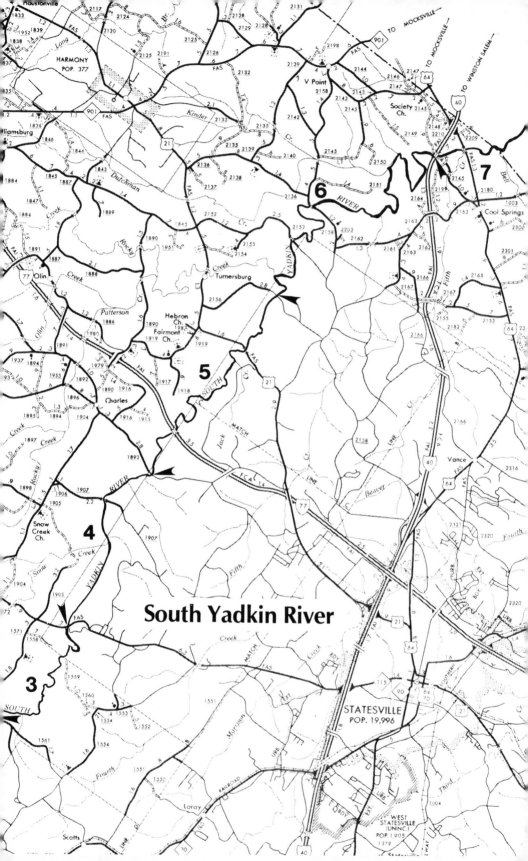

South Yadkin River

Difficulties   Water intake unit just below the put in should be approached cautiously. This is at the lower end of Col. R. L. Tatum Water Plant. At slightly higher than normal levels, there are a number of downed trees that could be dangerous.

(3)   Iredell Co. Rt. 1561 bridge to N.C. 115 bridge

Drop	Difficulty	Distance	Time	Scenery	Water Quality
29'	1	4.9 mi.	3 hrs.	B	Fair

Gage   6" below "0" for minimum.

Difficulties   Many downed trees that must be hauled over. A partially washed-out dam is about 4 mi. downstream, that might look tempting. Don't be misled, as there are steel reinforcing rods at the bottom of the chute. Carry it on the right. A drive across the bridge above the dam looks as if it would prove as hairy as trying the chute.

(4)   N.C. 115 bridge to Iredell Co. Rt. 1892 bridge

Drop	Difficulty	Distance	Time	Scenery	Water Quality
19'	C	4.5 mi.	1.5 hrs.	B	Fair

Gage   6" below "0." The river from this point downstream would very seldom be too low to run, other than during an extremely dry spell.

Difficulties   A few downed trees. An 8 ft. slanting dam just above the 1892 bridge. Easy take out or carry on the right, above the water treatment plant. This is one that might lure the neophyte into putting a little excitement into his life. If so, the very heavy hydraulic below won't allow him the opportunity to tell about it.

(5)   Iredell Co. Rt. 1892 bridge to Rt. 2156 bridge

Drop	Difficulty	Distance	Time	Scenery	Water Quality
19'	C	7 mi.	2.5 hrs.	A-B	Fair

Gage   See section (4).

Difficulties   Heavily clogged up below the US 21 bridge for a short distance.

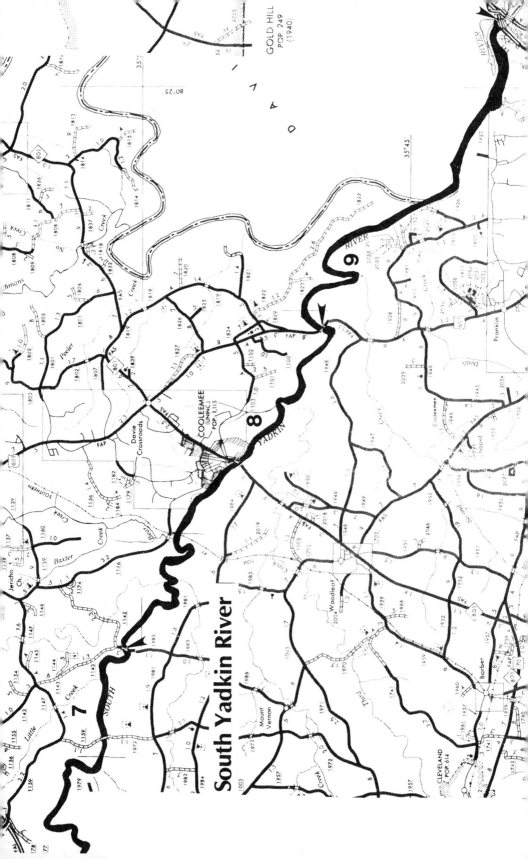

South Yadkin River

(6) Iredell Co. Rt. 2156 bridge to the side of Rt. 2145 (beneath the I-40 bridge)

Drop	Difficulty	Distance	Time	Scenery	Water Quality
28'	C	11.3 mi.	3.5 hrs.	A-B	Fair

Gage　　See section (4)

Difficulties　　None. Perhaps an occasional downed tree.

(7) Iredell Co. Rt. 2145 (beneath I-40 bridge) to Davie Co. Rt. 1143 bridge

Drop	Difficulty	Distance	Time	Scenery	Water Quality
21'	C	9.2 mi.	3 hrs.	A-B	Fair

Gage　　See section (4)

Difficulties　　Watch for possible downed trees.

(8) Davie Co. Rt. 1143 bridge to US 601 bridge

Drop	Difficulty	Distance	Time	Scenery	Water Quality
34'	-1/2	11.7 mi.	3.75 hrs.	A-B	Fair

Gage　　See section (4)

Difficulties　　Dam at Coolemee (7 mi. below the put in). Approach it on the right carefully. Take out is about 30 yds. above the dam in a low open area. A well defined trail leads around the dam, a carry of about 100 yds. A class 2 chute in the center below is runnable by approaching it from the right.

For those who don't wish to run the 2.5 mi. of slack water above the dam, a take out can be made at a ramp at Bear Creek, off Davie Co. Rt. 1116.

(9) US 601 bridge to N.C. 150 bridge over the Yadkin River

Drop	Difficuilty	Distance	Time	Scenery	Water Quality
5'	C	9.9 mi.	3 hrs.	A-B	Fair

Gage　　See section (4)

Difficulties   None, other than maneuvering around an occasional downed tree.

Directions   **Put In**—North on Alexander Co. Rt. 1001 off N.C. 90 in Hiddenite, then east on Alexander Co. Rt. 1461.
Take Out—N.C. 150 north of Salisbury.

R.B. Binegar at Watauga Falls, Watauga River. A D. Benner photo.

Steel Creek

Steel Creek is born in northeastern Burke County just east of Linville Gorge. The first several miles are a beautiful wilderness run then the creek begins to parallel Hwy 181. The entire drainage lies within Pisgah National Forest ensuring excellent water quality. Below the put in, this section is continuous Class 3 for two mi. after which the gradient subsides somewhat down to the confluence with Upper Creek. The natural slalom course is provided by the boulder garden nature of the river bed. This is strictly a high water run with a window of one to two days at best.

Topo Maps   Chestnut Mtn., Oak Hill

County   Burke

(1)   Forest Rd. 228 to S.R. 1405 (Adako Rd.) bridge

Drop	Difficulty	Distance	Time	Scenery	Water Quality
400'	3	6.0 mi.	2.5 hrs.	AA-B˙	Excellent

Gage   Upper Creek gage on Forest Rd. 982 [see section (1) on Upper Creek] should read 3" above "0" for a minimum level.

Difficulties   There are no major drops and everything can be boat-scouted. Eddy hopping and ferrying abilities will be strongly tested because the upper part of this run is very fast and tight. Below the first two mi. the gradient gradually decreases to the take out. Beware of one low-water bridge approximately 3.5 miles into the run. Carry on right.

Directions   Put in—Take N.C. 181 north of Morganton. Go 4.5 mi. beyond S.R. 1405 and take left onto Forest rd. 228. Follow this road until it literally runs into the creek.
Take out—S.R. 1405 bridge.

Upper Creek

Upper Creek originates in the Jonas Ridge area of northern Burke County. The upper stretches are within Pisgah National Forest, which ensures excellent water quality. The creek flows through one unrunnable gorge in the Jonas Hole area before entering the long abandoned Greentown community where the remains of an old railroad track are still visible. Downstream of Greentown is the Raven Cliff Gorge section. Below section (1) the creek progressively slows down and runs through rural areas before its confluence with the Catawba River, just above Lake Rhodhiss. Upper Creek is reportedly one of the best small-mouth fishing streams in the southeast.

Topo Maps   Chestnut Mtn., Oak Hill, Morganton North

County   Burke

(1)   Greentown trailhead to Forest Rd. 982

Drop	Difficulty	Distance	Time	Scenery	Water Quality
760'	3-4.2-5	4.3 mi.	4.5 hrs.	AA-A	Excellent

Gage   Located on river left piling of Forest Rd. 982 bridge. Minimum level is 3" above "0."

Difficulties   Due to the difficulty of the water, the hike to the put in, and the mandatory 45-minute portage, this section is only for dedicated experts in good condition. The gradient is somewhat skewed on this stretch due to the .4 mi. gorge, known as Raven Cliffs, where the river tumbles 280" (essentially unrunnable even by today's gnarly standards). At high water this is serious Class 4 with an occasional Class 5 drop thrown in to keep everyone honest. This section was first run at two ft. above the suggested minimum and things were somewhat out of control at times. Less than a mile into the run, the beautiful Burnthouse Branch Falls tumbles in on river left.

Approximately .5 mi. downstream, Raven Cliffs starts. Take out on the left well above to carry over the mountain. Entry into the Raven Cliffs section at high water is cheap thrills suicide. The water below Raven Cliffs is steeper than above. Pay particular attention to one long Class 4 rapid that feeds a drop with a major-league strainer, which one boater luckily survived on the first descent. Things don't ease up until you're about one mi. above the take out.

(2) Forest Rd. 982 bridge to S.R. 1405 (Adako Rd.) bridge.

Drop	Difficulty	Distance	Time	Scenery	Water Quality
240'	2-3	5.4 mi.	2.5 hrs.	A-B	Good

Gage Minimum level 1" above "0."

Difficulties Though there are no major drops on this section, there is plenty of maneuvering necessary at high water. A log dam, a few low-water bridges, and an 8-foot dam at Optimist Park are mandatory portages. This stretch meanders through pasture land for the last two mi. above Optimist Park and its subsequent confluence with Steel Creek.

Directions Section (1) Put in—Take N.C. 181 north of Morganton. Go 8.8 mi. beyond S.R. 1405 (Adako Rd.) to small sign on the right for Greentown/Upper Creek trailhead. Hike 1.1 mi. to the creek.
Take out—Take N.C. 181 north of Morganton. Go 4.5 mi. beyond S.R. 1405 (Adako Rd.) to Forest Rd. 982 on the right. Go to first bridge over the creek.
Section (2) Put in—See section (1) take out.
Take out—Take N.C. 181 north of Morganton to S.R. 1405. Go right 100 yds. to bridge.

(3) Rt. 1405 bridge (Adako Rd.) to Rt. 1439 bridge

Drop	Difficulty	Distance	Time	Scenery	Water Quality
25'	1/2	4.5 mi.	2 hrs.	B	Good

Gage Located on the southwest piling of Rt. 1405 bridge. Minimum for solo is 6" below "0."

Difficulties One ledge about .5 mi. below the put in. Watch for downed trees throughout all sections.

(4) Rt. 1439 bridge at Worry (Henderson Mill Rd.) to Rt. 1440 bridge

Drop	Difficulty	Distance	Time	Scenery	Water Quality
21'	1/2	3.5 mi.	1.5 hrs.	B	Good

Gage Located on a concrete slab under Rt. 1439 bridge on the east side. Minimum for solo is 7" below "0."

Difficulties   One fast narrow chute about halfway down the section. Watch
for downed trees.

(5)   Rt. 1440 bridge (Bost Rd.) to N.C. 18 bridge on the Catawba River

Drop	Difficulty	Distance	Time	Scenery	Water Quality
Flat	1	3.5 mi.	1.5 hrs.	C	Good

Gage   Minimum for solo is 7″ below "0."

Difficulties   None

Directions   **Take Out**—N.C. 18 bridge over the Catawba River north of
Morganton. The bridge is immediately below the confluence of
Upper Creek with the Catawba.

Leonard Baker at Upper Creek. A D. Benner photo.

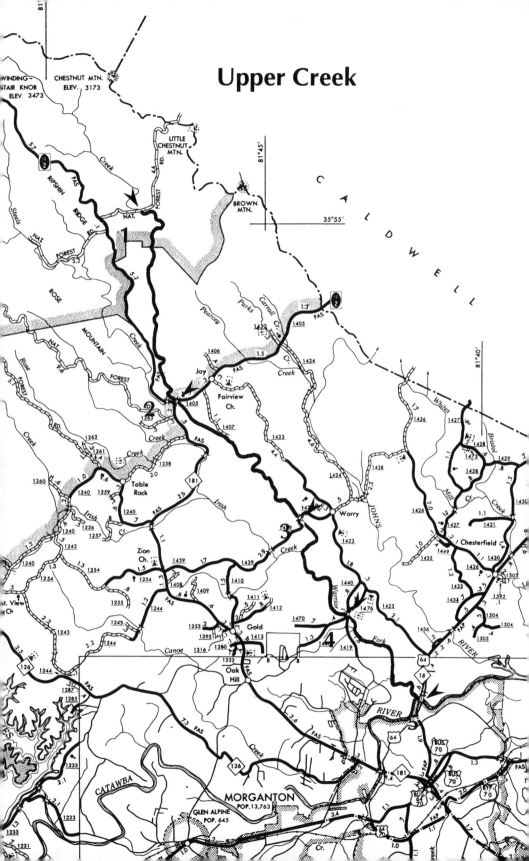

Upper Creek

Uwharrie River

The Uwharrie heads up west of Asheboro and flows generally south through the Uwharrie Mountains and across portions of the Uwharrie National Forest before it flows into Lake Tillery. The river meanders greatly through small floodplains and steep valley walls, which present some very scenic bluffs. The bed is primarily one of long pools with occasional ripples.

The area is widely known for its gold mining activity. North Carolina's first deep gold mines were found in Montgomery County in the early 1820s. In fact, several mines were worked along the river itself late in the nineteenth century. The largest of these was the Coggins Mine, just up Rt. 1301, west of the river. This was the most important mine in the state from 1915 until the late 1920s. The paddler may want to bring along a pan and take a longer than usual lunch break. It may pay for the gas to run the shuttle—one way, that is!

Note to hikers: A hiking trail, referred to as GUMPAC, has been developed in a corridor along the ridges paralleling the river. The trail, developed primarily through the efforts of a group of private citizens (Greater Uwharrie Mountains Preservation and Appreciation Committee) will hopefully be included soon as a component of the State Trails System.

Topo Maps   Asheboro, Albemarle

Counties   Randolph, Montgomery

(1)   N.C. 49 bridge to Randolph Co. Rt. 1143 bridge

Drop	Difficulty	Distance	Time	Scenery	Water Quality
22′	C-1	11.5 mi.	4 hrs.	A-B	Fair

Gage   U.S.G.S. gage 100 yds. downstream from N.C. 109 on the north bank. Minimum for solo is 1.6. Runnable year round except during extremely long dry periods.

Difficulties   Watch for an occasional downed tree. A 5 ft. dam located just above Rt. 1143 bridge can be carried fairly easily on the left side. Approach cautiously at higher water levels. Some two miles of back water will be found above it.

(2)   Randolph Co. Rt. 1143 bridge to Montgomery Co. Rt. 1301 bridge

Drop	Difficulty	Distance	Time	Scenery	Water Quality
24′	1-2	7.7 mi.	2.75 hrs.	A	Fair

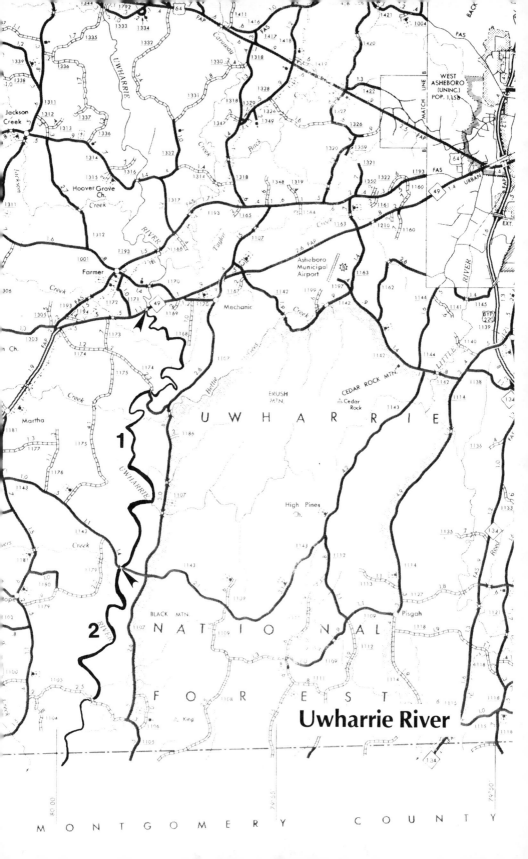

Uwharrie River

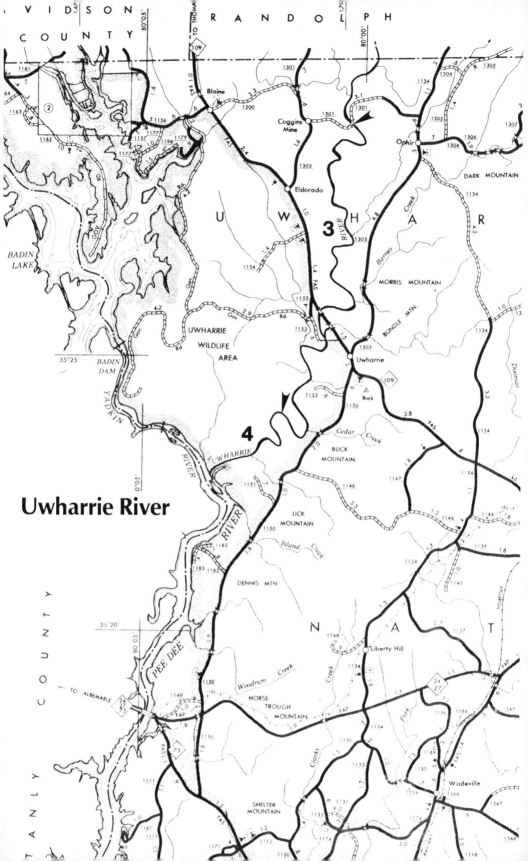

Uwharrie River

Gage   See section (1)

Difficulties   None.

(3) Montgomery Co. Rt. 1301 bridge to side of Forest Service Rd. 555 (Cotton Place Rd.), 2.9 mi. below N.C. 109 bridge

Drop	Difficulty	Distance	Time	Scenery	Water Quality
46'	1-2	10.6 mi.	4.5 hrs.	A	Fair

Gage   See section (1)

Difficulties   None.

(4) Forest Service Rd. 555 to Morrow Mountain State Park, directly across Lake Tillery from the mouth of the Uwharrie

Drop	Difficulty	Distance	Time	Scenery	Water Quality
23'	1-2	6.6 mi.	2.75 hrs.	A	Fair

Gage   See section (1)

Difficulties   None.

Directions   **Put In**—N.C. 49 bridge east of Asheboro.
                  Take Out—Morrow Mountain State Park, off of N.C. 740, northeast of Albemarle. For those who wish to extend the trip some 6 mi. down the lake, a boat launching ramp is located on the east side below N.C. 24-27-73 bridge, southeast of Troy.

Watauga River

The Watauga heads up on the eastern slope of Sugar Mountain. It winds along N.C. 105 for several miles before entering a short, steep section. After leaving 105, it meanders through hilly pasture and then through spectacularly rugged Watauga Gorge before reaching Watauga Lake in Tennessee.

Section (3) is a very pleasant, easy float trip, while section (5) is anything but. After its emergence from a deep gorge below Wilbur Dam, section (6) moves on through more pastoral country. Sycamore Shoals, just above the take out, is where the Over Mountain Men began their historic march to Kings Mountain.

Topo Maps   Boone, Valle Crucis, Sherwood (N.C.), Elk Mills, Watauga Dam, Elizabethton (Tenn.)

Counties   Watauga (N.C.), Johnson (Tenn.)

(1)   S.R. 1557 bridge to N.C. 105 bridge

Drop	Difficulty	Distance	Time	Scenery	Water Quality
180'	2-3-4.2	2.0 mi.	2 hrs.	B	Good

Gage   Gage is on river right concrete abutment of S.R. 1557 bridge. Minimum level should be 2" below "0."

Difficulties   This run is Dr. Jekyll/Mr. Hyde in character. The first half, down to the washed-out bridge, is composed of fun Class 2 water. Then the river changes nature immediately and becomes a Class 4/5 (depending on water level) challenge for the best boater. The one-mi. section down to the dam is recommended as a warm-up for what waits below. Known to the locals as the "Red Roof" run, this has for several years been a late afternoon adrenaline pumper due to its ease of access and short paddling time. This section must be caught during or shortly after heavy rains for adequate water.

The lower portion of the run is steeper and less forgiving than most anything in the gorge downstream. Well into the hard stuff, there is one house-sized boulder with a ledge spanning the river. Run far right. Below is a small island which should be run down the left side. Routes through most other drops are fairly obvious, if not pretty. Everything is blind and must be shore-scouted. At levels of 0 and below this is hard Class 4 water. Above "0" and the extra push increases the intensity to Class 5.

Directions   **Put in** Take N.C. 105 south of Boone to S.R. 1568 (Old Shulls Mill Rd.). Go .8 mi. to S.R. 1557 and take left to bridge over river.
Take out Take N.C. 105 south of Boone 4.8 mi. to bridge over river.

(2)   N.C. 105 bridge to N.C. 194 bridge at Valle Crucis

Drop	Difficulty	Distance	Time	Scenery	Water Quality
175′	1-2	4.5 mi.	2 hrs.	A-B	Good

Gage   U.S.G.S. gage is on the right bank 250 ft. upstream from Rt. 1121 bridge. Minimum reading for solo is 1.95. The river can be run throughout most of the year below section (1), except during long dry periods.

Difficulties   This section runs over a bed of rocks with some small ledges that can require a lot of maneuvering.

(3)   N.C. 194 bridge to U.S. 321 bridge

Drop	Difficulty	Distance	Time	Scenery	Water Quality
65′	1-2	7.5 mi.	2.5 hrs.	B	Good

Gage   U.S.G.S. minimum for solo is 1.85.

Difficulties   One low water bridge. Below Rt. 1121 bridge there is a 15 ft. dam that can be portaged on the right (50 yds.). A few gravel bars other than these.

(4)   U.S. 321 bridge to Watauga Co. Rt. 1200 (Guys Ford Rd.)

Drop	Difficulty	Distance	Time	Scenery	Water Quality
100′	2/3	4 mi.	2 hrs.	A	Good

Gage   U.S.G.S. gage. Minimum for solo is 1.85.

Difficulties   There is a drop of some 12 ft. within 20 yds. about .25 mi. below the put in. This can be seen from the highway. It can be run 2/3 of the way down, but the bottom is packed with boulders. A carry can

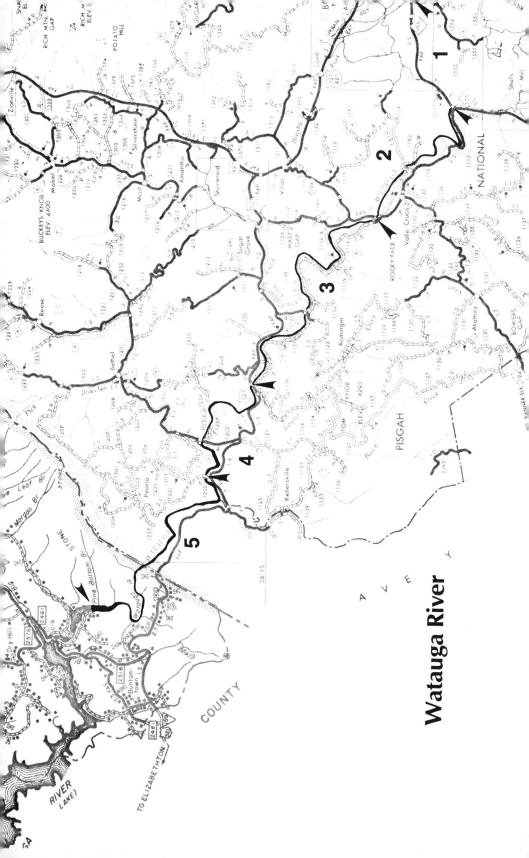

Watauga River

be made on the right. Other than this, it is primarily a run through gravel bars and small boulder fields.

(5)   S.R. 1200 (Guys Ford Rd.) bridge to Watauga Lake

Drop	Difficulty	Distance	Time	Scenery	Water Quality
515'	3-4-5/5.1	5.7 mi.	3.75 hrs.	AA	Good

* 3 parts drop at the rate of 200'/mi. for approximately .2 mile each.

Gage   Minimum level is 12" below the top of the river left (downstream) piling of the Guys Ford bridge.

Difficulties   The Watauga River Gorge has been a classic East Coast hardwater run since the East Tennessee Whitewater Club pioneered trips here in the early 70s. Though it has dropped several rungs on the hair boating ladder due to comparison with today's banzai runs, it remains a pre-eminent steep creek for advanced to expert boaters.

From Guys Ford bridge there is .7 mi. of Class 2-3 warm-up water before the first boulder clog, which can be eddy hopped. Below here are three major drops within .5 mi. The third, and most dangerous rapid on the river, Hydro, should definitely be scouted (on the left). Hydro, a hard Class 5 at medium and high water, is quite demanding technically, as well as dangerous due to a boulder strainer at the top and a strong keeper at the bottom. Rescue is questionable because it's hard to place ropes. From here the river alternates between reasonably open water and frequent blind drops squeezed between huge boulders. Downstream vision is generally very limited. Vernon's Folly, Edge of the World, and Blowjob are a few of the more significant drops. Heavy Water, another Class 5, is noted by a steep, complex entry, as the river narrows and disappears to the right around a macro boulder with the current tending to shove boats into one or two nasty holes below the turn. Scouting is advised here.

Approximately one mi. below Heavy Water is the Class 5 Watauga Falls. The Falls is a 16-ft. vertical drop with 60% of the water going over the right center. It is seriously aerated because there is a boulder that is slightly above the surface at the bottom. A distinct horizon line will tell you to take out on the left to carry or scout, about 75 yds. above the drop. If planning to run, it's a good idea to catch the eddy directly above the drop. Cut a hard right angle to boof the drop and hopefully avoid collision with said boulder at the bottom.

From here a house-sized boulder can be seen 200 yds. downstream. Run the nine-ft. drop just to the right of the boulder. Things start to ease up from here down to Watson Island where there is a possible take out on the left of the island. Don't count on taking out here because the landowners generally have the road shut down to boaters. Instead, run down the right side at Watson Island and continue on easy Class 2 water to the lake. A .5 mi. paddle across the lake will bring you to Phillips Campground, where boaters can leave shuttle cars for two bucks per vehicle.

Directions   **Put in**—Take U.S. 321 north out of Boone to S.R. 1200. Take a right on S.R. 1200 and go .25 mi. to river.

Take out—Take U.S. 321 north out of Boone to the first paved road on the right beyond the NC/TN state line. Keep bearing right on this road until the deadend at Phillips Campground.

(6)   Wilbur Dam to .5 mi. west of Sycamore Shoals on U.S. 321

Drop	Difficulty	Distance	Time	Scenery	Water Quality
158'	2-3	11.5 mi.	5.5 hrs.	A-B	Good

Gage   U.S.G.S. gage is on the left bank at 19E (Bristol Highway) bridge. Minimum reading for solo is 2.68. There is no regular schedule for water releases from Wilbur Dam, as power is furnished on demand. The only apparent pattern of release occurs on Saturdays shortly after 12 noon during the summer.

Difficulties   At lower water levels, when the dam isn't operating, there are no dangerous areas, but Sycamore Shoals should be approached with caution. At higher levels the picture changes. About 300 yds. downstream from the overhead foot bridge in the gorge, a series of ledges build up 3-4 ft. standing waves in a bend to the left. If not prepared to handle this, stay close to the left bank.

Downstream from 19E bridge the Beaunit Plant on the left and the Elizabethton sewage palnt on the right of the river dump waste into the river, which gives one added motivation to stay upright through Sycamore Shoals. It can be recognized by a long flat stretch and the fort on the left side. The shoals can best be scouted from the left. It consists of a series of ledges on the right, running diagonally downstream from right to left. The safest passage is to the right of the main channel.

Put In—Section (5) Take Tenn. 91 north from Elizabethton to the community of Hunter (alongside river) and take the first main road to the right after 91 leaves the river. Proceed approximately 4 mi. to the dam.

Take Out—Go west on U.S. 321 from Elizabethton approximately .5 mi. beyond Sycamore Shoals Historical Area.

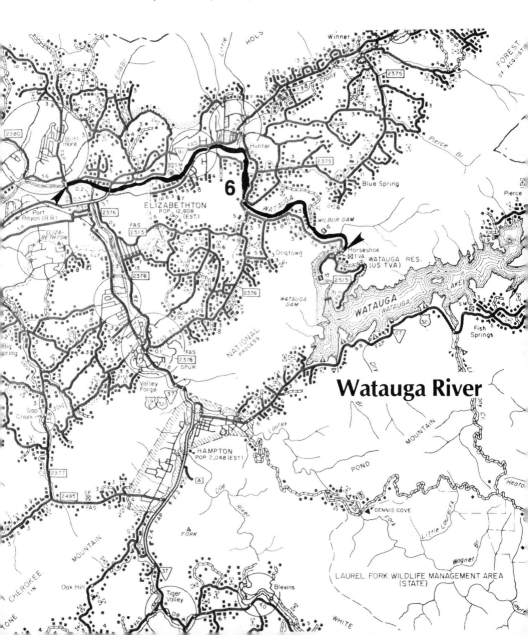

Watauga River

Wilson Creek

Wilson Creek has its headwaters on the eastern slopes of Grandfather Mountain. With its watershed primarily within the Pisgah National Forest, it has exceptional water quality. This quality quite often fools even the experienced paddler into underestimating water depth.

Section (1), which is quite technically challenging, can only be run after heavy rains, and has a small window during which it can be paddled. Sections (2) and (3) drop over the occasional ledge and stubble field and are suitable for low intermediate skill levels. Section (4) drops through a ruggedly beautiful gorge with several memorable rapids. It is one of the more popular advanced runs in the southeast. After leaving the gorge at Brown Mountain Beach, the creek slows down considerably upon its confluence with John's River. The gorge, as well as most of the creek, can be enjoyed by everyone, not only those with the skill to paddle it. Wilson Gorge is highly recommended to all—whether boating, mountain biking or just driving. Be aware that the creek, especially through the gorge, has become a very popular area.

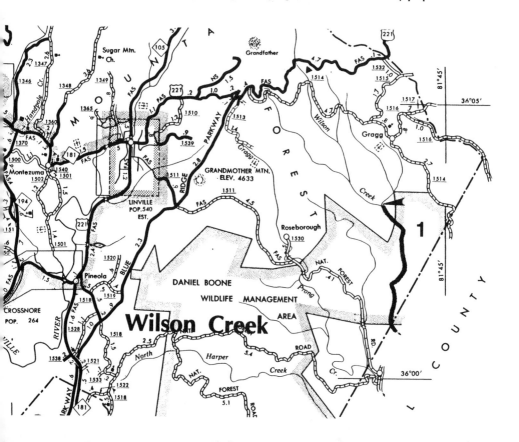

The traffic on the narrow road is quite heavy on weekends from late spring through the summer.

Topo Maps   Grandfather Mtn., Chestnut Mtn., Collettesville

Counties   Avery, Caldwell

(1)   Forest Rd. 45 to intersection of S.R. 90 and Forest Rd. 981

Drop	Difficulty	Distance	Time	Scenery	Water Quality
520'	3/4	4.9 mi.	3 hrs.	A-B	Excellent

Gage   Located on the river left piling of S.R. 1405 (Adako Rd.) bridge. A minimum level is 1.5 ft.

Difficulties   This is a bang-up section of almost continuous grade 3 water. Though not as impressive as the popular gorge downstream, this stretch requires excellent boat control, as there are many tight moves. With the exception of one rapid, everything can be boat-scouted. Approximately .75 mi. into the run is a steep Class 4 rapid which is best scouted and entered on the right. There is a potentially nasty undercut at the bottom of the drop. There is a trail on the left paralleling most of the run. The scenery, while not outstanding, is pristine, down to the first bridge. Be aware of the private property (owned by a hunting club) that is posted throughout the lower portion of the run, and precludes taking out at the first bridge you come to.

Directions   **Put in**—Take S.R. 90 north from Mortimer. S.R. 90 turns into Forest Rd. 45. Stay on Forest Rd. 45 to .5 mi. south of intersection at Gragg, where the trailhead is on the left. Hike in approximately 1.5 mi. to creek.

Take out—Take S.R. 90 north of Mortimer to intersection of S.R. 90 and Forest Rd. 981. Bridge is on the right 50 yds. up from the intersection.

(2)   Intersection of S.R. 90 and Forest Rd. 981 to low-water bridge in Mortimer on S.R. 1328.

Drop	Difficulty	Distance	Time	Scenery	Water Quality
100'	2	2.5 mi.	1 hr.	A-B	Good

Gage   The gage at Adako Rd. bridge should be a minimum of 9" above "0."

Difficulties   None.

Directions   **Put in**—See section (1) take out.
Take out—Go north on S.R. 1326 to low-water concrete bridge south of Mortimer.

(3)   Rt. 1328 concrete low water bridge to point 150 yds. south of National Forest boundary sign

Drop	Difficulty	Distance	Time	Scenery	Water Quality
120'	1-2/3	5 mi.	2.5 hrs.	A-B	Excellent

Gage   Located on river left of Rt. 1337 (Adako Rd. bridge). Minimum for solo is 5" below "0." Call the store at Brown Mountain Beach (704) 758-4257 for a rough estimate of the water level.

Difficulties   Most of sections (4) and (5) can be scouted from the road.
About .5 mi. below the put in, as the creek bends to the right, there is a low foot bridge that can be missed by a quick move to the left.

Lunch Stop Rapid, a Class 3, narrows down, piling the water against it and forcing it to the left of a rock wall. This should be scouted on the left and run on the inside. The rock makes for an excellent stopping place for lunch.

There are several ledges and stubble fields below the steel bridge that may require scouting depending on the water levels. Be sure that the take out is checked out and that it can be easily recognized, or the gorge may see you before you see the gorge.

(4)   National Forest Boundary sign to Brown Mountain Beach

Drop	Difficulty	Distance	Time	Scenery	Water Quality
220'	3-4.2	2.4 mi.	3 hrs.	A	Excellent

Gage   Minimum level is 3" below "0".

Difficulties   Wilson Gorge is primarily a drop/pool run, although there are several boulder gardens that provide natural slalom courses. There are five major drops on this section and plenty of good action between them. They are (in order) Ten Foot Falls, Boatbuster/Thunderhole, Triple Drop, Razorback, and Huntley's Retreat. These rapids are all Class 4 at levels of "0" and below. At levels of "0" and "1" foot, they progress to hard Class 5. Above 1 foot they are quite intimidating with sketchy lines and big keeper hydraulics that invite unwilling boaters back in for an extended chat.

With a road following the river closely for most of the run, scouting or aborting trips is a simple matter. As car break-ins are not uncommon, valuables should be left at the take out because that area is less secluded. Boaters have maintained good relations with the owners of Brown Mountain Beach by leaving cars parked across the road from the store and not driving through the property to the beach. Let's continue this practice.

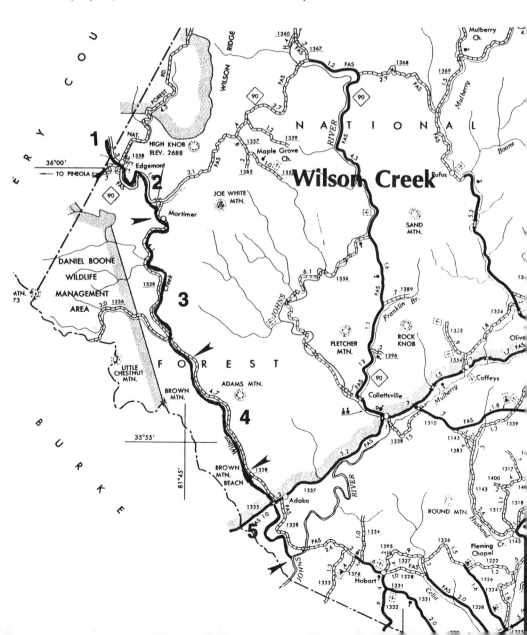

(5) **200 yds. above Rt. 1337 bridge on Rt. 1328 to Burke Co. Rt. 1438 bridge over the Johns River (refer to map on page 118)**

Drop	Difficulty	Distance	Time	Scenery	Water Quality
42'	1-2	8 mi.	3.5 hrs.	B-C	Good

Gage Minimum for solo is 6" below "0."

Difficulties There is one rapid, "Eddie's Icebox," approaching Class 3 in difficulty at higher water levels, about .5 mi. below Adako bridge, which requires a hard right turn. It will carry the unwary paddler directly onto the rock ledge straight in front. Step out on the small island to the left to scout.

One other rapid between Perkins Park and Playmore Beach can be trouble at lower water levels. Most of the water runs off a ledge on the far right, which is where it should be run.

Directions **Put In**—Caldwell Co. Rt. 1328 north of Rt. 1337 1 mi. northeast of Burke-Caldwell Co. line. Low water bridge is .6 mi. south of Mortimer.

Take Out—West on Rt. 1337 (Burke Co. Rt. 1405) 2.2. mi. from Wilson Creek bridge, to Burke Co. Rt. 1424 (Grade Rt.). Go south on it to Rt. 1438, then east to Corpening Bridge.

Section 4

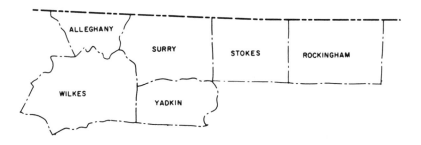

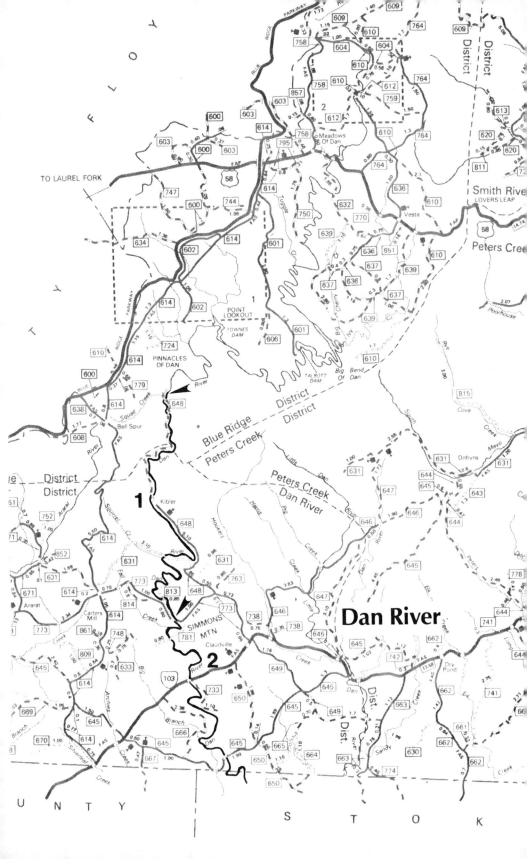

Dan River

The Dan River flows off the crest of the Blue Ridge beneath the Pinnacles of Dan. It is piped down the mountains through the turbines of the City of Danville Power Plant above the community of Kibler. From the power plant, it wanders southeast through hills of laurel and rhododendron before turning northeast and entering Virginia just east of Eden. It then flows generally east until it confluences with the Roanoke River.

The Dan was named after Danaho, a Saura Indian chief. The Saura Indians lived along the river, with Saura Town situated near the junction of the Smith and Dan and lower Saura Town located near the former town of Draper.

As one paddles the upper section in North Carolina, he will catch glimpses of the Sauratown Mountains to the South. This range is one of the most easterly mountainous areas in the state and is home to Hanging Rock State Park. The park consists of rugged mountain terrain and has excellent camping facilities. The Dan is now a North Carolina State Water Trail.

Topo Maps: Claudville, Stuart S.E. (VA), Hanging Rock, Danbury, Ayersville, Belews Lake, Walnut Cove, Mayodan, South West Eden, South East Eden, Draper (NC-VA), Brosville (NC-VA)

Counties: Patrick (VA), Stokes, Rockingham (NC)

(1)   City of Danville Power Plant at Kibler to Patrick Co. Rt. 773 bridge

Drop	Difficulty	Distance	Time	Scenery	Water Quality
255'	1-2	8 mi.	3.5 hrs.	B	Excellent
1 mi. @ 65'/mi.					

Gage   None. To check on the water flow, call Pinnacles Hydroelectric Station, 703-251-1255 and ask for the water flow. 5,600 k.w. would be a minimum. Maximum possible flow is 9,600, at which open canoes can run safely. The plant will run 7,500 k.w. on Saturdays July through October from 9 AM to 3 PM unless unusual conditions exist.

Difficulties   The first .5 mile below the put in drops very fast. About 200 yds. below the first bridge, a 3 ft. drop pushes much of the water into a large boulder on the right. If entered too far to the right, much of the boat is also pushed against the boulder. This rock is undercut, so be very cautious in trying to dislodge a broached canoe.

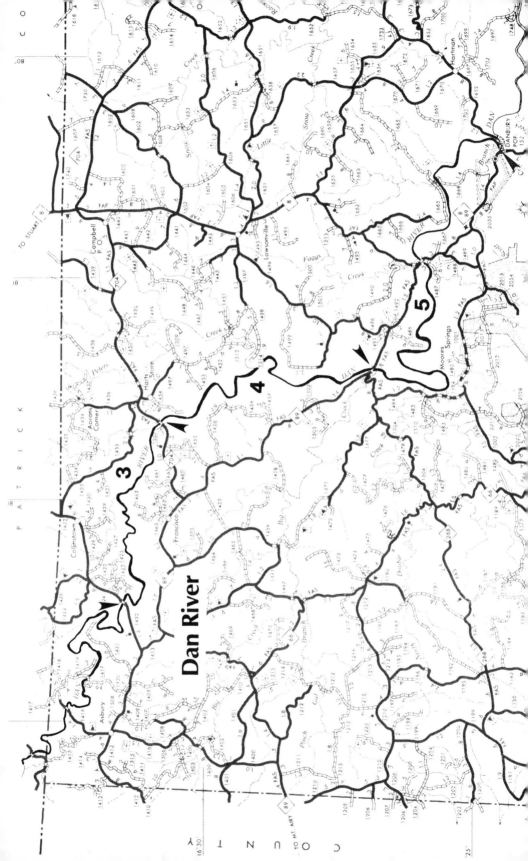

Dan River

(2)   Patrick Co. Rt. 773 bridge to Stokes Co. Rt. 1432

Drop	Difficulty	Distance	Time	Scenery	Water Quality
224'	1-2	12.5 mi.	5.5 hrs.	A	Good

Gage   U.S.G.S. gage located 75' above N.C. 704 bridge on the north
                bank. A reading of 1.7 is minimum for solo, or phone Pinnacles
for a reading (5,600 k.w. minimum).

Difficulties   Primarily fast water approaches through small rock gardens and
                over small ledges.
    Following the second bridge (Stokes Co. Rt. 1416) below Va. 103 bridge
there are a series of ledges ending in a tight "S" turn presenting a high Class 2.
Scout on the left. Old Route 1417 (Joyce Mill Rd. which is now closed) is immediately downstream.

(3)   Stokes Co. Rt. 1432 bridge (Collinstown Rd.) at Jessups Mill to N.C. 704 bridge (Hart's Access)

Drop	Difficulty	Distance	Time	Scenery	Water Quality
128'	1-2	8.5 mi.	4 hrs.	A	Good

Gage   U.S.G.S. is 1.7 minimum for solo.

Difficulties   One rapid where the river drops abruptly over a bed of rocks
                and narrows down between two large boulders. Easily recog-
nizable. An excellent lunch stop.

(4)   N.C. 704 bridge (Hart's Access) to Whitts Highway 89 Access at N.C. 89

Drop	Difficulty	Distance	Time	Scenery	Water Quality
72'	1-2	7 mi.	3 hrs.	A	Good

Gage   U.S.G.S. gage is 1.55 minimum for solo.

Difficulties   Many small gravel bars at lower water levels.

(5-A) N.C. 89 bridge (Whitts Access) to Hanging Rock State Park Access off County Rt. 1487)

Drop	Difficulty	Distance	Time	Scenery	Water Quality
52'	1-2	7.4 mi.	4 hrs.	A-B	Good

Gage U.S.G.S. gage is 1.55 minimum for solo.

Difficulties None, other than one sharply undercut bank in a sharp bend to the left, just below the put in.

Directions **Put In**—Va. Rt. 103 northeast of Mt. Airy, N.C., to Patrick Co. Rt. 773, northeast to Rt. 648, then north to the end of road at city of Danville Power Plant.

Ask permission at the plant to launch below. There is not much parking space in the immediate area, so be very careful not to block driveways in any way.

(5-B) Hanging Rock State Park Access off County Rt. 1487 to Moratock Park Access at Danbury off County Rt. 1695

Drop	Difficulty	Distance	Time	Scenery	Water Quality
29'	1	5.5 mi.	2.5 hrs.	A-B	Good

Gage U.S.G.S. gage is 1.55 minimum solo.

Difficulties None. Below the second bridge, be on the lookout for some caves on river right. The more ambitious paddler may be tempted to climb up to them. The problem is the great clusters of poison ivy growing at the entrance. Moratock Park located east of Danbury has water and restrooms. Overnight campsites are available with reservations through Stokes County Recreation Department in Danbury.

(6) Moratock Park to Hemlock Golf Course Access of Power Dam Road (Rt. 1712) on Rt. 1732

Drop	Difficulty	Distance	Time	Scenery	Water Quality
53'	1-2	8.6 mi.	3.5 hrs.	A	Good

Gage Runnable year round except during dry seasons.

Difficulties   The remains of a dam that was blown up with dynamite is located just above the take out and could prove dangerous. Scouting is easy from river right.

(7)   Hemlock Golf Course Access off Power Dam Road (Rt. 1712) on Rt. 1732 to N.C. 772 bridge Access in Pine Hall

Drop	Difficulty	Distance	Time	Scenery	Water Quality
51′	1-2	9.7 mi.	4 hrs.	A	Good

Gage   Runnable year round except during dry seasons.

Difficulties   Shoals above island. Best run on the left.

(8)   Access Area at N.C. 772 bridge in Pine Hall to Rockingham Rt. 1138 (Lindsay Bridge Rd. Access)

Drop	Difficulty	Distance	Time	Scenery	Water Quality
37′	1	6.5 mi.	2.5 hrs.	B-C	Good

Gage   Runnable year round except during dry seasons.

Difficulties   A six-ft. dam located just above 1138 and opposite the brick yard can best be carried on river right (40-yd. carry).

(9)   Rockingham Rt. 1138 (Lindsay Bridge Rd. Access) to Rt. 2145 bridge Access

Drop	Difficulty	Distance	Time	Scenery	Water Quality
42′	C-1	10.8 mi.	4 hrs.	A-B	Fair

Gage   Runnable year round.

Difficulties   Only a series of small, washed-out dams downstream from U.S. 220 bridge. They extend for some 100 yds. with steel rods exposed; however, the center is clear.

(10)   Rt. 2145 bridge to Wildlife Access area off Rt. 2309 south of Lakesville

Drop	Difficulty	Distance	Time	Scenery	Water Quality
21′	1-2	11.5 mi.	4.5 hrs.	A-B	Fair

Gage   U.S.G.S. gage 100 yds. downstream on right. Minimum for solo is a reading of "1.50."

Difficulties   None.

(11)   **Wildlife Access area off Rt. 2039 south of Lakesville to Rt. 1761 bridge (VA Rt. 880) at Virginia state line**

Drop	Difficulty	Distance	Time	Scenery	Water Quality
29′	C-1	10.6 mi.	4 hrs.	A-B	Fair

Gage   Runnable all year except during extremely dry seasons.

Difficulties   A six-ft. high dam located 1.2 mi. downstream from N.C. 14 bridge has a fairly strong hydraulic. A short carry on the right will be necessary.

■

I went to the woods because I wished to live deliberately, to front only the essential facts of life, and see if I could not learn what it had to teach, and not, when I came to die, discover that I had not lived.   *Thoreau*

Elk Creek

Elk Creek cuts through the deep valley below Elk Ridge on its way to join the Yadkin River just below Elkville. It is a small, fast moving stream meandering through farm lands before making a last dash, dropping through a beautiful gorge above Elkville.

Topo Map   Grandin

County   Wilkes

(1)   Rt. 1162 above Darby to N.C. 268 bridge

Drop	Difficulty	Distance	Time	Scenery	Water Quality
194'	1-2	8.4 mi.	4 hrs.	A-B	Good

Gage   U.S.G.S. gage is located 100 ft. above the last ledge on stream, above 268 bridge on the east bank. Minimum reading for solo paddling is 1.15. This is a low water stream which can be run in the spring and during or following rains.

Difficulties   Many small pebble fields and rock gardens. The last 600 yds. through the gorge drops rather fast over ledges that will require a lot of maneuvering. Much of the gorge can be scouted from Rt. 1162 when the foliage isn't too thick. With higher water levels (above 1.55), scouting closely will become a necessity.

Directions   **Put In**—Wilkes Co. Rt. 1162 off N.C. 268 at Elkville, to where the road touches the river just above the community of Darby. At low water levels, put in can be made 4.3 mi. above N.C. 268 alongside the road. This cuts the trip almost in half.

Take Out—Below the last ledge, about 100 yds. above N.C. 268 bridge, on the east bank. This is private property; ask permission at the building above.

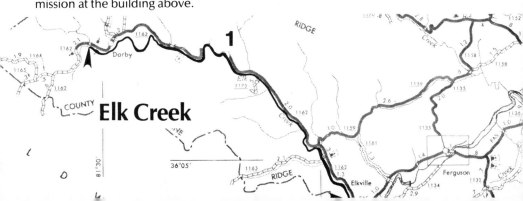

Fisher River

The author feels the Fisher is the ideal stream for the novice to begin his fast water paddling. It presents no really difficult rapids, primarily small riffles, but does require one to maneuver the craft and read the water well. The banks are pretty with many hillsides solid with rhododendron and for the most part there is little evidence of habitation. In the spring the Fisher appears to team with wildlife. For a nice leisurely paddle, try the Fisher.

Topo Maps   Dobson, Copeland

County   Surry

(1)   Old U.S. 601 bridge to N.C. 268 bridge

Drop	Difficulty	Distance	Time	Scenery	Water Quality
86'	1-2	8.5 mi.	4 hrs.	A-B	Good

Gage   U.S.G.S. gage is at the N.C. 268 bridge, 500 ft. upstream on the east bank. Minimum level for solo run is 2.20'.

Difficulties   Shallows and pebble fields.

(2)   N.C. 268 bridge to the community of Rockford, on the Yadkin River

Drop	Difficulty	Distance	Time	Scenery	Water Quality
78'	1-2	11.5 mi.	5 hrs.	A-B	Good

Difficulties   Shallows and pebble fields, except for a washed-out dam just below the put in, which should be approached cautiously. A Class 2 located between the second and third bridges can be recognized by the large flat rock blocking most of the stream. Best passage at lower levels is on the far left. At 2.90 or above, the right side of the left channel can be run. If one looks closely one will find the large rock is pock-marked with garnets.

Watch out for the low water bridge at higher water levels after entering the Yadkin.

A slightly shorter run can be made by combining the last part of section (1) and the major part of section (2). Put in at Rt. 1100 bridge, and take out at Rt. 2233 bridge (approximately 8 mi.)

Direcitons   **Put In**—Old U.S. 601 bridge northeast of Dobson.
            Take Out—Surry Co. Rt. 2221 south, off N.C. 268 (.3 mi. west
            of the 268 bridge) to Rockford Community Park, .3 mi. south of
Rockford. This will be 200 yds. downstream from Yadkin Co. 1510 low water
bridge on the north bank. If Yadkin is high, take out on the north bank just
above the low water bridge.

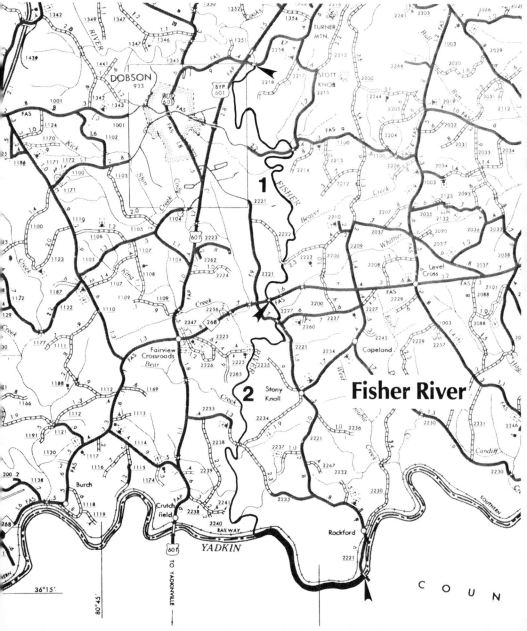

Fisher River

Lewis Fork, North Prong

The North Prong of the Lewis Fork heads up on the slopes of the Blue Ridge, and winds its way through the valley between Yates Mountain on the south and Judd Mountain on the north, before joining the South Prong and running on into Kerr Scott impoundment. The stream is primarily one of ledges, presenting a natural slalom course in several stretches. Most of the run is through a secluded area, until the last mile or so, where it becomes more pastoral.

Topo Map   Purlear

County   Wilkes

(1)   Wilkes Co. Rt. 1304 bridge to Rt. 1307, just below the confluence of the South Prong

Drop	Difficulty	Distance	Time	Scenery	Water Quality
141' .6 mi. @ 66'/mi.	2-3	4.2 mi.	2.5 hrs.	A	Good

Gage   On the east side of Rt. 1304 bridge, at the put in. Minimum for solo is a reading of 5'' below the "0." Generally runnable during wet seasons. A reading of 1'' or 2'' above the bottom of the "0" is probably maximum.

Difficulties   About 10 yds. below the first ledge, extending across the entire river bed, are two strands of barbed wire. The first can be raised and the second can be paddled over at a decent water level.

In the second mile, just beyond a bend to the right, there is a drop of some 20' within 80 yds. This stretch can best be scouted from the left.

A few hundred feet above the take out, a large tree blocks the passage at Rt. 1311 bridge. This can become a dangerous spot at higher water levels. At lower levels a boat can be worked around on the left side.

Directions   **Put In**—Go west on U.S. 421 approximately 8 mi from Wilkesboro, to Rt. 1307 (just beyond the 421 bridge over the Lewis Fork), then north to Rt. 1304 and right for approximately 1 mi. to the 1304 bridge. There is limited parking area, so be careful not to park in yards.

Take Out—(See put in.) The take out is a couple of hundred yards north of U.S. 421 on Rt. 1307.

A run of an additional 4 mi. can be made by extending the trip down the Lewis Fork into Kerr Scott Lake, and taking out at Smithey's Creek Public Use Area. This can be reached by going east 1 mi. from Rt. 1307 on U.S. 421, to Rt. 1145 and then south.

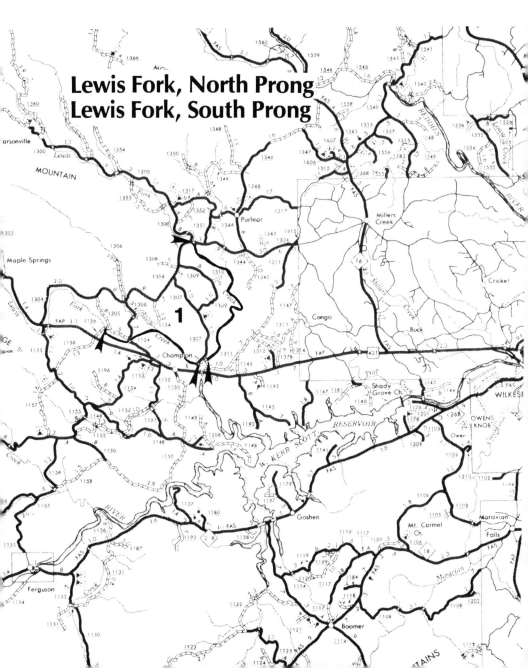

Lewis Fork, North Prong
Lewis Fork, South Prong

Lewis Fork, South Prong

The South Prong of the Lewis Fork runs along U.S. 421 between Dividing Ridge and Yates Mountain, to join the North Prong before entering Kerr Scott Lake. The run here is primarily over small gravel bars interspersed with an occasional ledge, through a fairly remote wooded area.

Topo Map   Purlear

County   Wilkes

(1)   Wilkes Co. Rt. 1156 bridge to Rt. 1307, just below the confluence of the North Prong

Drop	Difficulty	Distance	Time	Scenery	Water Quality
89' .4 mi. @ 50'/mi.	1-2	3.5 mi.	2 hrs.	A	Good

Gage   On the south side of Rt. 1154 bridge. Minimum for solo is a reading of 6'' below the "0." Generally runnable during wet seasons.

Difficulties   There is one slanting ledge, easily recognizable, which should be approached rather cautiously at higher water levels. The overall drop throughout the entire run is fairly gradual.

Directions   **Put In**—West on U.S. 421 approximately 9 mi. from Wilkesboro, to Rt. 1154; then northwest to the bridge, left beyond the bridge on Rt. 1305 for .6 mi. to the put in.
Take Out—See directions for Lewis Fork, North Prong.

Little River

The Little heads up on the slopes of Peach Bottom Mountain and winds its way through the foothills of the Blue Ridge to join the New River in Grayson County, Virginia. The entire run of the river is quite remote and very scenic.

Topo Map   Sparta East

Counties   Alleghany (N.C.); Grayson (Va.)

(1)   Alleghany Rt. 1424 bridge to Rt. 1433 bridge

Drop	Difficulty	Distance	Time	Scenery	Water Quality
147'	1-2/3	7.8 mi.	3.5 hrs.	A	Good

Gage   On the northwest side of Rt. 1424 bridge. Minimum level for solo is 5'' below the bottom of "0." Runnable primarily during wet seasons.

Difficulties   Watch for cables and barbed wire below the second bridge (Rt. 1426). About 2 mi. below this bridge, at a point just upstream from where Rt. 1428 comes down to the river on the south side, the river narrows down. About 50 ft. below is a 3.5 ft. ledge, forming a natural dam, followed immediately by a 2 ft. ledge. Carry on the right. At higher levels move right immediately below the narrow chute, since a strong hydraulic is formed below.

Approximately 1 mi. below the confluence of Glade Creek there is a 3 ft. ledge that should be scouted on the far left. Approach it cautiously.

(2)   Alleghany Rt. 1433 bridge to N.C. 18

Drop	Difficulty	Distance	Time	Scenery	Water Quality
53'	1-2	3.4 mi.	1.5 hrs.	A	Good

Gage   Minimum level for solo is 6'' below "0."

Difficulties   At slightly higher levels the stretch from below the confluence of Brush Creek down to N.C. 18 can become rather heavy.

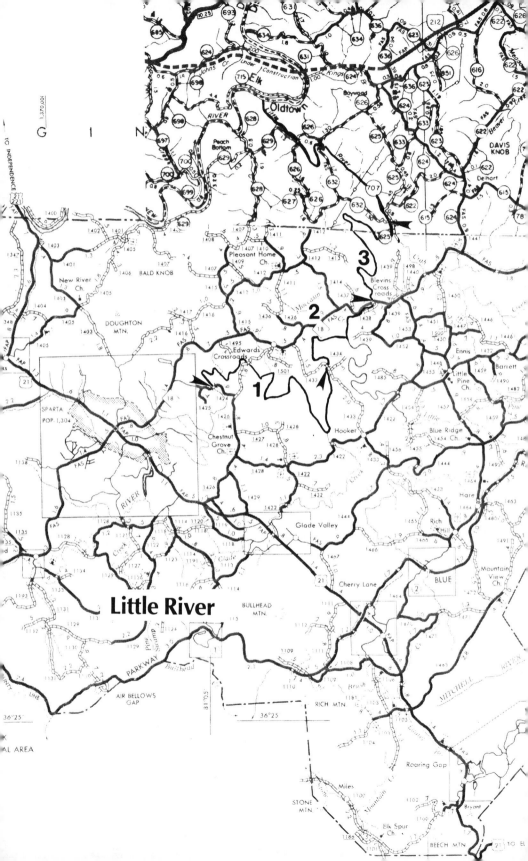

(3)   N.C. 18 to Grayson Co. Rt. 632 bridge

Drop	Difficulty	Distance	Time	Scenery	Water Quality
126'	1-2	7.7 mi.	3 hrs.	A	Good

Gage   Minimum level for solo on the gage at Rt. 1424 is 7" below "0."
There is also a roughly painted gage on 18 bridge. Minimum for
solo can be judged as the same distance below the bottom of the "0" as the
distance between numbers 1 and 2. Measurement between the numbers
varies considerably.

Difficulties   At one point about halfway down this stretch there is a natural
weir which funnels most of the water through a rock garden on
the inside of a hard bend to the right. It should be approached cautiously.

Directions   **Put In**—Northeast on N.C. 18 from Sparta for 1.1 mi., to Rt.
1424, then east for 1.1. mi. to the bridge.
Take Out—From N.C. 18, go north on Alleghany Rt. 1414,
turn right on 1412, cross the state line, and turn right again
on Grayson Rt. 632 to the bridge.

For those who might like to extend the trip on into the New River, there is a
run of 3 mi. to U.S. 58-221 bridge west of Galax, VA.

Mayo River, North Fork

The North Fork of the Mayo flows through heavily woded hills after leaving the pasture lands at the beginning of the section. It has more gradient than the upper reaches of the South Fork, thus providing a more interesting trip. Once it joins the South Fork, the Mayo is formed and it drops over a series of ledges that give the effect of a natural staircase. The latter part of the trip contains some of the best white water available to paddlers in the northern Piedmont and eastern North Carolina. It makes for an excellent training course.

Unfortunately, two murders were committed on the beach at the preferred take out and it has been posted. The Rockingham County Sheriff's Department has been requested to enforce the regulations vigorously by the land owners. You can take out above the last ledges at Rt. 1358 bridge. Run on down through the good stuff and take your chances at the old take out or continue on down to N.C. 770 bridge.

Topo Map   Price (Va.)

Counties   Henry (Va.); Rockingham (N.C.)

(1)   Henry Co. Rt. 629 bridge to Rockingham Co. Rt. 1359

Drop	Difficulty	Distance	Time	Scenery	Water Quality
56'	2-3	4.2 mi.	2.5 hrs.	B	Good

Gage   U.S.G.S. gage is 400 ft. south of Rt. 629 bridge, on the east bank. Minimum level for solo run is 1.55. Maximum for lower part of section is 2.6.

U.S.G.S. gage is 300 ft. downstream from Rockingham Co. Rt. 1358 bridge, on the west bank. Minimum for solo is 1.38, maximum 2.3. Can be run except during long dry spells.

Difficulties   Two ledges on the upper section might require scouting. Both are recognizable before getting too close. Both can generally be run on the far left.

Below the confluence, the staircase will require a great deal of maneuvering to locate the best passage in low water, and a great deal of care in high water. Below Rt. 1358 bridge, a 3 ft. ledge has a wide open chute on the left. Thirty yds below it, a series of ledges drop some 8 ft. within 15 yds. This is best entered at left center and by angling diagonally right across the current, before dropping through a slot not much wider than a canoe. A hard left turn must be made immediately, in order to miss the rock in the center of the bottom of the passage. The gradient averages 20 ft. per mile through this last mile.

Directions **Put In**—From Rockingham Co. Rt. 1358 (the extension of Rt. 1381), go north on Rt. 1360 and Henry Co. Rt. 693 (1.1 mi. east of Rt. 1358 bridge) to Henry Co. Rt. 629, west to the bridge. Old homestead northeast of the bridge has a road down it, which leads to the riverside. This is private property. If in doubt, check at the house across the river before entering.

Take Out—Rockingham Rt. 1360, west off U.S. 220 to Rt. 1381; then west to Rt. 1359, which runs down the east side of the river. Go .4 mi. to where Rt. 1385 cuts east.

For an extended trip, one may wish to paddle on down the Mayo to N.C. 770 bridge (distance is 6 mi.; time is 2-2.5 hrs.; Class 1, easy take out directly under the bridge on the east side). Take N.C. 770 west of U.S. 220 at Stoneville, NC.

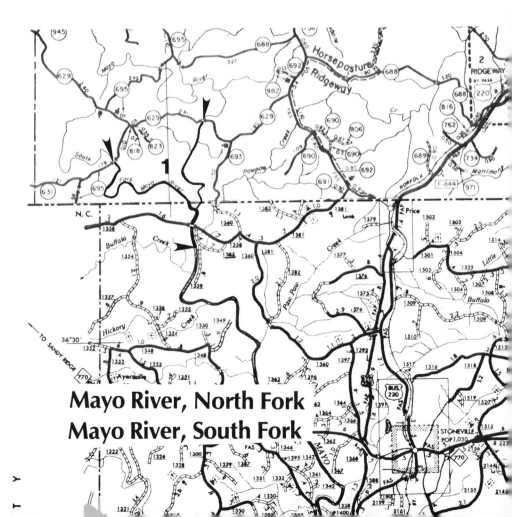

Mayo River, North Fork
Mayo River, South Fork

Mayo River, South Fork

The South Fork of the Mayo meanders through woodlands, presenting the paddler with easy riffles, until it confluences with the North Fork. From there down to the take out the river drops faster over a series of ledges, and gives a more challenging course.

Topo Maps   Spencer, Price (Va.)

Counties   Henry (Va.); Rockingham (N.C.)

(1)   Henry Co. Rt. 695 bridge to Rockingham Co. Rt. 1359

Drop	Difficulty	Distance	Time	Scenery	Water Quality
54'	2-3	5 mi.	3 hrs.	A-B	Good

Gage   U.S.G.S. gage is 300 ft. downstream from Rockingham Co. Rt. 1358 bridge, on the west bank. Minimum level for solo run is 1.38; maximum for lower part of the section is 2.3. Can be run except during long dry spells.

Difficulties   None in the range of levels mentioned as maximum and minimum. Primarily a run of easy riffles. For more information on the area below the confluence, refer to the Mayo River, North Fork.

Directions   **Put In**—Go west on Rockingham Co. Rt. 1358 bridge (Stokes Co. Rt. 1625) to Stokes Co. Rt. 1630, north to Henry Co. Rt. 695, then northeast to the bridge. Rt. 695 can also be reached from Rt. 629 west of North Fork bridge, and then southwest on Rt. 695.

Take Out—Reverse the above directions and refer to the directions for take out on the North Fork of the Mayo.

R. Braswell on Elk Creek. Photo by Bob Benner.

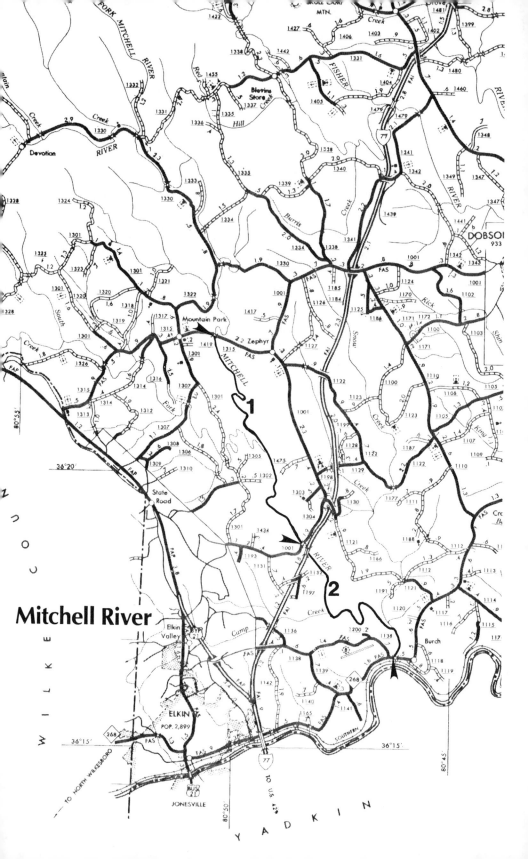

Mitchell River

Mitchell River

The Mitchell flows off the foothills of the Blue Ridge to join the Yadkin. It is a fast low water stream flowing over small ledges and through rock gardens. The water quality is generally quite clear, while the heavily wooded banks give the impression of complete wilderness. If the water table remained at a high enough level much of the year, this would surely be one of North Carolina's most popular float streams.

Topo Map   Elkin North

County   Surry

(1)   Rt. 1315 bridge to Rt. 1001 bridge

Drop	Difficulty	Distance	Time	Scenery	Water Quality
131'	1-2	6 mi.	3 hrs.	A	Excellent-Good

Gage   U.S.G.S. gage is located at the end of Co. Rt. 1498 just off Rt. 1001 and west of the bridge. A minimum reading of 2.5 is necessary for solo running. Can be run during the spring and after rain.

Difficulties   None, other than fast water running through rock gardens.

(2)   Rt. 1001 bridge to N.C. 268 bridge

Drop	Difficulty	Distance	Time	Scenery	Water Quality
69'	1-2	4.5 mi.	2 hrs.	A	Excellent-Good

Gage   Minimum reading of 2.18 for solo.

Difficulties   Bed is similar to the above, with the exception of one 3 ft. ledge located just above the take out. This can present a hydraulic at higher water levels.

Directions   **Put In**—Surry Co. Rt. 1315 bridge, east off U.S. 21 and 1 mi. east of the town of Mountain Park.
Take Out—N.C. 268 bridge 4.5 mi. east of Elkin city limits, and just above its confluence with the Yadkin River. A run of an additional 4.5 mi. can be made by extending the trip into the Yadkin and taking out at U.S. 601 bridge at Crutchfield.

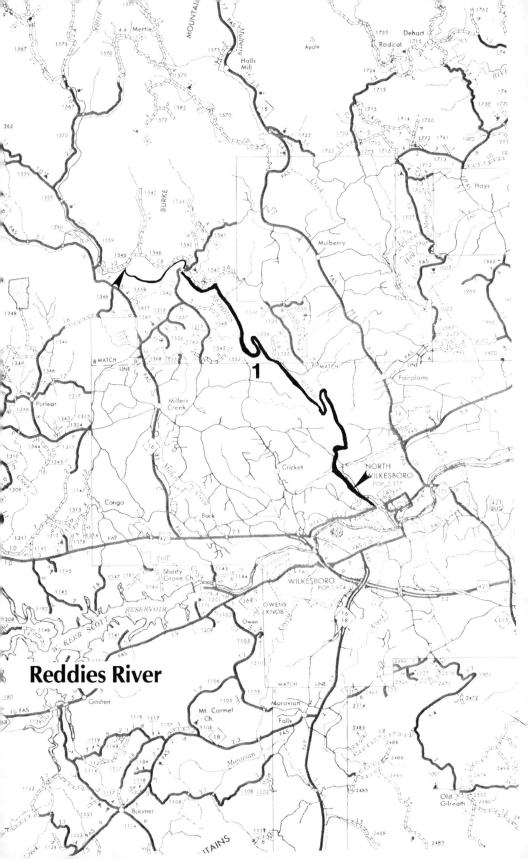

Reddies River

Reddies River

The Reddies flows out of the Blue Ridge Moutains between Judd Mountain and Burke Mountain to North Wilkesboro, where it joins the Yadkin River. Mostly it flows through forested land interspersed with farm land. The first two miles, with a 20 ft. per mile gradient, is where it's at—the white water, that is— but the entire section, except for the last mile, will give the paddler a pleasant float trip. A dam has been authorized on the lower part of the section, which will impound some 2,056 acres of water, so one may not have much to paddle in the future.

Topo Map   Wilkesboro

County   Wilkes

(1)   Rt. 1546 to city limits of North Wilkesboro

Drop	Difficulty	Distance	Time	Scenery	Water Quality
115′	1-2/3	10 mi.	4.5 hrs.	A-B	Good

Gage   U.S.G.S. is on the east bank 400 ft. upstream from Rt. 1517 bridge. Minimum for solo is 1.30. Can be run throughout most of the year, except during prolonged dry spells.

Difficulties   The Class 3 rapid is in the first mile, where a series of three ledges drop about 12 ft. within 20 yds. Scout on the left and enter on the left. This stretch of 2 mi. from the put in to Rt. 1540, which includes the Class 3, can be run in less than 1 hr.

Directions   **Put In**—N.C. 16 about 8.5 mi. north of U.S. 421, to Rt. 1546 and then east about .5 mi. to a gravel pit. This is private property, so observe it as such.

Take Out—Grade road immediately east of U.S. 421-A bridge, and north to North Wilkesboro city limits, which is beyond city sewage treatment plant.

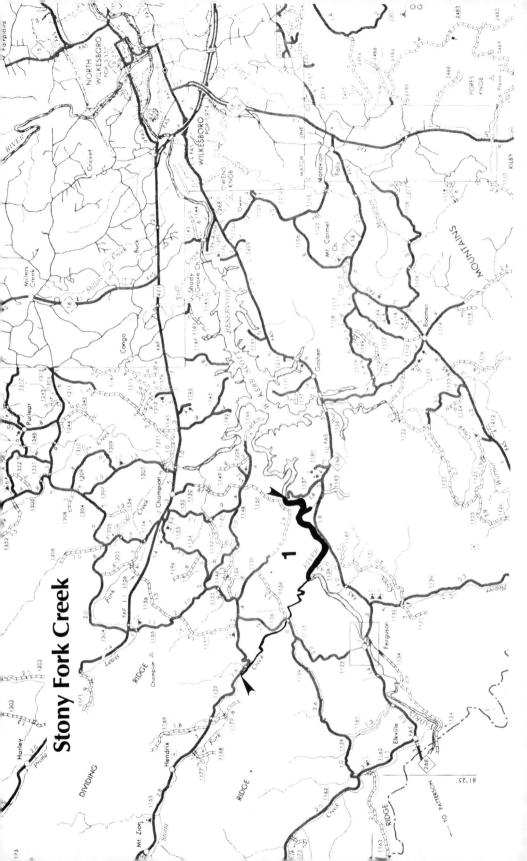

Stony Fork Creek

Stony Fork Creek

The Stony Fork runs off of the slopes of Tompkins Knob, off the Blue Ridge Parkway, and winds its way between Dividing Ridge and Elk Ridge, before confluencing with the Yadkin River above Kerr Scott Reservoir.

It is a small, fast moving stream, dropping over many small ledges.

It might be worth noting that it was in this area, between the Stony Fork and Elk Creek, that Tom Dula of "Hang Down Your Head" fame supposedly did his dastardly deed.

Topo Map   Grandin, Boomer

County   Wilkes

(1)   Wilkes Co. Rt. 1155 (Mt. Zion Rd.) to Rt. 1137, on Kerr Scott Lake

Drop	Difficulty	Distance	Time	Scenery	Water Quality
89'	1-2/3	6 mi.	3 hrs.	A	Good

Gage   On the northeast side of Rt. 1135 bridge (Mt. Pleasant Rd.) facing west. Minimum for solo is 6" below the bottom of "0." Generally is runnable during wet seasons.

Difficulties   Primarily ledges of 1 ft. to 18 in. high, until just above the Yadkin, where it drops considerably faster. This can be recognized by a large tree, which blocks most of the river. Directly behind it on the right, most of the stream pours down a 4 ft. drop into a great deal of turbulence and continues on down through a boulder garden. The total drop is some 9-10 ft. within about 50 ft.

Directions   **Put In**—From U.S. 421 go approximately 9 mi. west of Wilkesboro, to Rt. 1154, then south to Rt. 1155 and left approximately 2 mi. to the put in, just above a bridge crossing a small stream coming into the Stony Fork.

From Ferguson on N.C. 268 go northwest on Rt. 1135 (which becomes 1158 after crossing the Stony Fork) to Rt. 1155 and left approximately 2mi.

Take Out—3.9 mi. east of Ferguson on N.C. 268 to Wilkes Rt. 1137, and north 1.5 mi. to the lake.

Approximately .75 mi., mostly backwaters, can be eliminated by taking out up a rather steep bank along N.C. 268, about 2.5 mi. east of Ferguson.

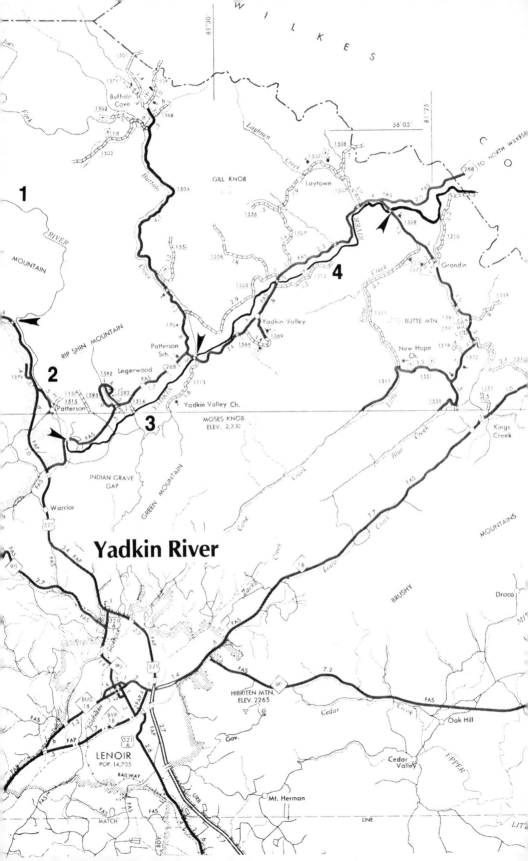

Yadkin River

Yadkin River

The Yadkin heads up in the mountain resort town of Blowing Rock and flows through a remote mountainous area of Caldwell County before coming alongside U.S. 321 about 3 mi. north of Patterson. It moves generally northeasterly through Happy Valley into Kerr Scott Lake, and then meanders through 5 counties before entering the impoundment at High Rock Lake in Davidson County. Two additional impoundments, Badin and Tillery, follow immediately after which the Yadkin becomes the PeeDee and flows into South Carolina.

The river is primarily pastoral down from Patterson, moving over occasional low ledges and through shallow rock gardens. Below Kerr Scott dam it continues on much the same, although considerably wider and with fewer rapids, until it makes the big bend to the south below Siloam. Here, it drops fairly fast for a couple of miles over a series of shoals, which can become formidable in medium high waters.

The one other point of difficulty on the river is Idols Dam, which is downstream from I-40 bridge and just below Tanglewood Park. Water flows over the dam and it should be approached with great caution.

Naturally, a water way crossing as much of a state as the Yadkin does carries with it much history—in fact, too much to delve into here in any detail. However, in section (3) it is of interest to note that the Daniel Boone family had two home sites in the vicinity in the 1760s. The first was near Beaver Creek, about .75 mi. south of the river, where the hearth still stands; the second was on the north side of the river just below the mouth of Beaver Creek. It was from here that Boone left on his trek to Kentucky in April 1775.

Topo Maps   Buffalo Cove, Lenoir, Grandin, Boomer

Counties   Caldwell, Wilkes

(1)   S.R. 1372 (Richland Rd.) bridge to U.S. 321

Drop	Difficulty	Distance	Time	Scenery	Water Quality
440'	3-4/4.2	7 mi.	3 hrs.	A	Good

Gage   Check first wooden plank bridge .5 mi. downstream of take out. Gage is on river right piling and water should be 4" below the bottom of "0" for a minimum level.

Difficulties   The upper Yadkin is strictly a high-water run. As with any tiny watershed, it must be caught during or after major rainfall. The river, like most headwater tributaries, picks up volume quickly. The scenery is quite pleasant, though not as spectacular as many gorges in the area. The stream flows through pasture land for the first half mile, making the bulls on shore the largest danger. The first 1.5 mi. are Class 1 and 2 and then there is a six-ft. drop that is best run in the center. The meat of the run begins in 1.5 mi.

In the next 1.8 mi., the river drops 200 ft. and is somewhat reminiscent of the Chauga Gorge. The entrance to the steep section is noted by a very constricted run through large boulders. This is followed by an eight-ft. drop into a boulder choke that is best run on the left. Below this drop are several long, steep boulder gardens that will test any boater. The steepest drop on the river, Main Squeeze, is quite undercut and should only be attempted at higher levels due to bow pin possibilities. Beware of downed trees, some in very critical places. About .75 mi. above the take out, the gradient slows down to Class 2. This stretch is well worth your time if you can catch it with water.

(2)   U.S. 321 to N.C. 268 bridge

Drop	Difficulty	Distance	Time	Scenery	Water Quality
80'	1-2	3.1 mi.	2 hrs.	B	Fair

Gage   See section (1)

Difficulties   None. One portage around a 12-ft. dam about 1.75 mi. into the run.

Directions   **Section (1) Put in**—Take U.S. 321 north of Lenoir to S.R. 1372 (Richland Rd.). Take a right on S.R. 1372 and go 1.7 mi. to bridge over river.
Section (1) Take out—Take U.S. 321 north of Lenoir to Annes Country Cubbard. Take out 100 yds. upstream of store on old roadbed.
Section (2) Put in—See Section (1) take out.
Section (2) Take out—N.C. 268 N.E. off U.S. 321 north of Lenoir.

(3)   N.C. 268 bridge at Patterson to N.C. 268 bridge

Drop	Difficulty	Distance	Time	Scenery	Water Quality
53'	1-2	4.2 mi.	2 hrs.	B	Fair

Gage   U.S.G.S. gage is located 50 yds. above N.C. 268 bridge in Patterson, on the east bank. Minimum reading for solo is 1.28.

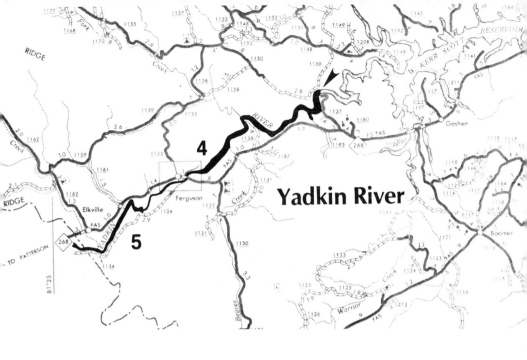

Yadkin River

Difficulties   None, but the river narrows considerably just below the put in, so the possibility of blocked passages always exists.

(4)   N.C. 268 bridge northeast of Patterson School to Rt. 1552 bridge

Drop	Difficulty	Distance	Time	Scenery	Water Quality
59′	1-2	6.2 mi.	2.5 hrs.	B	Fair

Gage   Can be run all year. Would be tight through a couple of shoals in very dry periods.

Difficulties   None.

(5)   Caldwell Co. Rt. 1552 bridge to the end of Wilkes Co. Rt. 1137 on Kerr Scott Lake

Drop	Difficulty	Distance	Time	Scenery	Water Quality
29′	1-2	9.5 mi.	4 hrs.	B	Fair

Gage   Can be run all year.

Difficulties   None.

Directions   **Put In**—N.C. 268 N.E. off U.S. 321 north of Lenoir.
Take Out—3.9 mi. east of the community of Ferguson, on N.C. 268 to Wilkes Co. Rt. 1137 and north 1.5 mi. to the lake.

David Benner at Main Squeeze, Yadkin River. A Dennis Huntley photo.

Section 5

Chattooga River

Chattooga River

The Chattooga rises as a sparkling mountain stream near Cashiers, N.C., in the vicinity of Whitesides Mountain. It flows 10 mi. before leaving North Carolina, and continuing on for some 40 mi. as the boundary line between South Carolina and Georgia, before entering the impoundment at Lake Tugaloo. In this 50 mi. the river drops 2,469 ft., for an average drop of 49.3 ft./mi.

The river cuts down the magnificent Chattooga Gorge, providing many rugged white water cascades through an area which is almost totally wild and natural. Upon reaching Nicholson Fields, above Rt. 28, it becomes a more pastoral area and continues as such to Turn Hole. Beyond there, it slowly begins to revert back to its wild and rugged characteristics and is accessible at only five points within the next 24 mi.

It is one of the longest and largest free flowing rivers in the southeast and is the only mountain river in a four state area without substantial development along its banks. Its outstanding scenery and unspoiled wilderness will now be protected with its inclusion as the second National Wild and Scenic River, under Public Law 90-542. With this protection the river hopefully will be preserved in a natural state for generations to come, so that they may see what their forefathers saw—a wild and free flowing river. In order to continue this preservation, certain conditions must be followed:

1. Each float party leader must register.

2. All floaters, including innertubers, must wear a life jacket rated "Coast Guard Approved."

3. All persons in decked craft, and ALL floaters below Woodalls Shoals, must wear a helmet.

4. Minimum party size:
   Above Earls Ford—2 persons, 1 craft
   Below Earls Ford—2 persons, 2 craft

5. Innertubes are prohibited below Earls Ford

6. Rafts must have a minimum of 2 air chambers

7. All floating is prohibited north of S.C. Hwy. 28.

8. Air mattresses, motorized craft, or other craft deemed unsuitable by the U.S. Forest Service, are prohibited.

The following conditions have been established for camping:

1. 50 ft. from river, stream, or hiking trail

2. .25 mi. from a maintained road

3. 200 yds. from any other occupied site

4. 15 persons maximum occupancy.

The stream that heretofore had been known to a few trout fishermen, backpackers, and canoeists has been made famous by the film "Deliverance." It brings many canoeists and rafters to the river, who know little of what to expect and who quite often are ill equipped to handle what they find. It is for this reason that the author has gone into greater detail in describing certain rapids in the river than has been done on other rivers. Hopefully such knowledge will persuade the unprepared adventure seeker to reconsider and arm himself with the skill that the Chattooga demands of those who seek her unspoiled beauty.

Topo Maps   Satolah, Rainy Mtn., Tugaloo Lake (Ga.); Whetstone (Ga.-S.C.)

Counties   Oconee (S.C.); Rabun (Ga.)

Section (1)

The stretch from Burrels Ford to Rt. 28 bridge, usually referred to as Section (1), has not been included because of the extreme gradient of the upper part of the section. Also, floating above Rt. 28 is prohibited at this time by the Forest Service.

(2)   Rt. 28 bridge (Russell Bridge) to Earls Ford

Drop	Difficulty	Distance	Time	Scenery	Water Quality
80'	1-2/3	7 mi.	3.5 hrs.	A	Good

Gage   Metal gage on Georgia side of Rt. 28 bridge. A minimum reading of .72 and a maximum of 2.23 indicate the optimum levels.

Difficulties   The water is generally shallow and slow to the mouth of the West Fork where the current picks up.

Long Bottom Bridge, about 2.5 mi. downstream, must be carried, so the novice paddler should approach with care.

Turn Hole is the first rapid of any consequence. Here the water pushes the canoe into the left bank and a strong pull to the right is necessary in order to stay out of the branches. Following Turn Hole is a series of rapids which require one to maneuver back and forth across the streambed.

Big Shoals, the Class 3, can be recognized by the big rock ledges which appear to block most of the center and left side. The run is to the far right through an open chute which twists slightly to the left at the bottom. The drop is about 5 ft. Scout from the ledge in the center and carry over there is necessary.

Small riffles and shoals continue on down to just above Earls Ford where passage becomes a little more complex. Beginners and novices should not attempt to continue beyond here.

Directions　　**Put In**—S.C.-Ga. 28 bridge.
　　　　　　　Take Out—From Mountain Rest, S.C. on S.C. 28 go southwest on Rt. 258 which becomes Rt. 196 to the first 4-way stop intersection and bear right to the end of pavement and beyond on graded road to the river and Earls Ford. There is a 1,400 ft. carry from the river to the parking area.

(3)　Earls Ford to U.S. 76 bridge

Drop	Difficulty	Distance	Time	Scenery	Water Quality
370'	3-4/5	12.5 mi.	6 hrs.	AA	Good

Gage　　U.S.G.S. gage 75 yds. downstream from 76 bridge on the S.C. side. A reading of 1.3 to 2.0 is considered a minimum and maximum for open boats.

Difficulties　The second rapid below Earls Ford should be entered on the
and Points　left side of the river, then turn hard left dropping over a 3 ft.
of Interest　ledge which in lower water levels puts the bow on a rock just under the surface at the bottom. This gives the paddler a quick idea of whether he should be here or not. If trouble occurs here it is not too late to head back, for several rapids follow that are much more difficult.

About 400 yds. beyond, the river passes through Rock Gardens, where great slabs of angular rock stick up out of the river. Several scenes in "Deliverance" were filmed here.

The next rapid of any consequence is Dick's Creek ledge, which is recognized by Five Finger Falls cascading down on the Georgia side. Scout on the right center, which is also the best place to portage. For those wishing to run this, an "S" turn is required. The first drop should be entered with the bow angled to the right as the canoe slides down the ledge and drops into the small pool above the next ledge. Do not attempt to enter from the left side at the top.

The next two rapids should be run to the right of the respective islands. Below these rapids is Sandy Ford, which is the last place to take out for those who find the river more than they can handle. There is a very rough road negotiable only by four wheel drive vehicles, on the Georgia side.

Mild rapids follow, and then a calm pool before the river bears left. Around the bend is the Narrows, where three concentric ledges funnel the river into a constricted canyon. Enter toward the left. Two more drops follow as the river narrows down even more. Beware of the turbulent cross currents below these drops. More canoes swamp here than at any other point on the river. It is very difficult to get through the entrance ledges without swamping if paddling tandem. A beautiful cliff overhangs the river below the last drop. This makes an excellent lunch stop.

Second Ledge is around the next bend. Scout or portage it on the right. This can be run on the left side by sliding down across the face of the falls, not too easy by any means. At higher levels, a run down right center, if possible, with a hard right turn into the pool, eddy turn, then drop through a small slot in the bottom ledge.

Eye of the Needle, about 1.5 mi. beyond Second Ledge, is entered on the extreme left. A rock ledge extends about halfway across the river from the right, forcing most of the water through a twisting chute dropping to the right. Don't lean to the right and you'll arrive upright. Note to decked boats: there is a good spot for "pop ups" at the bottom.

There are some four miles of easy rapids before arriving at Fall Creek Falls, entering on the left.

Just below the falls is the Roller Coaster, a delightful ride through a series of big waves, and also a very good place for the unwary to fill the craft.

The next rapid is a large ledge called Keyhole. Scout on the left. Enter on the right center and cut to the right. A very large boulder sits on the left center in the bottom. If entering to the left, a mishap can push a boat square into the rock.

There are several interesting ledges and shoals in the next 3 mi., before arriving at a bend to the left. A huge rock formation extending from the right bank is just beyond. This marks the entrance rapid to Bull Sluice, a series of two falls totaling 10 ft. in height. The rock formation and large boulders block the "Sluice" from view, so immediately upon spotting the bend and the rocks pull out on the right. Portage on the right also.

The entrance rapid to Bull Sluice is a class 3, which can splash a great deal of water into the canoe before ever arriving at the first falls. The hydraulic below the first falls can easily hold a body or a boat in, so give it all due respect. The second has a rock just under the surface which is generally well hidden. What appears as a fast open chute isn't. The author broke a rib bouncing off this rock, and on another occasion saw a swamped 17 ft. Grumman do an end over end when the bow met with said rock. So if attempting to run Bull Sluice, don't assume that it's been made if one makes it beyond the hydraulic. Keep in mind that several drownings have occurred here.

U.S. 76 bridge is about 300 yds. downstream around the bend. For those who wish to see the "Sluice" before or without running the river, a trail leads up along the S.C. side.

Directions   **Put In**—From U.S. 76 bridge, go east approximately 2 mi. to the
first paved road on the left (S.C. 196). Proceed north approximately 6 mi. to the first 4-way stop intersection. Bear left there on S.C. 193, which becomes a graded road, until reaching the parking area, some 1,400 ft. above Earls Ford and the river. You guessed it, neighbor, you get to warm up before you reach the water.

From S.C. 28 go west on S.C. 193 (2 mi. south of the intersection of 28 and S.C. 107), and proceed to the river on 193.

Take Out—From the put in, backtrack on the above directions.

(Take the first two paved roads to the right, coming from Earls Ford Parking Area). Hopefully, you've got a little energy left, for now you get to "cool down" with your second 1,400 ft. hike of the day, to the parking area at 76 bridge.

Chattooga, Section (4)

---

(94)   U.S. 76 bridge to Tugaloo Lake

Drop	Difficulty	Distance	Time	Scenery	Water Quality
275'	3-4-5	7.5 mi.	5 hrs.	AA	Fair

Gage   U.S.G.S. gage. A reading from 1.1. to 1.9 is considered a minimum and a maximum for open boats.

Difficulties This section offers the paddler some of the most beautiful
and Points of and challenging white water in the east. There are many rapids
Interest   throughout the stretch which an intermediate would find difficult, but only the major falls and rapids will be discussed. In other words, only those rapids that will prove difficult to even the advanced canoeist will be mentioned.

The first, Surfing Rapid, is entered from the right after coming around the first bend of the river below the put in.

Some distance downstream, a large sandbar appears on the Georgia side. About 200 yds. below is Rock Jumble, a single drop which is clutted with rock. Scout to determine the best place to run.

About .5 mi. downstream, where the river bends left, a large rock ledge extends out from the S.C. side, forcing the water to the right. Pull out on the ledge before the current does the same to the canoe, and scout. At the end of this ledge is the entrance falls to Woodall Shoals. It forms a strong, dangerous hydraulic at the bottom, which has kept boats, rafts, people, or anything else that floats, for extended periods of time. Due to the power of the hydraulic, this is probably the most dangerous spot on the river. It definitely is not the place to play. At lower water levels a slanting ledge on the far right might be run without the danger the hydraulic presents.

The rest of the Shoals is a twisting turning ride for another 60 yds. before ending in a quiet pool. A very rough forest road enters into Woodall on the S.C. side.

Below the Shoals the river enters a gorge containing two fairly long rapids with standing waves. Let this be the warning of Seven-Foot Falls coming up. Scout it on the right, where instead of the abrupt drop of the left, a slanting drop can be run.

Following several rapids, the river widens and Stekoa Creek drops in from the right, indicating the beginning of Stekoa Creek Rapids, a quarter mile of constant white water. The creek is the source of the pollution that has prevented the rest of the section from qualifying in the Wild, Scenic, or Recreation River class, but hopefully this will soon be remedied by a new sewage treatment plant. It has been listed in a Conditional Scenic River class.

Long Creek Falls, a beautiful waterfall which was shown in "Deliverance," enters on the left into the pool at the end of Stekoa Creek Rapids.

Following several ledges the river runs into a house-size boulder. It has become known as "Deliverance Rock" due to several scenes in the movie having been shot here.

A beautiful cliff, Raven Rock, rises on the left high above the river, as one paddles beyond "Deliverance Rock." Just above the cliff is Raven Rock Rapid, which should be scouted on the left and run on the far left across the face of the slanting rock.

For a little over a mile, the river courses over small rapids which appropriately enough have been called "Calm Before the Storm." Below here the river pulls out all stops as it enters The Five Falls, one of the most exciting stretches of water to be found anywhere.

1. First Fall is entered down a long stubblefield running diagonally left to far right into a small pool. At this point it is best to scout, perhaps the rest of the falls, before continuing. First Fall should be run on the right and angling to the

left. If trouble develops upon attempting First Fall, get to shore immediately, because 100 ft. downstream is

2. Corkscrew, which is the toughest rapid for an open boat on the river, and is a mass of surging cross currents.

3. Crack in the Rock, which in reality is 3 cracks, follows. The five foot crack on the right is the safest of the three, although it can be dangerous as it sometimes becomes partially clogged by logs and debris. Scout on the right. There is a good pool for rescue below the crack. Avoid "left crack" at all costs. Two boaters have drowned there in recent years.

4. Jawbone comes up next. Scout on the left. It should be entered from right center. Drop left into the eddy on the far left, make an eddy turn and then cut back into the main chute to be flushed out at the bottom. To the right and two-thirds of the way down the diagonal curler, there is a badly undercut rock to avoid. Below here Hydroelectric Rock bisects the current. Go left or right, but be aware there is water flowing through this boulder.

5. Sock 'Em Dog, a 7 ft. vertical drop on the far right. Jawbone in itself isn't terribly difficult, but with Sock 'Em Dog awaiting to chew up a swamped craft, one must consider carefully before attempting the run. The eddy on the left is the best spot to get out from to scout or to carry. The run is to the far right over a slight rise at the very top of the falls. For those who can't resist the temptation, there is a long pool to reassemble whatever needs be.

The last rapid of any consequence above the lake, Shoulder Bone, is at the end of the pool. Run it at left center. After that one can relax somewhat before the fun beings—a 2 mi. paddle down Lake Tugaloo.

Directions   **Put In**—At the U.S. 76 bridge.

Take Out—Go east on U.S. 76 to the community of Longcreek and take a right on S.C. 96. Proceed on 96, which turns to gravel and then back to pavement, until Damascus Church is passed on the left. Take the next right (Forest Rd. 754) and on to Tugaloo Lake, over one hellacious bumpy single lane road. In the event the above road is impassable due to inclement weather, take out can be made by paddling 2 mi. farther down the lake to the dam on the Georgia side. Off U.S. 23, about .5 mi. south of Tallulah Falls, go east on the road to the hydroelectric plant.

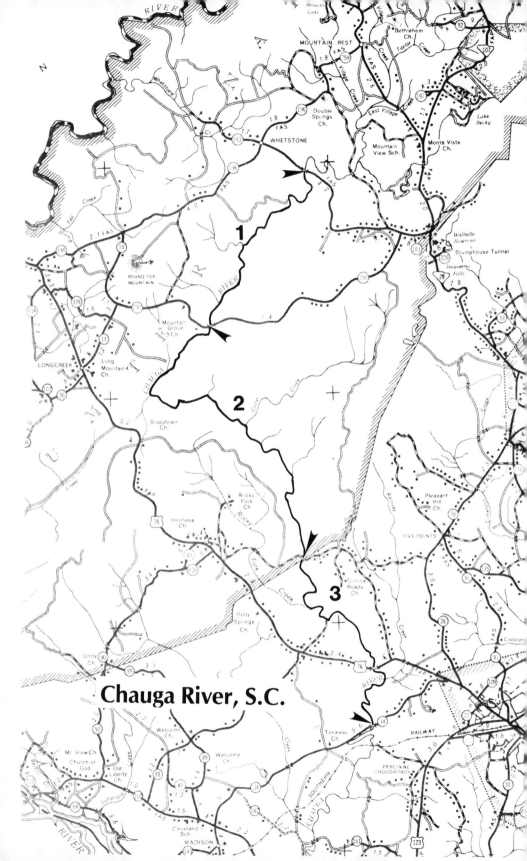

Chauga River, S.C.

Chauga River, S.C.

The Chauga heads up on the eastern slopes of Chattooga Ridge in Sumter National Forest, wherein flow the first two sections. It moves south, then sharply east and south again, until it reaches the backwaters of Lake Hartwell. On its way it cuts through several small gorges that rival the Chattooga River for spectacular beauty.

Section (2), known as the "Chauga Gorge," begins with gentle rapids in the first mile, before dropping quickly through a series of waterfalls and continuous fast water. Access is difficult so the paddler should be skilled enough to handle his boat under very rough water conditions as well as care for any emergencies that might arise.

Topo Maps   Whetstone, Holly Springs

County   Oconee

(1)   Oconee Co. Rt. 193 bridge (Blackwell Bridge) to Rt. 290 bridge

Drop	Difficulty	Distance	Time	Scenery	Water Quality
206'	2-3	5.4 mi.	3.5 hrs.	A	Good
2 mi. @ 63'/mi.					

Gage   Oconee Co. Rt. 290 bridge. Minimum run for solo is 2" above "0." The gage on U.S. 76 bridge on the Chattooga will require a reading of 2.3.

Difficulties   Within the first .5 mi. there is a 45 ft. waterfall, which can be carried on the right. It is followed by a 10 ft. sliding drop that can be run at slightly higher water levels. One should watch for downed trees throughout the section.

(2)   Oconee Co. Rt. 290 bridge (Cassidy Bridge) to Cobbs Bridge Road bridge. (Take the first right .75 mi. north of Holly Springs community)

Drop	Difficulty	Distance	Time	Scenery	Water Quality
417'	3-4-5	9.8 mi.	7 hrs.	AA	Good
1 mi. @ 140'/mi.					

Gage   Oconee Co. Rt. 290 bridge. Minimum for solo run is "0.". Maximum for a safe run is 6".

Difficulties   Watch for downed trees within the first mile. As one enters the gorge, watch for a waterfall which should be carried on the left. Approximately 1 mi. further on is another falls, that can possibly be run at a favorable level. The river continues to drop quickly as it turns toward the east. A slanting waterfall, which is best carried, is followed by continuous heavy water for close to 2 mi. Several Class 3 rapids are interspersed along the way, as the gradient eases up for a couple of miles. Then, some 2 mi. above the take out, a sheer falls is reached, that requires a carry on the right.

(3)   Cobb Bridge Rd. bridge to Co. Rt. 34 bridge (Horseshoe Bend Bridge)

Drop	Difficulty	Distance	Time	Scenery	Water Quality
135'	2-3/4	7.5 mi.	4.5 hrs.	A-B	Good

Gage   U.S. 76 bridge on the Chattooga. Minimum for a solo run is 1.8. Maximum for a safe run is 2.5.

Difficulties   Below the U.S. 76 bridge and just above the water pumping facility is Pumphouse, a Class 3 which can be scouted from the rocks in left center. Just downstream is the Class 4, Canopener—a steep 5 ft. slide with a sharp rock alongside the chute that can "open" one's boat up if not careful. Scout it before running.

Directions   **Put In**—N.E. on Oconee Co. Rt. 196 off U.S. 76, for 6.1 mi. to Whetstone and the intersection with Rt. 193. Take a right to the bridge.
Take Out—S.W. on Oconee Co. Rt. 34 off U.S. 76, west of Westminster.

Doe River

The Doe flows off Roan Mountain, through the town of the same name, and cuts through the spectacular Doe River Gorge on its way to join the Watauga in Elizabethton, Tennessee. The Gorge, between Fork Mountain on the south and Cedar Mountain on the north, is 800-1,000 ft. deep. There are several outstanding rock formations, the most prominent being Flagpole Point, jutting out sharply on the right, and Pardee Point, rising high on the left.

A small gage railroad, where the original "Tweetsie" of the East Tennessee and Western North Carolina ran, makes it fairly easy to scout the gorge on foot. In fact, this is recommended in order for one to fully appreciate the rugged beauty. A hike down the gorge is highly recommended for those who haven't the skill to paddle it.

Topo Maps White Rocks Mtn., Iron Mtn. Gap, Elizabethton (Tenn.)

County Carter (Tenn.)

(1) U.S. 19E at the confluence with Buck Creek to U.S. 19E bridge

Drop	Difficulty	Distance	Time	Scenery	Water Quality
55'	1-2	2.6 mi.	1 hr.	B-C	Good

Gage U.S.G.S. gage on section (2). Take the road east of Honeycutt Grocery. Minimum reading of 3.80 for solo run. Can be run all year except after dry spells.

Difficulties None.

(2) U.S. 19E bridge at Crabtree, to the bridge at Blevins

Drop	Difficulty	Distance	Time	Scenery	Water Quality
182' 1 mi. @ 65'/mi.	2-3	4.6 mi.	3 hrs.	A-B	Good

Gage Minimum reading of 4.14 for solo.

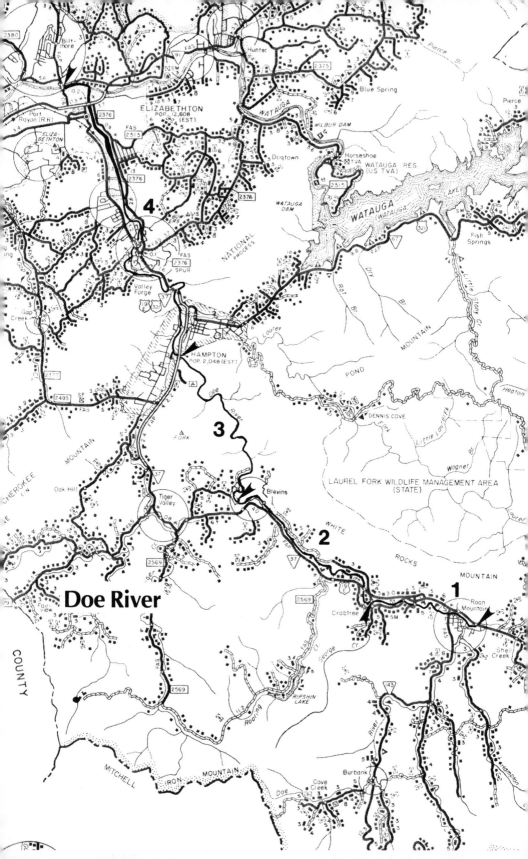

Doe River

Difficulties   There are two Class 3 rapids in the second mile. Both should be
approached cautiously and scouted to determine if a passage is
open. Each is strewn with boulders and has a difficult entrance.

(3)   Bridge at Blevins (off 19E at Whitehead Hill) to U.S. 19E bridge at Hampton

Drop	Difficulty	Distance	Time	Scenery	Water Quality
498'	3-4-5	6 mi.	6 hrs.	AA-A	Good
1 mi. @ 145'/mi.					
2 mi. @ 115'/mi.					

Gage   4.30 for solo. Maximum reading of 4.70. Due to the gradient
and tight passages the river courses through, not much leeway
between the minimum and maximum is left.

Difficulties   The road at the put in continues along the river for 2.5 mi. to
the head of the railroad tracks. The upper section can be
scouted from the road. There is one Class 4 above the first railroad bridge,
where the water piles up on a rock, requiring a hard left turn into a drop of 3-4
ft.

Below the first railroad bridge there are numerous rapids, many of which
require scouting. Be on the lookout for a point where the river bends to the
right, where the entrace is pretty well clogged up. Below here a 75 yd. carry
on the left must be made. This area is quite difficult in an open boat, but the
thrill seeker may wish to put back in just above the bottom to try the seven-ft.
falls on the right.

Following the falls, the next hairy rapid can be recognized by the rock wall
constructed to support the railroad tracks. Here a series of diagonal ledges
make for an extremely difficult course.

As the river approaches the next rock wall, the course splits into two channels with a Class 5 on the left, and on the right a jumble of boulders. Line
down on the right. One unwary paddler swamped twice here, just portaging.

From here to the take out, there are many exciting rapids remaining, several
of which should be scouted. This section is not recommended for the paddler
who is not in excellent condition. The stress and strain are sure to take their
toll on one who isn't.

(4)   U.S. 19E bridge south of Hampton to U.S. 19E bridge in Elizabethton

Drop	Difficulty	Distance	Time	Scenery	Water Quality
252'	2-3	9.5 mi.	4.5 hrs.	A-B-C	Fair
2 mi. @ 50'/mi.					

Gage   Minimum reading of 4.20 for solo.

Difficulties   A Class 3 directly beneath the first 19E bridge north of Hampton may require scouting. Beyond the second bridge a series of ledges form a staircase which will require a good deal of maneuvering to locate the best passage. Other than these there are a few stubblefields which one should watch for.

Directions   **Put In**—U.S. 19E below confluence with Buck Creek and east of Tennessee Rt. 143 in the town of Roan Mountain.
Take Out—Power Sub Station 100 yds. above U.S. 19E bridge over the Watauga River, on the south bank in Elizabethton.

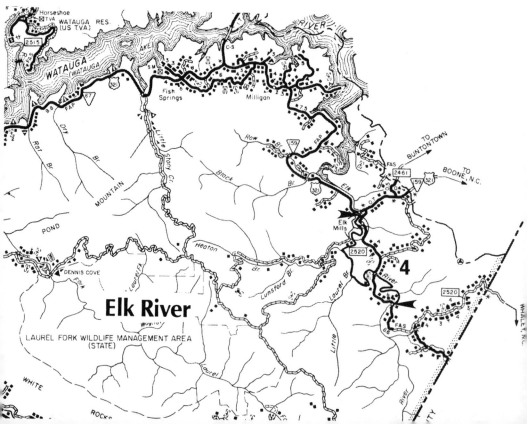

Elk River

The Elk originates in Avery County in the valley between Beech and Sugar Mountains, both popular ski resorts. The river flows generally west and north into Tennessee, eventually reaching the impoundment at Watauga Lake. The Elk Gorge [Section (3)] is very remote, beautiful, and difficult. Big Falls and Twisting Falls are found at the beginning and end of this section. Section (1) is neither remote nor particularly beautiful, except to the serious hard boater who finds beauty in extreme descents. Sections (2) and (4) are pleasant intermediate runs with fun ledge drops. Sections (1), (2), and (3) must be caught during or shortly after heavy rains for adequate volume.

Topo Maps   Elk Park (NC), Elk Mills (TN)

Counties   Avery (NC), Carter (TN)

(1)   S.R. 1326 bridge to S.R. 1305 bridge

Drop	Difficulty	Distance	Time	Scenery	Water Quality
460'	3-4-5.1	3.4 mi.	3.5 hrs.	B	Good
(1 mi. at 240')					

Gage   Located on river left piling of S.R. 1326 bridge. Minimum level is 5" below "0."

Difficulties   This run has two distinct, steep sections. After a .75 mi. warm-up, one enters a mile section that drops 240 ft. This piece ends above the N.C. 194 bridge and the other begins just downstream of the bridge. The highway parallels most of the hard water, so aborting trips is simple. You'll find yourself scouting Class 5 rapids in someone's backyard. There is one mandatory portage that comes toward the end of the run. It's a ten-foot drop choked down with boulders. Carry on the left. The rest of the run is complex, steep, and doable. The larger drops include a couple of 10-footers and an 18-ft. cascading slide. Bow pins have occurred in the middle slot of the lead-in rapid to the first 10-ft. water fall. High-volume creek boats are essential on this run. This section is more difficult than the gorge downstream and is only appropriate for groups of experts.

(2)   S.R. 1305 bridge to dead end of S.R. 1305

Drop	Difficulty	Distance	Time	Scenery	Water Quality
100'	2	3.6 mi.	105 hrs.	A-B	Good

Gage   Located on river left piling of S.R. 1326 bridge. Minimum level is 6″ below "0."

Difficulties   None. Just be sure to take out at the park because Big Falls (55 ft.) is 100 yds. downstream.

(3)   Dead-end of S.R. 1305 to bridge below Stone Mountain Church

Drop	Difficulty	Distance	Time	Scenery	Water Quality
560′	3-4-5.1	5.0 mi.	4.5 hrs.	AA	Good

Gage   See section (1) gage. Gage reading should be 5″ below for a minimum level.

Difficulty   The Elk River Gorge, from Big Falls to Twisting Falls, is truly a classic piece of water. It is seldom run due to a small watershed, mandatory (hard) portages, and general remoteness. This is experts only country that even the most jaded of hard boaters will enjoy. The gorge alternates between complex boulder gardens and steep, gnarly ledge drops. Few of the larger drops have crystal clear routes, but all can be run cleanly at medium or higher flows. Large volume creek boats are recommended.

From the put in, you can paddle 100 yds. before reaching Big Falls. Carry on the left around this 55-footer. For the next 1.5 mi. enjoy the scenery and easy gradient. A 12-ft. drop denotes the beginning of the "interesting water" and the end of paying attention to anything other than the confrontation of boat and water.

The 2.5 mi. of serious water ends with Twisting Falls, where the river cascades 160″ in .3 mi. The entrance to Twisting Falls is noted by the vertical rock walls that pinch the river down to a width of 20 ft. Prudent boaters will take out 100 yds. upstream to avoid a nasty entrance rapid that leads to a 15-ft. waterfall and an unrunnable 35-footer. Carry on the left, either up and over the mountain or along the rocks beside these first two falls.

Below here are other rapids and two more vertical drops of 16 and 45 ft. in succession. These drops have been run, but are not recommended unless you've been in some serious car wrecks and enjoyed the sensation. Below Twisting Falls there is fun Class 2 and 3 water for a mile down to the take out.

Directions   **Put in section (1)**—Take N.C. 194 west of Banner Elk to S.R. 1326. Take a left 200 yds. to the river.
                Take out—Go to Elk Park and take a right on S.R. 1305 (Elk River Rd.) and go to first bridge over the river.

Put in section (2)—See section (1) take out.
Take out—From U.S. 321 go south on the first paved road east of 321 bridge over the Elk. Go through the community of Elk Mills to the second bridge.

(4) Bridge below Stone Mountain Church to U.S. 321 bridge

Drop	Difficulty	Distance	Time	Scenery	Water Quality
212'	2-3	5.5 mi.	3 hrs.	A	Good
1 mi. @ 55'/mi.					

Gage Northeast side of U.S. 321 bridge. Minimum for solo run is 6'' below "0.". Runnable most of the year, except during long dry spells. Best in spring and early summer.

Difficulties There are several ledges that may require scouting through the area of the greatest drop. This stretch is located downstream from the second bridge and can be recognized by the bluffs which rise some 300 ft. above the river.

Directions **Take Out**—Below U.S. 321 bridge at Elk Mills.

■

Like winds and sunsets, wild things were taken for granted until progress began to do away with them.   *Aldo Leopold*

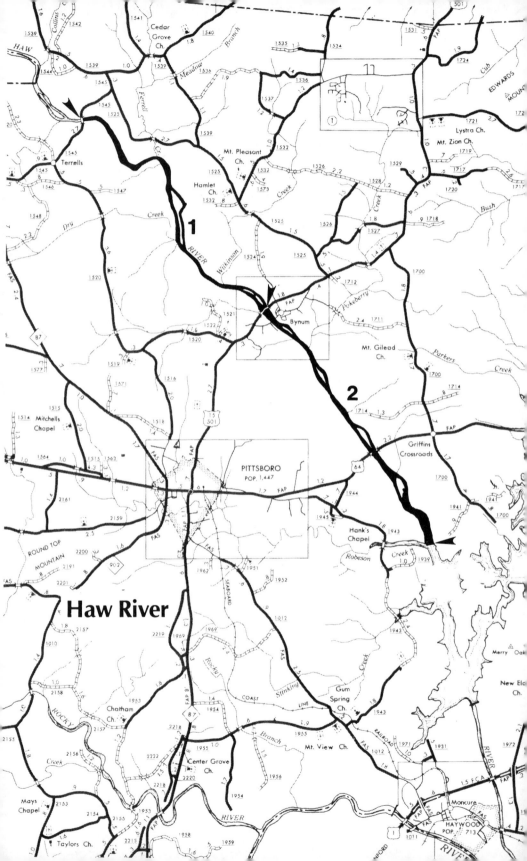

Haw River

Haw River

The Haw River begins in the northwest corner of Guilford County, and flows east around Greensboro and Burlington before turning generally southeast. It meets the New Hope River in Chatham County, where the Cape Fear River is born. The Haw varies greatly in width—from 50 ft. in some sections to as much as 1,000 ft. at the dam at Bynum.

The river flows through farm lands, forested hills, and some residential areas. As with most rivers in the lower Piedmont, there are long stretches of flatwater, as well as many rapids. There are places where the river branches into two or more channels, each island looking very much like the last one— long, narrow, and heavily covered with trees, shrubs, brambles, and poison ivy.

The creation of Jordan Lake at the end of Section (3) was controversial due to expected poor water quality, among other things. Over time, the quality of water has improved, although it remains threatened by demands for riverside and watershed development by upstream communities. Citizen watchdog groups maintain a high profile level of activity working to protect and improve the river corridor and its water.

Topo Maps   Bynum, New Hope Dam

County   Chatham

(1)   Chatham Co. Rt. 1545 bridge ("Chicken Bridge") to the dam, just upstream of U.S. 15-501 bridge

Drop	Difficulty	Distance	Time	Scenery	Water Quality
50'	102	6.5 mi.	3 hrs.	A-B	Fair

Gage   A gage has been painted on the bridge piling closest to river right. Minimum for solo open canoe is about -1.5, but at this level the river is low and the trip will be long — 4 hrs. not including a lunch stop. If no rocks are visible downstream from the bridge, this section will be pushy, with many holes and waves and few eddies — not good for novices. This section can generally be run all year, except during periods following an unusually long, dry season.

Difficulties   There are three places of any consequence on this section — Sawtooth Ledge, Lunch Stop, and Final Solution. After about 1.5 mi. of flatwater, a small boulder garden appears and the river bends from river right towards center around a small island. Enter on the right of and as close to the island as the overhanging branches will permit and run straight through, eddying on either right or left at the bottom of the chute.

Sawtooth Ledge is just around the corner, about a mile downstream. This is a rock garden, runnable on the left at normal levels. As the river splits into two channels, stay right in the one with more water. (The left side is unrunnable at low water.) Follow the bend to the left; and on the backside of the island, stay left to avoid rocks in the center of the channel. Then move back to center to avoid rocks at the bottom.

The next rapid, Lunch Stop, is about 4 mi. into the trip. It is a long rock garden spanning the width of the river. At lower water, run it left of center; and once past the island, traverse to river right. At higher water, run center to avoid large holes and swamping waves on the left. (Also at higher water, look for great surfing waves in the heavy flow or else you'll be swept by them before you realize they are available to you.)

After Lunch Stop, the river splits into four channels. Either of the two center channels are runnable; the preferred route is just left of center. After the entrance rapid at the head of the channel, find a slot and paddle over to the next channel on the right for a cleaner route to rejoin the main flow.

Final Solution, the last rapid, is below the wave field just downstream of the gas pipeline right of way. It can be entered left or right of a large boulder that marks the entrance just left of center. Eddy behind this boulder for a look at how to run the chute below. The lake created by the dam at the take out starts just downstream from Final Solution. When the river channelizes, stay left for a take out on river left above the dam.

(2)   U.S. 15-501 bridge, on the south side of the river, to U.S. 64 bridge

Drop	Difficulty	Distance	Time	Scenery	Water Quality
73'	1-2	4.1 mi.	3.5 hrs.	A-B	Fair

Gage   See section (3)

Difficulties   This section is excellent for skills practice of water reading, eddy hopping, peel-outs, surfing, and ferrying (depending on water levels). Ferry from river left just below the dam (and well clear of the backwash) and start your descent right of the island. Paddle this side to enjoy the delightful rock garden until you pass under the Bynum bridge.

Once past Bynum bridge, traverse the river back to the left side of the island. About one mi. downstream, the river channelizes further, separated by several islands. Stay with the most flow and widest sections. If you take the far left channel, you'll run Crystal Falls, a shallow ledge "S" turn entered left of center and run left to right with a subsequent and immediate hard left turn. If you choose to enter the channels in the center, look out for strainers. You'll be rewarded with the channels' intimacy, a channel-wide surfing wave at reasonable water levels, and Thunder Falls, a tight Class 2 "S" turn chute. Enter it right of center and turn back left in the chute to avoid being swept into the right bank.

The river becomes wide and flat again where all the channels converge. When it again is separated by islands, stay right for the most interesting run through rock gardens, tiny islands, and finally, a quick "S" turn chute. If you take the middle channel, you will have to portage the long islands on either side to access river right or river left under the U.S. 64 bridge.

(3) U.S. 64 bridge to Jordon Lake

Drop	Difficulty	Distance	Time	Scenery	Water Quality
44'	2-3	2.1 mi.	2 hrs.	A-B	Fair

Gage   A gage is painted on the U.S. 64 bridge pilings and visible from the access on river right. Minimum for solo open canoe is about -6 in. Six in. to two ft. on this gauge is an excellent level for eddy hopping and surfing. Above two ft., the river gets pushy, especially in Gabriel's Bend. For example, at three ft., extremely strong currents, huge waves, and keeper holes form throughout, thus transforming this section into a run for only properly equipped advanced to expert boaters.

The National Weather Service gives a reading of the U.S.G.S. gauge [located about one mi. below the Bynum bridge in Section (2)] in the mornings—usually until 11:00 am. It can be obtained by listening to a weather radio or calling the National Weather Service in Raleigh, NC. A U.S.G.S. reading of 4.0 is minimum.

Difficulties   This is the most difficult section. The higher the water, the less margin for error and the greater the chance for a long, bumpy swim. The section packs a lot into a short run—often paddled after work by locals looking for a one to two hr. workout before dark. And if darkness comes prematurely, you need not worry as long as you clear the last rapid with daylight because the final 30 to 45 minutes is paddled across the lake.

For the best run and the most action, take the right channel from U.S. 64 bridge. Within 200 yds., you will enter Lunch Stop, a boulder garden with all the flow to the left of large rocks jutting out into the river from river right. Run the first part just right of center and eddy right just below the rocks if you're not interested in playing. From the eddy, stop at the channel-wide wave below and practice ferring, surfing, and elevator moves. At two ft. and above, try for enders behind the large boulder in the middle. There is flat, slow-moving water below for roll practice.

50 yds. below the ender boulder, paddle through a break in the island to

enter the center channel. This is Ocean Boulevard. Ocean Boulevard ends on far river right in a small rock garden that boasts a great side-surfing wave. The river pools briefly in the approach to the most difficult rapid on the entire river. Gabriel's Bend, a bona fide Class 3 at most levels, is identified by a high rock wall on the right. You may pull over and shore scout, although you cannot see the entire run from shore. The best scouting is from an eddy, (entered from left or right) in the center of the channel at the top of the rapid.

For a down-river run, stay just left of center, avoiding large, potentially nasty holes to the right. The large, channel-wide wave at the bottom is a very forgiving side-surfer at many water levels, which willingly lets its victims go.

Just below Gabriel's Bend, you have three options. At a level of 1' or more, Moose Jaw Falls on the far right is runnable. At all levels, you can run The Maze, a rock garden at the head of the center channel that requires turning immediately to the right and threading your way through a rock garden descent where the channel joins the right below Moose Jaw Falls.

The most open, least technical run after Gabriel's Bend is Harold's Tombstone — on the far left shore. Traverse the entire river and as you approach the overhanging trees and work your way left to avoid being washed into the rocks on the right and prevent being slammed into a jagged rock in the channel just left of center. All three channels rejoin about a quarter mile downstream where the current ends and the Jordan Lake begins, burying forever some of the finest rapids on the river. Paddle to the take out on river left (approximately 1.5 mi. — 30-45 minutes).

Directions   **Section (1) Put in**—From U.S. 15-501 bridge, take 15-501 north to the first intersection and turn left onto Hamlet Chapel Road (S.R. 1525). Go about two mi. and turn left onto River Rd. (Continuation of S.R. 1525). Cross the bridge and park on the pavement to the left of the road.

Section (2) Take out—From U.S. 15-501 bridge, take U.S. 15-501 north to the first intersection and turn right onto Durham-Eubanks Road (S.R. 1524). At the stop sign, turn left onto Bynum Road and go about one-half mi. and turn right onto Bynum Bridge Road (S.R. 1711). At the stop sign, turn right onto Mt. Gilead Church Road (S.R. 1700). At the stop sign, turn right onto U.S. 64 West and cross the bridge and turn left onto the dirt road access.

Section (3) Take out—Take N.C. 64 west from put in and go .7 mi. to a left onto S.R. 1943. Go to stop sign and take left on Hanks Chapel Rd., then go one mi. and turn left onto gravel road to the take out. Note: if running left channel below Gabriel's Bend you will have to paddle back upstream 100 yds. to reach the take out.

North Tyger and Tyger River

The north Tyger heads up in northern Spartanburg County and flows practically the length of the county, to where we pick it up just upstream of the confluence with the South Tyger. It drops through the Fall Line, presenting several miles of interesting white water. This area is composed of long pools, with occasional sharp drops and long shoals.

Topo Maps   Spartanburg, Enoree

Counties   Spartanburg

(1)   Spartanburg Co. Rt. 231 bridge over the North Tyger to Spartanburg Co. Rt. 113 bridge over the Tyger

Drop	Difficulty	Distance	Time	Scenery	Water Quality
76'	2-3	7.6 mi.	3.5 hr.	A	Good-Fair

Gage   Spartanburg Co. Rt. 231 bridge at the northwest corner. Minimum for solo is 8" below "0."

Difficulties   This stretch is primarily a series of pools interspersed with ledges and long shoals, several of which can be quite formidable at higher water levels (above 1 on the gage). The second rapid drops 7 ft. in some 25 yds. and has a rather sneaky hydraulic in the center that one must punch through.

Nesbitt Shoals runs for about 200 yds. above Rt. 50 bridge. Below the bridge one encounters another 150 yds. of shoals which should be run right of center, due to a number of large rods in the middle and far left immediately below the first ledge. The last shoals run .25 mi. down to the take out. It has many possible passages.

(2)   Spartanburg Co. Rt. 113 bridge to S.C. 56 bridge

Drop	Difficulty	Distance	Time	Scenery	Water Quality
45'	C-1-2-3/4	6.2 mi.	3 hrs.	A	Good-Fair

Gage   Spartanburg Co. Rt. 113 bridge on the southwest corner. Minimum for solo run is 8" below "0."

Difficulties   A series of shoals run for almost a half mile, providing many choices of channels. This stretch ends with a natural 6 ft. vertical dam. Approach with great caution, for at higher levels, one will have a very difficuilt time scouting this ledge. Beyond this point, one will encounter primarily fast flatwater.

Directions   **Put In**—S.C. 86 south of U.S. 221 to Spartanburg Co. Rt. 231, then east across I-26 to the bridge.
Take Out—South off S.C. 50 on Spartanburg Co. Rt. 142, then northeast on Spartanburg Co. Rt. 113 to the river.

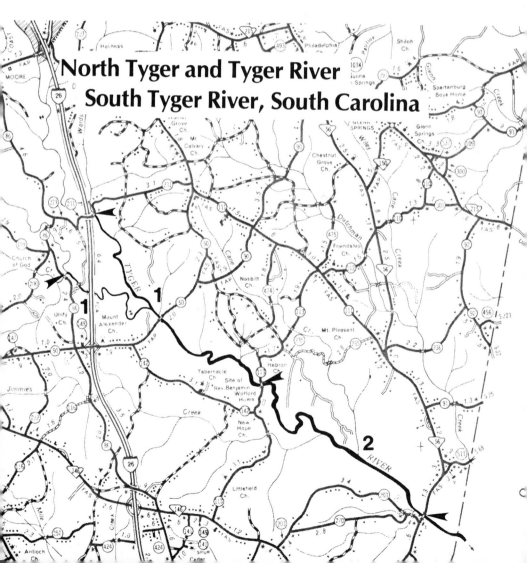

North Tyger and Tyger River
South Tyger River, South Carolina

South Tyger River, South Carolina

The South Tyger heads up in the foothills and cuts across the Piedmont Plateau before making its final plunge where we pick it up. This section has long pools with occasional sharp drops, that make the flatter stretches worth paddling.

Topo Maps   Spartanburg, Enoree

County   Spartanburg

(1)   Spartanburg Co. Rt. 86 bridge over Fergusons Creek to S.C. 50 bridge over the Tyger

Drop	Difficulty	Distance	Time	Scenery	Water Quality
36'	2-3	5.2 mi.	1.75 hr.	A	Fair

Gage   Spartanburg Co. Rt. 231 bridge on the North Tyger at the northwest corner. Minimum for solo run is 8" below "0."

Difficulties   Susan Thomas Shoals drops 5.5 ft. in about 30 yds. It can be scouted at right center. The next shoals, Chesnee, now known as "Stingemdog" due to an experience Jack and David Powell had with their canine companion, presents a very technical run. The rapid drops 7 ft. within 50 yds. It can be scouted far left. Nesbitt Shoals runs for some 200 yds. just below the confluence with the North Tyger and continues on to the take out.

Directions   **Put In**—Go north on Spartanburg Co. Rt. 86 off S.C. to Fergusons Creek bridge, and put in alongside 86.
Take Out—S.C. 50 bridge east of I-26. For an extended trip of 3.3 mi. down the Tyger to Spartanburg Co. Rt. 113, see Section (1) of the North Tyger and Tyger.

Section 6

Introduction

This section includes primarily flatter water suitable for canoe camping trips. Over the years the author has been asked about suitable stretches of water that beginning and novice paddlers can handle in canoes loaded with camping gear. The Broad and two of its tributaries—the Enoree and the Tyger—contains approximately 220 mi. from which beginner and novice paddlers can select trips. The description of the tributaries continues into the Broad in order to give Boy Scout troups two separate streams for possible 50-miler trips.

The Enoree is the easiest of the three rivers. The Tyger requires slightly more river skill, while the Broad is more difficult, from the standpoint of both skill and strength needed to negotiate the rapids as well as the dams.

All three flow through remote areas for most of the distance, with little signs of civilization evidenced except at bridges and dams. Wildlife is exceptional along the Enoree and the Tyger in particular. The author has observed as large a variety of wildlife along these stretches as any he has paddled, and in great abundance.

For those considering a trip on the tributaries or one including the lower Broad, we recommend obtaining a map of the Enoree and Tyger Districts of the Sumter National Forest, which is available from the District Ranger in either Newberry or Union, South Carolina.

Please note that paddle times listed are conservative, and don't include time taken for portage, for lunch breaks, or for scouting. The drop listed is for paddling waters only. It does not include the amount of gradient at dam sites.

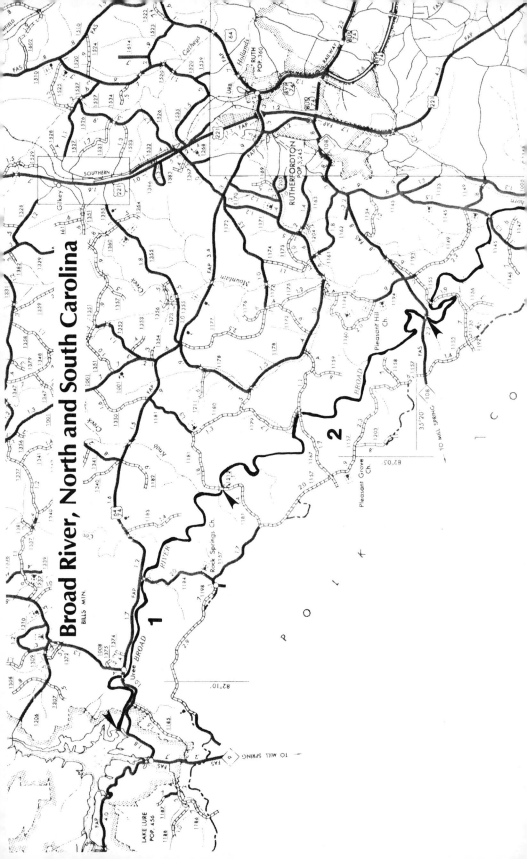

Broad River, North and South Carolina

Broad River, North and South Carolina

The Broad, below section (1), winds its way east across southern North Carolina before bending sharply south into South Carolina. Although several dams have been constructed on the river, there are no long stretches of slack water behind them. Total mileage below section (1) is approximately 113 mi.

Topo Maps   Lake Lure, Rutherfordton South, Cowpens, Boiling Springs South, Blacksburg North (N.C.-S.C.); Blacksburg South, Kings Creek, Hickory Grove, Lockhart, Leeds, Carlisle, Blair, Pomaria, Jenkinsville (S.C.)

Counties   Rutherford, Cleveland (N.C.); Cherokee, Union, Newberry (S.C.)

(2)   Rutherford Co. Rt. 1181 bridge to N.C. 108 bridge

Drop	Difficulty	Distance	Time	Scenery	Water Quality
42'	1-2	7 mi.	3 hrs. .	A	Good

Gage   None. Runnable year round, except possibly following an extremely long dry spell.

Difficulties   Watch for downed trees. Note: On certain days about halfway down this section those with keen ears may hear the startling scream of the "Wild Flat Chested Broad Bird," although the more discerning paddler of the wild will recognize this unusual sound as the call of the Pea Fowl.

(3)   N.C. 108 bridge to N.C. 1004 bridge

Drop	Difficulty	Distance	Time	Scenery	Water Quality
49'	1-2	9.8 mi.	4 hrs.	A	Good

Gage   None.

Difficulties   None. There are a few riffles on this section, but nothing of any consequence.

Note: The Green River enters on the right .9 mi. above the take out.

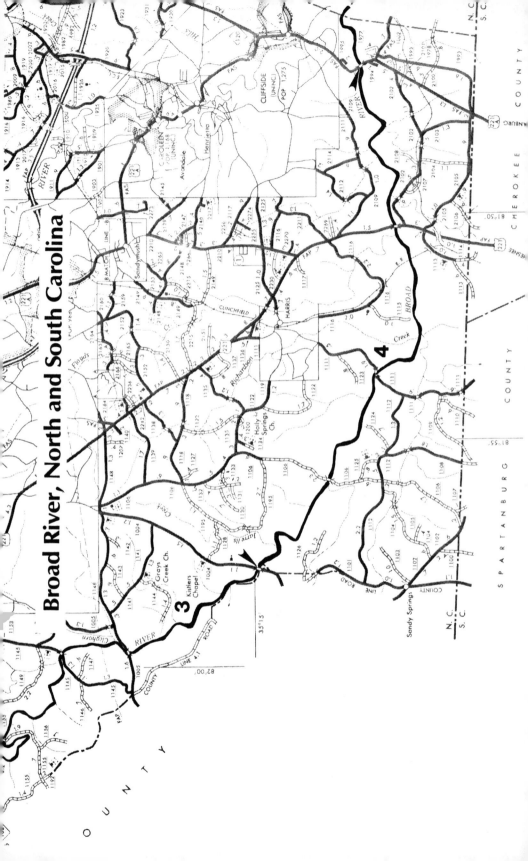

Broad River, North and South Carolina

(4)   N.C. 1004 bridge to U.S. 221A bridge

Drop	Difficulty	Distance	Time	Scenery	Water Quality
35'	1	13.6 mi.	5.5. hrs.	A	Good

Gage   None.

Difficulties   None.

(5)   U.S. 221A bridge to N.C. 150 bridge

Drop	Difficulty	Distance	Time	Scenery	Water Quality
52'	1-2	7.6 mi.	3 hrs.	A-B	Good

Gage   None.

Difficulties   A Duke Power dam is located 1.5 mi. below the put in. Begin moving right after passing under the bridge at the power plant. Pull out on right and carry to bottom of hill. Watch the backwash below the dam, being sure to put in well below it. A few small shoals will be encountered occasionally from here on down to N.C. 150.

(6)   N.C. 150 bridge to S.C. 18 bridge

Drop	Difficulty	Distance	Time	Scenery	Water Quality
28'	1-2	10.6 mi.	4 hrs.	A-B	Good

Gage   None.

Difficulties   Gaston Shoals or Gravo Dam is reached after some 40 min. of slack water. The dam is constructed in three sections, with the easiest portage to the left of the section on the right (the first section to be approached). Pull out about 30 ft. upstream from the highest concrete. Carry into the small ravine, up to the top and directly down the trail (total carry of 100 yds.) There is an excellent campsite on the right bank below the dam. In low water there will be slow going for some distance below the dam, due to sand deposits.

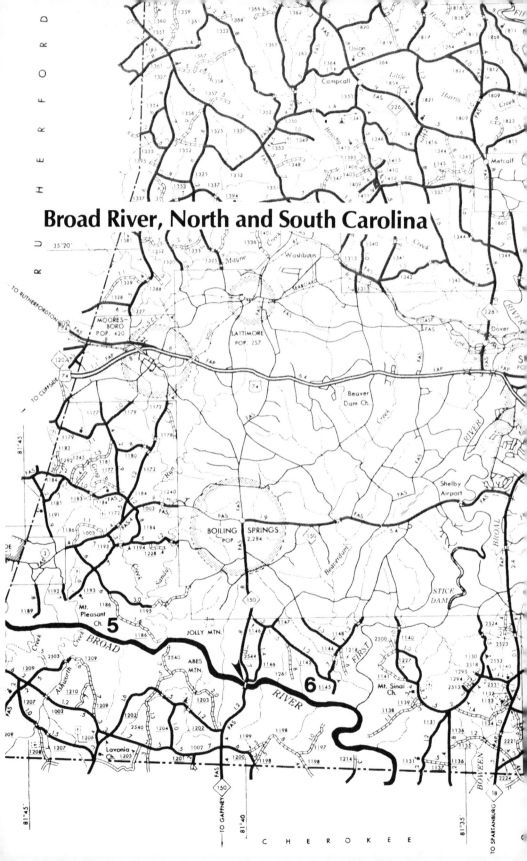

Broad River, North and South Carolina

(7) S.C. 18 bridge to S.C. 211 bridge

Drop	Difficulty	Distance	Time	Scenery	Water Quality
57′	1-2	17.9 mi.	7 hrs.	A	Good

Gage   None.

Difficulties   Approximately 1 mi. below U.S. 29 bridge there is an area of shoals running for 200 yds., which should be approached rather cautiously—especially at levels even slightly higher than normal. There is a launching ramp on the right at the head of the shoals.

Cherokee Falls Dam is downstream a short distance from the two islands with the old bridge pilings. Water runs over the top, so move to the right as quickly as possible and take out far enough above the dam to prevent being caught by the current. The carry here is fairly short. Following is a series of ledges interspersed among rock gardens, which can prove quite difficult at higher water levels. At normal to lower levels it is best to work to left center and down. Keep to the right channel after the rapids. Note: Cherokee Nuclear Power Plant is a short distance west of the river and some 2 mi. downriver from Cherokee Falls.

There are many large sand bars suitable for camping between Cherokee Falls and the up-coming No. 99 or Ninety-nine Island Dam. It can be recognized by the high, narrow rocky dam on the left. Paddle around the island to the right of this rock dam while staying as close as possible to the island. Bear left around the island and above the face of the dam. Hug it closely for water flows over the dam. Proceed to the left bank, behind the rock dam, to the dock. If the Duke Power staff is on duty, arrangements may be made for a shuttle around the dam and power plant. Otherwise a 600-700 yd. portage along the fence to the side road on the left of the entrance gate and thence down the road to the riverside will be necessary.

(8) S.C. 211 bridge to Dam at Lockhart

Drop	Difficulty	Distance	Time	Scenery	Water Quality
16′	1	13.6 mi.	5.5 hrs.	A	Good

Gage   None

Difficulties   None until arriving at Lockhart. Move to the extreme right and take out above the log boon. Carry along the fence. The pool

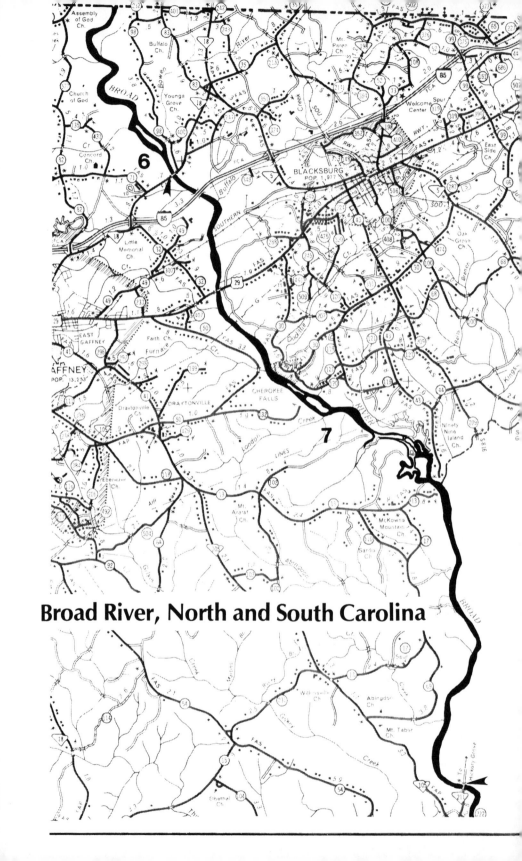

Broad River, North and South Carolina

and sluice running along the right here is closed for any water traffic. There is a distance of 1.4 mi. from here to the next point below the Lockhart Power Company Plant where one can re-enter the river. One alternative, which is questionable as far as ease of accomplishment, is to stay to the left of the dam. This will require a carry through a boulder field below the dam. Paddle the pool below and then carry across the boulders at the opposite end, and paddle the left side of the island from the Power Plant. Whatever the decision, the character building session for the day will begin here and now.

(9) Lockhart Power Company Powerhouse to S.C. 121 bridge

Drop	Difficulty	Distance	Time	Scenery	Water Quality
27′	1	17.2 mi.	6.5 hrs.	A	Good

Gage **None**

Difficulties Neal Shoals Dam is 11 mi. down from Lockhart. Approach on the far left, where a good 60 yd. portage can be made. Watch the slippery rocks! Be sure to put in far enough below the backwash from the dam, and work your way carefully back into the main current. Note: Get permission to drive onto Lockhart Power Company property. Put in about 90 yds. below the power plant at a break in the wall, where a small sand bar is located.

Woods Ferry Recreation Area in Sumter National Forest is 8 mi. below the put in on the east bank. In fact, the National Forest Boundary is just below Lockhart, and the paddle will be within its boundaries down to S.C. 34.

(10) S.C. 121-72-215 bridge to S.C. 34 bridge

Drop	Difficulty	Distance	Time	Scenery	Water Quality
37′	1-2	15.2 mi.	6 hrs.	A	Good

Gage None.

Difficulties There are some riffles along the Shelton Island area (the island is 2 mi. long), the tip of which is located 4 mi. down from the bridge. They aren't difficult, but one may become complacent after a few miles of fairly flat water.

Note: The Tyger enters at 7.4 mi., just above Henderson Island.

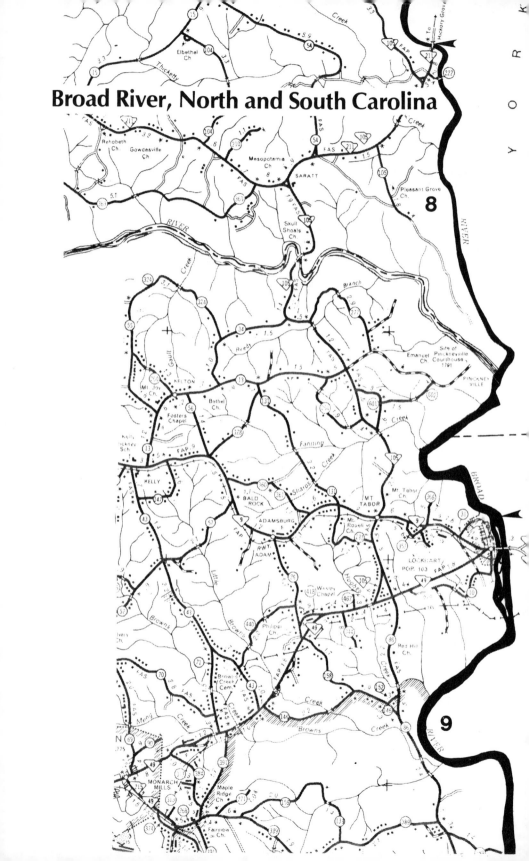

Broad River, North and South Carolina

8

9

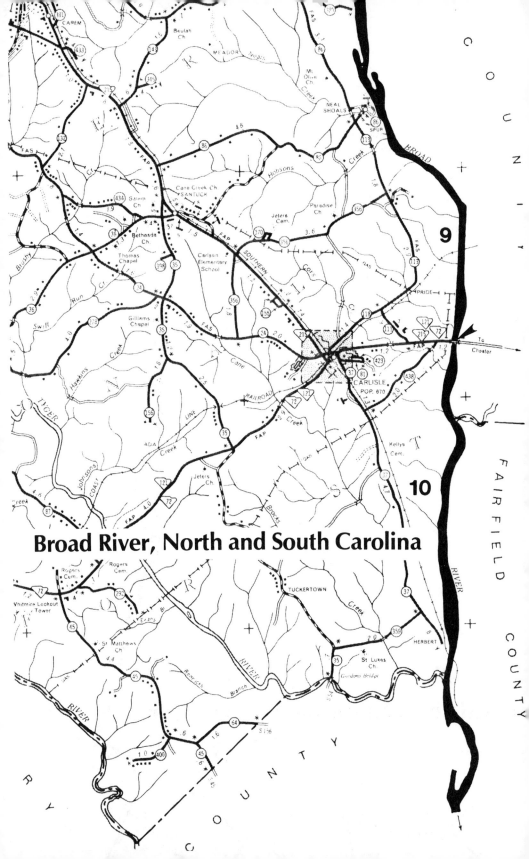

Broad River, North and South Carolina

There are a few shoals immediately above and along Henderson Island. Just below the island an area of shoals extends for close to 200 yds. Approach with caution.

Note: The Enoree enters at 12.4 mi.

Below the Enoree the flow slows appreciably, especially so if power isn't being generated at Parr Shoals. The wind then becomes the only difficulty to be encountered on the remainder of the trip.

Note: Take out at a small launching area about 100 yds. below 34 bridge on the left bank. To reach here, take first right after crossing the bridge going east. Go down the hill and bear hard right across the railroad tracks.

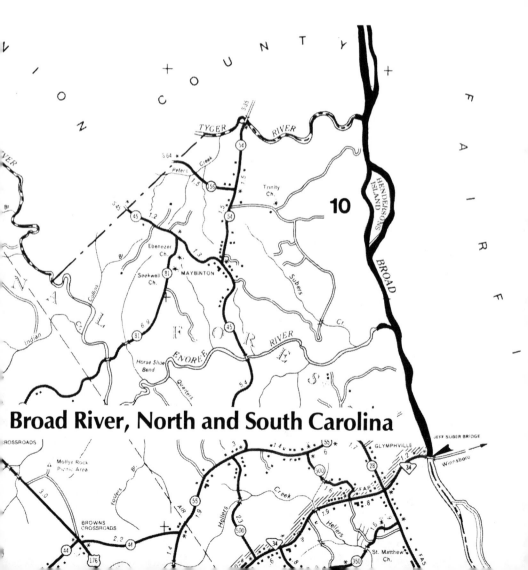

Broad River, North and South Carolina

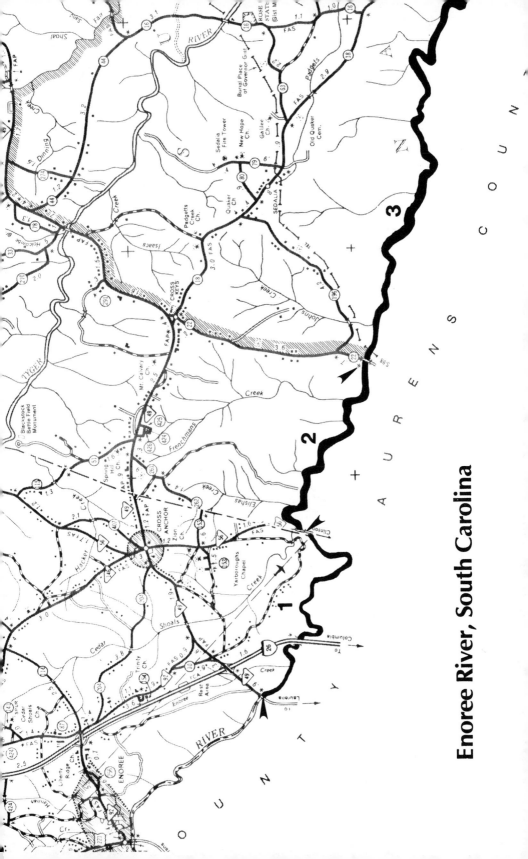

Enoree River, South Carolina

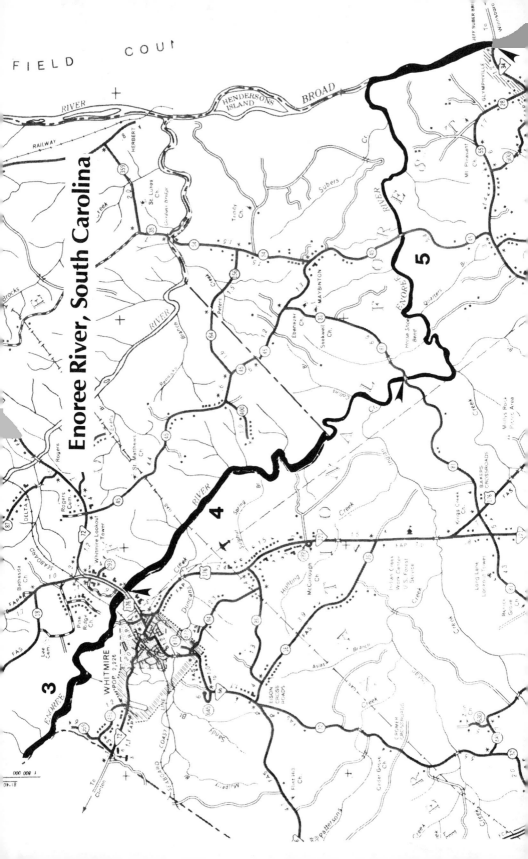

Enoree River, South Carolina

Enoree River, South Carolina

The Enoree heads up on the Piedmont in Greenville County and winds its way southeasterly to confluence with the Broad, northeast of Newberry. On its way, it cuts through the Fall Line, offering a short stretch of interesting white water before reaching Sumter National Forest and the coastal plains.

From the put in to the take out at Parr Shoals on the Broad, one encounters very little evidence of civilization other than highway bridges. It is a most scenic run through rolling hills.

Topo Maps Ora, Philson, Crossroads, Sedalia, Whitmire North, Whitmire South, Pomaria, Jenkinsville

Counties Spartanburg, Union, Newberry

(1) S.C. 49 bridge to Spartanburg Co. Rt. 10, where it comes alongside the river (.3 mi. above S.C. 56 bridge)

Drop	Difficulty	Distance	Time	Scenery	Water Quality
52′	C-1-2/3	6.8 mi.	3 hrs.	A	Fair

Gage U.S.G.S. gage is on the east bank 20 yds. above S.C. 49 bridge. Runnable year round. A reading of 3.0 will require a lot of skill and experience to handle the stretch below Rt. 49.

Difficulties The river drops very quickly within the first .75 mi., with a series of shoals. This fast stretch ends with a drop of some 8 ft. within 100 yds. At higher levels (above 3.0) pull out well above on the left and scout.

(2) S.C. 56 bridge to Union Co. Rt. 22 bridge

Drop	Difficulty	Distance	Time	Scenery	Water Quality
22′	1	4.5 mi.	2 hrs.	A	Good

Gage None. Runnable all year. May be a little scratchy following extremely long dry spells.

Difficulties Downed trees. With water levels following rains extreme care should be taken, expecially with gear-loaded canoes.

Enoree River, South Carolina

(3)   Union Co. Rt. 22 bridge to U.S. 176 bridge

Drop	Difficulty	Distance	Time	Scenery	Water Quality
53′	1	17.2 mi.	7 hrs.	A	Good

Gage   None.

Difficulties   See (1).

(4)   U.S. 176 bridge to Newberry Co. Rt. 81 bridge

Drop	Difficulty	Distance	Time	Scenery	Water Quality
33′	1	10.4 mi.	4 hrs.	A	Good

Gage   None.

Difficulties   See (2).

(5)   Newberry Rt. 81 bridge to S.C. 34 bridge on Broad

Drop	Difficulty	Distance	Time	Scenery	Water Quality
24′	1	12.5 mi.	5.5 hrs.	A	Good

Gage   None.

Difficulties   Winds can become a problem once entering the Broad. If power isn't being generated at Parr Shoals, one will encounter slack water in this area.

(6)   S.C. 34 on the Broad to Parr Shoals Dam

Drop	Difficulty	Distance	Time	Scenery	Water Quality
10′	A	10 mi.	5 hrs.	A-B	Good

Gage   None.

Difficulties   Primarily winds. This may become the "character building" part of the trip.

Directions   **Put In**—S.C. 49 bridge west of I-26.

Take Out—Approach the dam (Parr Shoals is the first nuclear power plant in the southeast) on the right, where a graded road runs down and take out. Carry about 100 yds. to the gate. If locked, carry around it. No problem! To drive to the take out go north on S.C. 28 from S.C. 213 for .7 mi. to the first gravel road on the right. Proceed .4 mi. to the gate.

Tyger River, South Carolina

The Tyger is formed in Spartanburg County after the confluence of the North, Middle and South Forks. It then flows generally south and east to meet the Broad east of Whitmire. As it drops through the Fall Line it presents a stretch of rather fast and difficuilt white water before it flattens out in the plains and meanders across Sumter National Forest. Other than the occasional bridges spanning the river, one sees little signs of habitation. The entire stretch is fairly wild and scenic.

Topo Maps   Cross Anchor, Union West, Sedalia, Whitmire North, Blair, Pomaria, Jenkinsville

Counties   Spartanburg, Union, Newberry

(3)   S.C. 56 bridge to S.C. 49 bridge

Drop	Difficulty	Distance	Time	Scenery	Water Quality
38'	1	7 mi.	2.5 hrs.	A	Good

Gage   None. Runnable all year.

Difficulties   Downed trees, although the channel apears to stay fairly clear. Take care at higher than normal levels.

(4)   S.C. 49 bridge to U.S. 176 bridge

Drop	Difficulty	Distance	Time	Scenery	Water Quality
51'	1	11.9 mi.	5 hrs.	A	Good

Gage   None.

Difficulties   See (3). For information: Rose Hill State Park (at S.C. 16) is 4.9 mi. down from the 49 bridge.

(5)   U.S. 176 bridge to Union Co. Rt. 35 bridge

Drop	Difficulty	Distance	Time	Scenery	Water Quality
41'	1	12.7 mi.	5 hrs.	A	Good

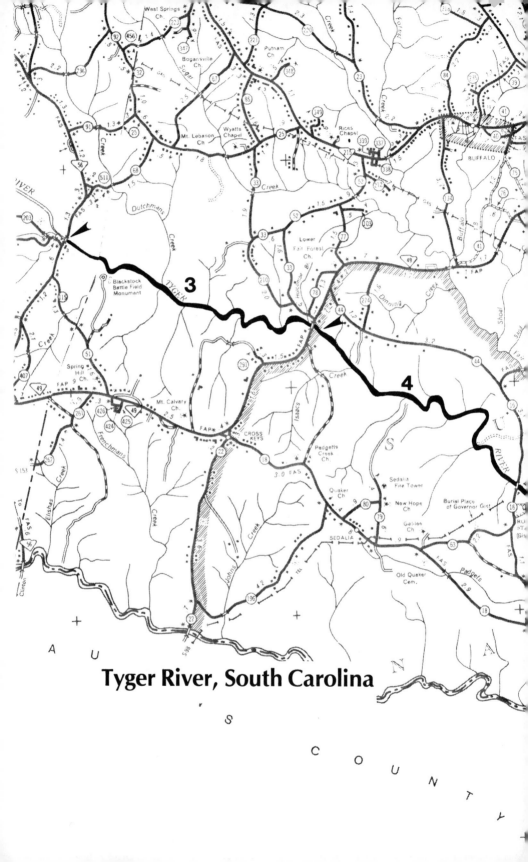

Tyger River, South Carolina

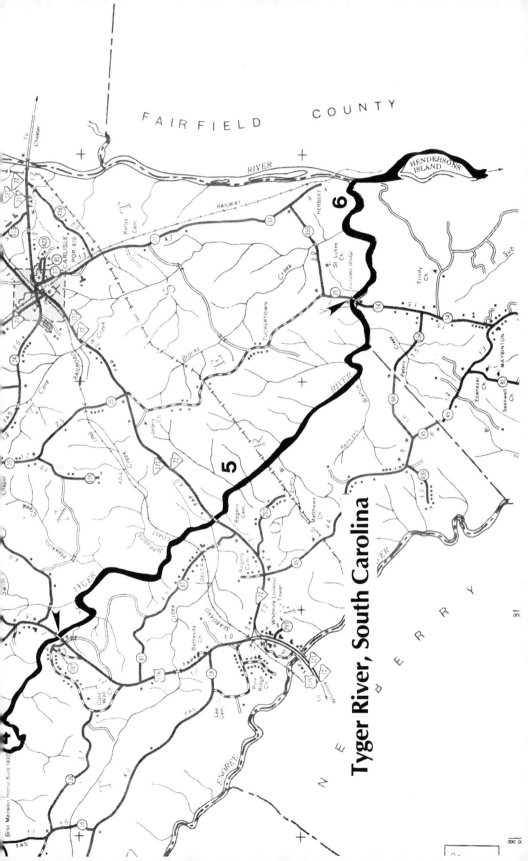

Tyger River, South Carolina

Gage   None.

Difficulties   See (3).

(6) Union Co. Rt. 35 and Newberry Co. Rt. 45 bridge to S.C. 34 on the Broad

Drop	Difficulity	Distance	Time	Scenery	Water Quality
25′	1-2	11.6 mi.	4.5 hrs.	A	Good

Gage   None.

Difficulties   After entering the Broad one will hear a rather ominous sound as Henderson Island comes into view. It's only a small shoals extending across the river, but following all the peace and quiet it makes quite a roar. Best passage is probably 20 to 30 ft. off the right bank. There are a few rock gardens on the way down to the end of the island, where shoals run for 150-200 yds. This area should be approached with caution, especially with canoes loaded with gear and inexperienced paddlers.

(7) S.C. 34 bridge to Parr Shoals Dam

Drop	Difficulty	Distance	Time	Scenery	Water Quality
10′	A	10 mi.	5 hrs.	A	Good

Gage   None.

Difficulties   Primarily winds.

Directions   **Take Out**—Approach the dam on the right where a graded road runs down to the water and take out. Carry about 100 yds. to the gate. If locked, carry around it. No problem! To drive to the take out go north on S.C. 28 from S.C. 213 for .7 mi. to first gravel road on right. Proceed .4 mi. to the gate.

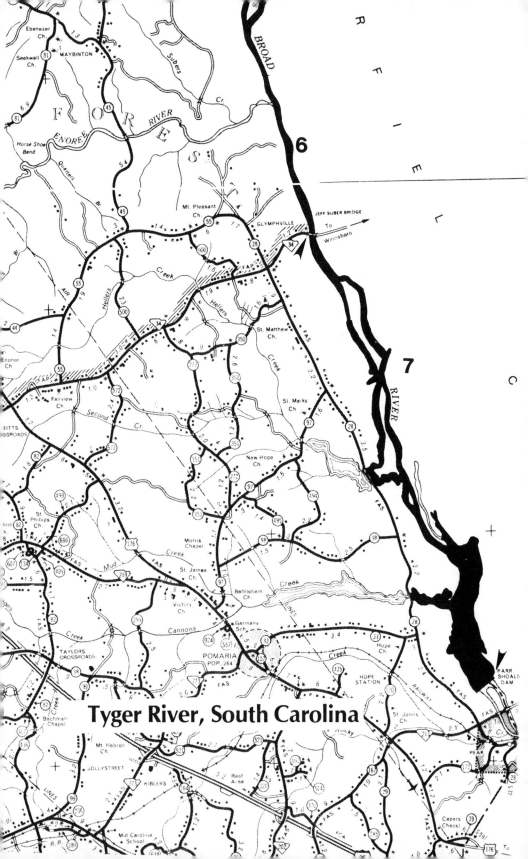

Tyger River, South Carolina

Suggested Reading

INSTRUCTIONAL

A White Water Handbook for Canoe and Kayak
by John Urban
Appalachian Mountain Club
5 Joy Street
Boston, Massachusetts 02108

The Complete Wilderness Paddler by John Rugge
and James West Davidson
Knopf
400 Hahn Road
Westminister, Maryland 21157

Canoeing and Kayaking by Laruie Gullion
American Canoe Association
P.O. Box 1190
Newington, Virginia 22122

Basic River Canoeing by Mary McNair,
Robert McNair, and Paul Landry
American Camping Association
Bradford Woods
Martinsville, Indiana 46151

River Rescue by Les Bechdel and Slim Ray
Appalachian Mountain Club
5 Joy Street
Boston, Massachusetts 02108

Canoeing Wild Rivers by Cliff Jacobson
ICS Books Inc.
One Tower Place, 107 E. 89th Ave.
Merryville, Indiana 46410

The New Wilderness Canoeing and Camping by Cliff Jacobson
ICS Books Inc.
One Tower Place, 107 E. 89th Ave.
Merryville, Indiana 46410

Canoeing by Dave Harrison
Sports Illustrated Winners' Circle
Time-Life Building
1271 Avenue of the Americas
New York, New York 10020

Path of the Paddle by Bill Mason
Northwood Press Inc.
Box 1360
Minocuqua, Wisconsin 54548

Song of the Paddle by Bill Mason
Northwood Press Inc.
Box 1360
Minocuqua, Wisconsin 54548

■

. . . an so there ain't nothing more to write about, and I am rotten glad of it, because if I'd'a knowed what a trouble it was to make a book I wouldn't 'a' tackled it, and ain't a-going to no more.

Mark Twain, from The Adventures of Huckleberry Finn

'73

It is said that time heals all wounds but I wonder in amazement how in two short years my memory failed to retain the feelings of how the good Mr. Twain had so aptly expressed my sentiments upon completion of the first edition.

—The Author

'76

. . . and here we are again!

—The Author

'80

Index